THE FILTHY TRUTH

ANDREW DICE CLAY

WITH DAVID RITZ

A TOUCHSTONE BOOK
Published by Simon & Schuster

New York   London   Toronto   Sydney   New Delhi

Touchstone
An Imprint of Simon & Schuster, Inc.
1230 Avenue of the Americas
New York, NY 10020

First Touchstone paperback edition April 2016

TOUCHSTONE and colophon are registered trademarks of Simon & Schuster, Inc.

For information about special discounts for bulk purchases, please contact Simon
& Schuster Special Sales at 1-866-506-1949 or business@simonandschuster.com.

The Simon & Schuster Speakers Bureau can bring authors to your live event. For
more information or to book an event, contact the Simon & Schuster Speakers
Bureau at 1-866-248-3049 or visit our website at www.simonspeakers.com.

Interior design by Robert E. Ettlin

Manufactured in the United States of America

3   5   7   9   10   8   6   4   2

The Library of Congress has cataloged the hardcover edition as follows:
Clay, Andrew Dice.
The filthy truth / Andrew Dice Clay with David Ritz.
pages   cm.
1. Clay, Andrew Dice.   2. Comedians—United States—Biography.
3. Actors—United States—Biography.   I. Ritz, David.   II. Title.
PN2287.C5449A3   2014
792.702'8092—dc23   [B]
2014010723

ISBN 978-1-4767-3471-2
ISBN 978-1-4767-3474-3 (pbk)
ISBN 978-1-4767-3475-0 (ebook)

This book is in memory of my parents, who had me,
raised me, loved me, and taught me to always believe in myself.
Fred and Jackie Silverstein, you are missed every second of every day.

FOREWORD

DECEMBER 1988. I'M twenty years old, home from college for winter break. I'm with my boys, the boys I've known since I was six (the boys whose interactions I will steal from many times when I write *Entourage*).

They all know that my going to college is a farce. I'm never gonna be a lawyer. I'm either too dumb or too lazy. But I'm gonna be in comedy. Somehow. Some way.

My boys know this. One of them, Frankie Giovanello, tells me that I have to see this new comic on the Rodney Dangerfield special.

Frankie swears that "you're gonna shit your pants when you hear this guy."

His name: Andrew Dice Clay.

So we all sit down.

We bust open some Jack (my parents are out).

And we wait. For the Diceman.

Now, I'm a punk at the time, a hater. Comics I don't already know and idolize all suck. So I wait, anxious to tell my boys how much the Diceman sucks. How when I'm older, I'm gonna be much funnier.

And then he comes on.

Leather jacket.

Hair to the ceiling.

Cigarette in his mouth.

I remember this like it's yesterday. Seriously.

And I'm thinking, *What the fuck is this?*

And then he starts.

He puts his arm around his neck and takes a toke off his cig.

To this day I have no idea why that was funny, but I didn't stop laughing for the next ten minutes.

Neither did my boys.

Vulgar nursery rhymes.

Sex jokes.

Aggressive.

Raw.

Nasty.

But you could feel, or at least I could, that it was a put-on. There was something lovable about this guy.

I was sure he was going to be a giant star. Two years later, the same crew and I were at Madison Square Garden, screaming along with twenty thousand other maniacs at "Little boy blue. He needed the money."

I was right. Dice had blown up.

Every guy I knew could recite his entire act.

He made movies and TV shows. He seemed to be everywhere.

And then he disappeared. Poof.

I always wondered what had happened.

I didn't know that nearly twenty-five years later I would have a chance to help resurrect one of the most dynamic performers I'd ever seen.

When Dice came to the set of *Entourage* to start work on our final season, it was as if I were a kid again, watching as a fan. He's such a force and a presence. The minute he started his scene, he just popped. I went over to him after and said, "You know, your whole life is about to change." And he just said, "Yeah. I'm ready."

I knew he was. And so did Woody Allen, and now Martin Scorsese. The Diceman is back with a vengeance!

Doug Ellin

INTRODUCTION

MOST CELEBRITIES WRITE their books to look good. If their necks were long enough, they'd bend over backward to kiss their own ass. Most people rewrite history to make themselves the fuckin' hero. Well, I do consider myself a hero, but not the kind that blows smoke up his butt. I'm a hero like Rocky is a hero, 'cause I've learned to take punches. I'm a hero because if you knock me down, I get right back up. I'm a hero 'cause the weasels who wanted me outta the game are outta the game themselves, and I'm still swinging. I'm a hero 'cause I got the balls to tell the filthy truth.

So I'm not gonna start at the top. I'm gonna start this at the bottom. I ain't playing the Garden or the Forum. I'm playing the back room of a sushi bar in Vegas. I'm broke, grinding through the toughest decade of my life. Two marriages have collapsed. Counting the cost of my divorces, my crumbling career, and a vicious blackjack jones, I've lost millions. If it wasn't for the fact that I was raising my two wonderful sons—the most beautiful human beings in the world—I might have lost it. But I haven't lost it. I still got it. I'm standing up tall in this little Japanese joint, performing in front of fifteen people when I used to perform in front of fifteen thousand. I'm saying, "You're watching history. You're watching Rocky training for the championship. You're watching the champ on the comeback trail. You're gonna remember this moment when you saw Dice in such a place, just like you remember the time you got your first hot fuck. When you're fucking, the dark clouds lift and the world goes away. You guys know what I'm talkin' about.

When you're slammin' into her soaking-wet pussy like a fuckin' freight train, you ain't worried about the rent or the price of gasoline. When you're about to bust wide open with your barrel of load, you got the energy of the gods. Well, I got that energy tonight. I'm coming at you with all I got."

That night was the beginning of the ride back. That night I also got a little spiritual. I talked about God. I said, "They say after you die you get a few minutes with God. Well, I can imagine God saying, 'Dice'—he's calling me Dice 'cause he's a fan—'Dice, what's the one thing in life that really bothered you?'

"And I say, 'Well, G, you're a great guy for asking. So, with all due respect, there is one thing I'd like to know.'

" 'What's that, Dice?'

" 'When men get older, why did you go and stretch the balls out like that? Why didn't you stretch out the cock? I mean, how great would it be when you go off to work to hear your chick say, "Honey, tuck your cock into your cuff." ' "

That small crowd in the back of the sushi bar got off. I got off. I made sure we had a good time. They laughed until they cried. They soaked up my take on life, which only gets richer with each passing day. They got all of me.

In this book, I'm giving you all of me. I'm making goddamn sure that you're gonna have a good time—the time of your life—in reading about my life.

I have every confidence that whether you begged, borrowed, bought, or stole this book, once you get done reading it, you'll wanna read it again. It's gonna be that fuckin' good. I say that because I was born and nurtured in the most colorful, beloved place in all the world, a place where storytelling is an art form—stories coming out of the candy stores and the playgrounds and the delis, stories in every apartment building and on every street corner, crazy stories, funny stories, but no story funnier or crazier than the one belonging to Andrew Silverstein, born September 29, 1957, in beautiful Brooklyn, New York, a kid so bold and eager to get going that when in the hospital the nurse put a plastic nipple in his mouth, he ripped open her shirt, watched her big, beautiful boobs pop out, and said, "Honey, I like it from the tap."

THE ORIGINALS

THE ORIGINALS ARE:

Jackie Silverstein, Supermom.

Fred Silverstein, Superdad.

Natalie Silverstein, Supersis.

And me—Superman.

BECAUSE SUPERMAN LOVED his neighborhood of Brooklyn, and because Superman knew it was his job to protect the neighborhood, Superman was taking his job seriously.

At six years old I was going to school wearing my Superman costume under my regular clothes. When my parents and sister were sleeping at night I was practicing flying, leaping from the couch to the floor in a single bound. Like the television Superman on my favorite show, I was faster than a speeding bullet and more powerful than a locomotive. If someone had told me that Superman was a figment of the imagination of two Jewish cartoonists from Cleveland, I wouldn't have believed it. I thought he was real. I thought he was me.

Without knowing I was wearing my costume, Mom one morning walked me to the corner where the school bus arrived to take me to PS 222. I climbed in and took a seat by the window. I watched Mom watching me and saw all the sadness in her eyes. She didn't like to be apart from me—not even for a few hours. That's the kind of mom she was.

At school I had a hard time sitting down. I was in the back of the room pacing back and forth.

"Andrew," said the teacher. "What in the world are you doing?"

"Pacing."

"Stop."

"I can't."

"Why?"

"I gotta go to the bathroom."

"Then go."

I went, and that's where I took off my street clothes and ran back to the classroom as Superman.

The kids loved it. They howled. They applauded. With my arms extended and my cape flowing, I was running around the room.

"Stop!" screamed the teacher.

"I can't. I'm Superman. I'm here to protect you. I gotta protect everyone."

I caused mayhem and chaos. I liked it.

Fifteen minutes hadn't gone by before Mom showed up in the classroom. Jackie Silverstein was a gorgeous woman with the looks of Liz Taylor who also had a mouth on her that could scare mountain lions. Not that there were too many mountain lions in Brooklyn.

The teacher started in on Mom. Big mistake. The teacher said, "Andrew not only has shown absolutely no interest in his schoolwork, now he's running around here in this costume and scaring the other children."

"They don't look scared," said Mom. "They look amused."

"There's nothing funny about this," said the teacher.

"Then why are they laughing?" said my mother.

"Mrs. Silverstein, let me be frank. The way Andrew is behaving, it's going to all go downhill from here. Your son's not going to have a future."

Mom stepped up to the teacher and stood as close to her as she could. They were jaw-to-jaw. Mom laid into her.

"That's what you want to say about my kid—right here in front of the other kids—that he has no future? I thought teachers were supposed to be smart. But this is not a smart thing to say. This is a stupid thing to say. Very stupid. So stupid I have half a mind to waltz you into the principal's office and tell him what you're telling me and these other bright little kids. You're telling them that having an imagination and a little fun is not only a terrible thing but it also means you're ruining your life. And you call yourself a teacher? Lady, you should be ashamed of yourself. You should resign your job and look for work down in the sewers—that's what you should do."

My jaw dropped. The same went for the other kids. They were stunned. Mom grabbed me by the arm and yanked me outta there. I wanted to thank her, I wanted to kiss her, but I didn't say anything, because as soon as we left school she was yelling at me. "What kind of kid puts on a Superman show in the classroom? Are you out of your mind, Andrew? Are you crazy?"

When Dad got home from work she told him the story and started yelling at me all over again. But I didn't mind. Because hearing what happened, my sister, Natalie—who's three years older—was laughing just like the kids had been laughing. And besides, even though I knew I may have messed up, I'd learned the biggest lesson of all: that my family was everything. My family was there to back me up. My family was there to defend me against the world, no matter what I did. My family was my protector, and I was my family's protector. We were the Originals. We were from Brooklyn. No one was gonna mess with me. No one was gonna intimidate me. I was free to fly.

My dad could do anything he put his mind to. He wasn't scared of going from one kind of business to another. In the earliest part of my life, when we lived in a garden apartment on Burnett Street, he owned a big toy store on Avenue U. If Mom had the mouth, Dad had the heart. He was a giver. He'd say, "Take any toys you want, Andrew."

I saw Dad as a combination of Santa Claus and Hanukkah Harry. At Christmas our living room was piled high with toys—board games and dolls, cowboy holsters and every ball known to mankind. Too bad I couldn't catch or throw the balls worth a shit. From childhood on, I sucked at all sports except for one—boxing.

This was another gift from my father, who'd been a Golden Gloves champ. He was so good they put up a statue of him in a park near Cunningham Junior High. Dad wasn't a loudmouth like Mom. He was a strong, good-looking man with no apparent fears. He didn't provoke fights, but he didn't back down. He made it clear that he was there to protect my mom, my sister, and me. His attitude was, *You don't gotta be afraid of the world; you can take on the world, and when you do, I got your back.*

Dad might have been calm, but our household wasn't. Our household was loud. There was a lot of screaming, not only because Mom expressed herself that way but also because her loud family was always around. There was my beautiful grandmother Shirley and her sister, Carol, and Carol's husband, Ernie, not to mention all the other aunts and uncles and cousins. I loved all this. I even loved the screaming. I came to believe that, for Jewish families living in Brooklyn, the more you screamed, the happier you were. The more you screamed, the more you loved your family. You didn't hold nothing back. You let your feelings fly.

Shirley and her daughters also lit up certain fancy New York nightclubs where they ran the cloakrooms. I remember my dad leaving the apartment at midnight to drive into the city to pick them up after work. This was our family's first venture into showbiz. Mom, Aunt Carol, and Grandma loved the bright lights of Broadway and wanted to be close to the action. Dad never objected and, because he was so sure of himself, never got jealous when Mom got the attention of other men.

I got everyone's attention early on. I didn't have to demand their attention—I got it 'cause they loved me. I got it 'cause I loved to carry on and entertain them, mimicking voices I'd heard on the radio or actors I'd seen at the movies. By the time I was six, I could do John Wayne. The living room was my stage, and my family, with sister Natalie as my biggest fan, cheered me on.

Brooklyn was the center of our universe. Brooklyn was heaven. I never imagined leaving. And then one day, much to my amazement, we got up and left.

THE ORIGINALS WERE ON THE MOVE

AFTER FIVE YEARS of construction, the Verrazano-Narrows Bridge, linking Brooklyn to Staten Island, was finally opened on November 21, 1964. This was the first day that cars could make the drive. Among those passenger cars was a Pontiac LeMans driven by Fred Silverstein. Jackie was sitting shotgun, with Natalie and seven-year-old Andrew in the backseat.

The Originals were making the short haul over the water from Brooklyn to Staten Island.

Back then Staten Island was wide open and ripe for development. Dad's dream was to create a whole neighborhood—fifty-two homes. He was calling it Silvertown Estates and moving us into the middle of the action. We'd be living in one of the first completed two-family houses in the development. We'd be living upstairs, and downstairs would be Aunt Carol and Uncle Ernie and their kids, my cousins Jamie and Lori.

As we drove off the bridge and exited onto Victory Boulevard, I craned my neck to look around. My little heart was beating like mad. I was excited but also wary. We were only a few miles from Brooklyn, but as far as I was concerned, we could have been on the fuckin' moon. Brooklyn was wall-to-wall apartment buildings. Staten Island was acres of empty farmland. Brooklyn had subways. Staten Island had cows.

Silvertown Estates was still going up. Some of the houses were half-built, some just framed, others just cement foundations. Only half the streets were paved. Our house, at 431 Canterbury Avenue, was a beautiful two-tone shingle home. The development was set in the middle of the woods. Just beyond that area, some two thousand feet away from our house, was a giant brick tower next to a complex of big old ugly brick buildings. It looked like a penitentiary.

"What is it, Dad?" I asked.

"Willowbrook. It's a mental hospital."

"What's a mental hospital?"

"A hospital for people who've gone mental."

"Crazy people?"

"They come there for treatment."

"And they lock 'em up?"

"They're locked up till they get better."

"And what if they escape?" I asked, feeling uneasy about these neighbors.

"You don't got nothing to worry about, Andrew. Look around, sonny boy. Staten Island is paradise."

I looked around, but my eyes went back to the ugly brick tower and those nasty-looking buildings. Crazy people. We were living down the road from an army of crazy people.

Other than living in the shadow of a loony bin, I liked Staten Island. The wide-open spaces made me feel free. I raced around on my first serious bike—a three-speed red Stingray with a big banana seat, thick motorcycle handles, and a fat sissy bar in the back.

Schoolwork still didn't thrill me. It never would. I was a third-rate student and first-rate class clown. My favorite parts of the school day were the fire drills.

"They're great," I was telling Mom. "The teacher lines us up outside, and if you're not in a straight line, he punches you in the arm to get you back."

"He *what*?"

"He walks up and down like John Wayne and punches you in the arm."

"He didn't punch you, Andrew, did he?"

"Well, yeah, kinda . . . 'cause I was outta line."

I realized I shouldn't have said nothing, because the next day Jackie Silverstein, dressed like she was attending the Academy Awards, showed up at school. When the door to our classroom opened, she walked through wearing her full-length mink coat. It was like she was making a personal appearance. As I said, my mom was a knockout, a dead ringer for Elizabeth Taylor. But you put her next to the real Liz Taylor, you'd think Liz Taylor was a skank. But more than beauty, my mom had charisma. When she walked into a room, it was like she had a spotlight following her. My teacher, Mr. Barketta, this tall guy in his thirties, he didn't have a chance.

"I'm Mrs. Silverstein," she said. A hush fell over the room. I could feel everybody staring at her. She smiled, but I wouldn't call it a happy smile. This smile gripped your heart and made you shudder. "So, Andrew told me you gave him a little punch in the arm, is that right?"

"It was just a little chuck." Mr. Barketta tried to look cool, but he mainly looked sick. He came over to me. "It was only a tap. I didn't hurt you, did I, partner?"

"I know you would never hit my kid." That smile again. Blazing cold. Turning Mr. Barketta to ice. "I see that now that we've met. I just had to check." Then Mom flipped that smile over, changing it from giving you the shivers to warming you up. "Andrew told me you do a pretty good John Wayne."

Mr. Barketta rotated his neck, hitched up his pants, narrowed his mouth and walked bowlegged across the room toward Mom. "No way I'd ever hurt your little boy, ma'am," he said, channeling John Wayne himself.

Everybody laughed, Mom the loudest. "Very good, Mr. Barketta. It's like I'm looking right at the Duke."

"Aw, shucks, Mrs. Silverstein."

Another huge laugh.

"Well, I'll let you all get back to class." My mother dipped her head daintily at Mr. Barketta, gave me a wave, and headed out of the classroom, her mink coat swishing as she walked.

"Very nice meeting you, Mrs. Silverstein," Mr. Barketta said, losing the John Wayne, going back to his goofy normal voice.

My mom waved again, tinkling her fingers over her shoulder, and left the classroom. For half a second, the room went quiet as a tomb. Then all the girls clapped and cheered, and all the boys whistled.

DON'T FUCK WITH AN ORIGINAL

I NEVER BEGAN fights, but I never shied away from them. There was this kid who lived down the street. He was a little nuts to begin with. We were trading baseball cards when he decided that he didn't like how the trades were going. So, without provocation, he knocked over a huge stack of cards and swiped at my face with his open hand. Before I could react, he ran off. When I got home, Mom took one look at me and started screaming.

"What happened to my Andrew?"

I went to the bathroom and looked in the mirror and saw why Mom was yelling. I looked like something out of a horror movie. The kid had taken his fingernails and raked my face from my forehead to my chin. That's when I flipped out. I ran out of the house and down the street to where the kid lived. I was gonna kill him. When I got there his big fat mother—she must have weighed three hundred fifty pounds—was blocking the door. The kid was hiding behind her. Trying to reach around her to grab her son, I was scream-ing, "You're dead! You're dead!" I was just about to get past the mother when my mother and sister showed up. They knew my temper and were scared I was going to kill the kid. But I wouldn't listen to reason. I was still going after him when I felt a hand on my shoulders.

"Okay, big shot," said my dad. "Time to stop."

So I did.

Next day Mom said I could skip school 'cause of the scratch marks on my face, but I went anyway. I was gonna get this fuckin' kid. I waited all day 'cause I knew we'd be on the same bus going home. I stared at him, letting him know he was gonna get it. He looked out the window, trying to ignore me. When we got to our stop, he got to the front of the bus in a hurry. I was in the back, but I blasted my way through the bus, knocking the other kids out of the way. He was already running down the street. I dropped my books to gain speed and quickly caught him right in front of our house. He tried to rake my face again. Not this time. He then tried to punch me in the balls. That's when I really went off. I don't mind a fight, but I do mind getting punched in the balls. I got him in a headlock and bashed his face with my knee. Aunt Carol heard the commotion and came running out.

"Beat the shit outta him, Andrew!"

I slammed him with his metal lunch box. By now he was a bloody mess. I didn't stop until Dad and a few other men arrived and put an end to the massacre.

An hour later I was back home with Mom and Natalie when we heard Aunt Carol screaming. We all ran downstairs to see what was wrong.

"That little bastard," she said, "the one Andrew beat up. He was just here. He pulled out his dick and pissed on my window."

The way Aunt Carol said that broke us up. It also broke up the mood. We couldn't stop laughing.

YOU CAN KEEP JOHN AND PAUL;
I WANTED TO BE RINGO

ANOTHER BEAUTIFUL THING about my childhood is music. I fell in love with rhythm before I fell in love with girls. I was crazy for the beat of a tom drum, the snap of a snare, and the brassy crash of a cymbal. The first grooves I heard that drove me wild came from a song called "Caravan," which Uncle Ernie loved and played on his phonograph over and over. Uncle Ernie loved the big-band beats, especially when the drummer was Gene Krupa, his favorite. Krupa's drum intro and later his solo in Benny Goodman's "Sing, Sing, Sing" did the trick: it turned me inside out and had me grabbing the spoons from Aunt Carol's kitchen and beating on the phone book.

"Sure, Krupa was the greatest," said Mom. "But they say he was a hophead. They say he took drugs. If I ever catch you taking drugs, Andrew, I'll murder you. Do you understand?"

"Yes, Mom."

"Promise me you won't."

"I won't."

And I never did.

Not long after my Krupa craze—a craze that has lasted until this day—I got even crazier one Sunday night when I was watching our Emerson console TV. Natalie and I were sitting on the floor, Mom and Dad were on the couch. Ed Sullivan came on. He looked like a corpse and talked like a tight-ass, but we loved Ed because Ed loved show business and always honored the old-timers. But tonight he didn't have no old-timers. He had this group of four shaggy-haired kids from England.

The one who got to me was the guy playing the drums—the guy sitting high on a riser above the other three, up there with his big nose, his head bobbing up and down while he beat the shit out of those tubs. While the girls in the balcony were screeching so loud for George, Paul, and John that you couldn't hear them sing or play their guitars, I could hear every sound Ringo made. Ringo was behind the whole operation. Ringo was the driver in the driver's seat. I loved Ringo. I wanted to be Ringo.

"I'm gonna be that guy!" I announced to the other Originals.

In another family—a family more normal than the Originals—I might have been told that I was nuts. Who is this little kid saying that he's gonna be a rock-and-roll star? But in my family the reaction was just the opposite.

"You'll be whoever you wanna be," said Mom.

"You'll be terrific at whatever you do," said Dad.

"Let's go get that Beatles record," said Natalie.

It wasn't long before I had my own toy drum set and was banging away to my heart's content. Turned out I was a natural. The rhythm flowed outta me. Also turned out that the drums were a great way for me to get out everything inside—frustrations at not doing good at school and anger at the bullies and gang members who thought they'd scare me off. They didn't.

FUCKIN' CUNT MOTHERFUCKIN' BITCH ASSHOLE GODDAMN BASTARD COCKSUCKER PIECE OF SHIT SONOFABITCH BASTARD SHITHEAD

I'D HEARD CURSING my whole life. You couldn't live in the Silverstein home and not hear a little cursing. My aunt Carol would call someone a "stupid bastard" or Mom would refer to some schmuck as a "dumb son of a bitch." They used those words with a certain rhythm that rang right. There was a poetry to the way they cursed.

Back then cursing wasn't what it is today. Certain words—like "fuck" or "cunt"—you'd never hear. They were off-limits. And of course as kids we were not allowed to curse at all. Even words like "goddamn" were not allowed. If I slipped up and said "Goddamn shit," my parents would get upset.

Mom would say, "Listen to that mouth on him, Fred."

Then Dad would say, "Where do you think he gets it from, Jackie?"

Either way, I was told, "Use language like that again and we'll wash out your mouth with soap."

All that brings me to one day when I was in the schoolyard during recess, a time when the other kids liked to gather around me because they never knew what I might do. I might get an old pail and start beating it like a drum, pretending I was Ringo Starr. I might climb on top of the tallest fence, announce that I was Superman, and fly off. I might do anything. But on this particular freezing-cold day I felt like being alone—an unusual condition for a kid like me 'cause I liked attention. I liked being noticed. But unnoticed, I went off by myself back to the school building, where I stood alone. No one was there. No one could see me. No one could hear me. I stood facing the closed doors of the school. While the kids were far away, running around the schoolyard and letting off steam, I opened my mouth, and a hurricane of curse words came storming outta me.

"Fuck!

"Shit!

"Cunt!

"Motherfucker!

"Bitch!"

I shouted out each word individually, and then I strung them together—"Fuckin' cunt motherfuckin' bitch asshole goddamn bastard cocksucker piece of shit sonofabitch bastard shithead . . ."

It was like I had Tourette's. I couldn't stop myself. It felt like diarrhea of the mouth. It went on for several minutes. But when it was over, it felt good. I felt free. Maybe those words had been bottled up in my mind and needed to explode. Those words had power. They came out of some deep part of me, and even as a kid, they felt good coming outta my mouth. To this day I can't believe that moment happened. I was only in the third grade.

THE KING

IT WAS 1968 and I was eleven. I was told to go to sleep but couldn't, because music was coming from the TV set in the living room that had me climbing out of my bed and crawling on the floor to crack open the door. I had to see who was making the music.

There he was. He was so explosive and dynamic that I couldn't stay put. I had to take a chance on pissing off my parents by walking into the living room and just standing there. Knowing me as they did, Mom and Dad let me stay. They let me sit right in front of the TV, understanding that the singing was so great that I'd never get back to sleep anyway.

"Stay, Andrew," said Mom. "You can hear a couple of songs, then straight back to bed."

I heard more than a couple. I stayed for all of them—"That's All Right," "Heartbreak Hotel," "Lawdy Miss Clawdy," "Blue Suede Shoes," "One Night with You"—one better than the other. The way he sounded fuckin' fractured me—that cocksure smoothness of his voice. The way he looked fuckin' fractured me—the tight leather pants and the leather jacket with the collar stuck up in the back. His sneer fractured me. His easy give-and-take with the audience fractured me. His absolute total not-insecure-for-a-second confidence fractured me.

I watched Elvis Presley that night—only later did I learn it was his comeback special—feeling that he was everything I wanted to be. Whatever he had, I wanted. But it was more than that. I felt that I already *had* what he had. I knew that Elvis was Elvis because he took over the stage and the room and the television audience around the world. He loved how everyone was looking at him. And everyone was looking at him because his every move was right. And his every move was right because he was in charge.

That was it!

His in-charge attitude was the attitude that lived inside me!

I didn't know how or when or even why, but goddamn it . . . I was gonna have that kind of in-charge look and feel and act. I was gonna take over. I was gonna command the fuckin' stage.

I was gonna be Elvis!

My parents saw that I was transfixed and did nothing to break my spell. Even though my parents related more to Frank Sinatra than Elvis Presley, they saw that Elvis had what Frank had: crazy charisma. By that age I'd heard enough Sinatra to love him myself. I loved when he sang "My Kind of Town" and "Come Fly with Me." I could fly with Sinatra. But Elvis had something that Frank didn't. Elvis had the leather. Elvis had the rebel look. While Elvis was singing, he was also saying, "Fuck you if you don't like me, 'cause I like me. I like me so much I'm gonna *make* you like me."

MIAMI FOR A MINUTE

I DON'T KNOW exactly why we left Staten Island and moved to Miami when I was twelve, because my parents didn't include my sister and me in discussions about their finances. But that's how it should be. With Silvertown Estates, I figured that Dad hadn't made the fortune he had expected, but that was okay because Dad had lots of skills. Dad always found a way to make a living. The man could do anything. And Mom, like millions of other Brooklyn Jews, had always wanted to live in Miami Beach.

So we moved.

Miami in those days was about the Fontainebleau Hotel, where Sammy Davis and Sinatra played; the Eden Roc, where Liz Taylor stayed; and the Miami Beach Auditorium, where they shot *The Jackie Gleason Show*. I remember the palm trees, the beach, the sunshine, and the Parkview Point, the high-rise where we lived.

I was still an innocent kid. For instance, my friend Mark, a year older than me, would talk about fucking girls, but I wasn't ready. I didn't know the territory. I hadn't studied the anatomy. I didn't really know what to do. I was shy. Yes, loudmouth class-clown jackass joker do-anything-for-attention Andrew Silverstein had a shy side. He wasn't ready to get down and dirty. It would take many more years for me to gain the courage to explore the sexual territory that I was dreaming about. At that point, the dreams would have to do.

• • •

My dad was my hero because he not only loved and protected his family, he always found a way to deal with the cold, cruel world, no matter what setbacks he faced. When he got to Miami Beach, he was a builder, supervising construction crews putting up high-rises. He'd go out and walk on those steel girders fifteen stories above the ground and not think twice about it. The man could do anything. I saw that when things didn't work out he never complained. When business at his Brooklyn toy store went flat, he just put a lock on the door and walked away. When the Silvertown Estates project didn't work out, he didn't moan or groan. He moved on. After eight or nine months in Florida, when Mom missed Brooklyn so badly we decided to move back, Dad walked out of his Miami Beach building business and started up a new business. This was the Royal Process Agency at 16 Court Street in downtown Brooklyn.

All the Originals were glad to be back in the borough we loved best. Staten Island was okay, Miami Beach was nice, but Brooklyn was home, Brooklyn was my heart. We moved in for a while with Grandma Shirley at Avenue M and East Twelfth—it was great living with a grandmother who treated me like a little prince—before we got a place of our own at 3202 Nostrand Avenue, apartment 4A.

FALLING IN LOVE WITH A PAIR OF FURRY GLOVES

I STILL REMEMBER my first time. You always remember your first. I was in my bedroom at my little desk making believe I was doing homework while my parents were sitting at the kitchen table on the other side of my door. My bedroom was right off the kitchen. I had an itch down there. And the more I scratched the itch, the itchier it got. Looking for something soft to rub the itch, I was rummaging through a box in my closet when I noticed a pair of furry gloves that Mom had bought me in the Brooklyn Kings Plaza shopping center.

I took one of the gloves and folded back the opening so the leather on the outside of the glove wouldn't hurt me. Hoping to stop the itch, I stuck my cock inside the little furry glove. The more I rubbed the glove up and down, the better it felt. More rubbing, better and better feeling, until all of a sudden an overwhelming feeling washed over me. I pulled the glove off to see that my cock was shooting out stuff like I'd struck oil. It wouldn't stop. I panicked. Making sure Mom and Dad weren't around, I made a beeline for the bathroom, my cock still shooting cum. I threw a towel over the dick head to catch the last of my load. Remember—I didn't even know what a load was. And I knew that it wasn't piss, 'cause taking a leak never felt that good. I figured I had broken my dick. Matter of fact, I didn't touch my cock again for months after. It wasn't until I heard the other boys talking about jerking off that I realized it was normal. That's when I went home and started seriously dating both those furry gloves. I was the only kid in the ninth grade dating twins.

With the help of Vaseline and Neosporin, I wound up fucking everything in the house—scarves, socks, blankets, earmuffs. I fucked my mom's fur coat so many times it didn't even need a hanger. I'm sure some scientist has figured out how many loads your average horny boy shoots in a day. Well, if the norm is two or three, I could double that. Whacking off became a religious ritual. It was my way of worshipping the Priestess of Pussy. It was where I put my energy and imagination. No one told me it was wrong. No one warned me that it would ruin me. My parents had to know what I was doing in the bathroom for thirty minutes at a time. If they objected, they didn't bug me. They figured it was normal, even healthy. In that respect, I was one of the healthiest kids on the block.

SLY AND THE STONES AT MY BAR MITZVAH

ONCE WE MOVED back to Brooklyn, Dad transitioned fast from picking up work serving summonses for different lawyers around the borough to starting his own company, the Royal Process Agency. He was done moving from business to business. He'd own and operate Royal Process for the next twenty years.

For me, the first big event of our return home was my bar mitzvah.

Because it happened soon after we'd returned from Florida, I hadn't had a lot of time to prepare. I was not exactly a star student with my Hebrew lessons, but I'd learned a couple of quick prayers and written a nice little speech in English. The big party was held at the Marquee Room, right there on Nostrand Avenue near Sheepshead Bay. Making it even stranger—and better—was the fact that it was happening on Halloween night. Dad honored the promise he'd made six years before when I saw Ringo Starr on *Ed Sullivan*. He presented me with a beautiful shiny new white Pearl drum kit that he bought at a music store down the street from Grandma Shirley's apartment. Drums spoke my language, and I'd been playing for almost half my life at this point. The kit was all set up and ready for me to sit in with the hired band, comprised of older guys who could really play. I kicked off with the Stones' "Honky Tonk Woman" and followed up with Sly Stone's "I Want to Take You Higher." Feeling like a million bucks, I crushed both songs. My family and friends cheered for me like I was John Bonham with Led Zeppelin or Carmine Appice with Vanilla Fudge.

Among my friends at the party was Jimmy D. Maria, one of my pals from Hudde Junior High, a six-foot-three hulk of a kid. He had red cheeks and red hair that told you right away he was 100 percent Irish. He was also a member in good standing of a gang called the Avenue M Animals. In the playground during recess, Jimmy D. was always playing craps. Maybe the reason I liked him was 'cause he was a gutsy gambler.

"Hey," I told Jimmy D. one day in the schoolyard, "I know what the 'D' in your name stands for."

"What?"

" 'Dice.' I'm calling you Dice."

He laughed it off. "Okay, I'm Dice."

The kid was a tough guy, and I liked it when the tough guys liked me.

"Hey, Dice," I told him. "I'm glad you showed up."

Jimmy was a little pissed off because he was in the middle of a giant Halloween egg fight when his parents called him in and made him come to my party. But once he got there, he had a ball. Everyone did.

The party went on till late that night, and I got home feeling terrific. When I woke up the next morning, I kept hearing the phrase "Now you're a man."

Funny, though—I didn't feel like a man. I still felt like a kid. A horny kid. But still a kid.

The sexual revolution came late to Brooklyn. When it did arrive, it skipped my neighborhood entirely. When I was fourteen or fifteen, a date meant taking a girl to see Sean Connery as James Bond in *Diamonds Are Forever* or Clint Eastwood in *Dirty Harry*. You'd buy the chick a box of popcorn and awkwardly throw your arm around her, hoping to get some side tit. You'd hope that the side tit would get her going, but that didn't happen, 'cause her tits were shoved into an industrial-strength bra made of material that felt like iron. If you happened to find a girl who was a little more liberal, after the movie she might let you dry-hump her in the stairwell of her building. In theory. I wasn't there yet. But that was my goal: coax a girl into a stairwell. For some reason, I always found the stairwells of Brooklyn buildings to be incredibly sexy places. Later on I had some of the best blow jobs of my life in those stairwells.

But let me be clear. I wasn't even close to actually touching a real live pussy. Between me and the wet box were overcoats and sweaters and blouses, pantyhose and leggings and all sorts of other shit. I was dying to get to it, but basically I was a nice Jewish boy chasing after nice Jewish girls or nice Italian girls whose niceness was icing me out. Besides, I was a gentleman.

THE BIG FIGHT

I HAD MORE than sexual frustrations. I had problems with an Irish gang at school. The trouble started the day that Mom asked me to run down to the German deli to pick up some groceries.

I was walking out carrying a bag of groceries when this gang was waiting for me. Must have been nine or ten of 'em.

"What you got in the bag?" asked one.

"What you think I got? I got groceries."

"Wiseass, huh?"

I didn't say nothing back. I just started walking home, and they were following me, right on my heels. I kept walking. They got even closer, and finally when I was close to our apartment building they started taunting me and calling me names. I wasn't really scared except I didn't want to get hit from behind, so I turned around and said, "Look, I don't even know you guys. So I don't know what the problem is."

"The problem is," said the gang leader, "we're gonna kick your fuckin' ass."

And just like that, they came at me. They circled me. Without my seeing what he was doing, one guy kneeled down behind me. Another guy told the leader, "Why don't you just take him in the grass and fight him?" I didn't have a problem with that. I welcomed it. But before that happened, the leader shoved me so hard that I fell back over the guy kneeling behind me. As I tried to get up, I felt a foot split my face open. Blood came pouring out like it was coming out of a faucet.

I barely made it up to our apartment, where Mom freaked and started screaming for Dad. Then we were in the family Pontiac rushing to the ER of Brookdale Hospital, where Mom was screaming, "My Andrew's not gonna be scarred for life! I'm not having some ER student practicing on his face! No one's laying a hand on my kid until I find the best plastic surgeon in this hospital!" Because Grandma Shirley worked at the hospital, we actually were able to get the best plastic surgeon. To this day you can't see a trace of a scar on my face.

Crazy as it sounds, a few months later it happened all over again. It was the same Irish gang. They were called the Shed because they hung out under a shed in Marine Park. When they saw me and my friends walking down Avenue S on our way home from a school carnival, they started chasing us. One of them caught me and flung me against a pointy fence that ripped open my hand. As I looked down at the blood streaming from my hand, another guy ran up behind me and hit me in the back of the head with a blackjack. I was back in the hospital, getting stitched up, and Mom was beside herself, pacing, planning; I could almost see her mind at work.

When we got home, I went into my room to sleep off my headache, and my mother started making calls. As I lay in bed, I heard her say a name, and it clicked. The lowlife piece-of-shit motherfucker who coldcocked me was in my gym class.

My head throbbing, I burst out of my room. "I know the kid," I said to my mother, who was still on the phone. "He's in my gym class."

She saw the rage in my face. She cupped her palm over the phone. "You stay away from him," she whispered urgently.

"Ma, I'm telling you—"

"It's handled, Andrew. You hear me?"

I couldn't speak. I just burned.

"Promise me you won't go near him," my mother said.

I bit my lip so hard I thought I'd drawn blood.

"I promise," I lied.

I didn't want my mother to worry.

I went back to my room, and Mom went back to making calls. I got into bed vowing one thing: that kid was a dead man. Then I heard my father on the phone, too. Both of my parents began talking with urgency. I couldn't hear everything they were saying, but I got the gist. Because my parents were from the neighborhood, they had connections all over the community. They knew who to call. I was a curious kid and I knew something was happening that concerned me, so I stayed up. I listened to all the calls and conversations between Mom and Dad. I learned that their connection told Mom—not Dad—to make a call to the father of the kid who fucked up my head and slammed me with the blackjack.

I got out of bed, tiptoed across my floor, and put my ear to my bedroom door. I heard Mom on the phone. "This is Jackie Silverstein, Andrew's mother," she said. "The boy your son beat up *twice*. With all due respect, your son is an animal. First he kicked Andrew in the face and sent him to the hospital, and then he blindsided him with a blackjack. Two different beatings, two trips to the hospital, surgeries, stitches, a nightmare. I also want to mention that it was ten kids against one. Now, I'm not calling you because I want you to pay the hospital bill, because I don't. We don't need your money. I'm calling you because I want you to hold up the phone as you go in his bedroom, wake up your animal of a son, and beat the shit out of him. I want to hear him crying and yelling for you to stop. And then I want you to beat him up some more. If you ask me why you should do this, look out your window. Look right now. Parked outside you'll see a white Lincoln. Inside are three men who also want to hear the sounds of you beating up your son. If they don't hear those sounds, they'll kick down your door. You don't want that to happen. Trust me. You do not want these gentlemen inside your home. You just wanna go and beat the crap out of your son."

Mom must have taken the phone off her ear and held it up so Dad could hear as well. Even behind my bedroom door I could hear the sounds of the screaming kid. That was enough for Mom.

But it wasn't enough for me.

• • •

I had my share of fights. I kicked plenty of ass. I also got my ass kicked plenty of times. I get my head split open in a street fight? I could live with that. But getting coldcocked from behind? No way. I didn't give a crap if this kid's old man, old lady, brothers, sisters, uncles, aunts, cousins, grandparents, and *dog* took turns beating the shit out of him every night while they watched *Wheel of Fortune*. This gutless fuck hits me from behind? I didn't care what Mom arranged. I was gonna repay the favor.

I didn't really have a plan. I just felt a wave of rage. I waited nearly three weeks for the kid to recover from his father beating the hell out of him and for him to think that the incident was over. One day we had "free play" in gym class. I kept to a corner of the gym, hanging with my boys, playing badminton or some shit while the kid and his buddies shot hoops across the way. I went over to the gym teacher, Mr. Harper, and told him I had to take a squirt. I ducked into the hall, waited ten seconds until I saw Mr. Harper turn away, then snuck back into the gym and went straight for the rack that held the baseball bats. I grabbed the first one and, my neck pulsing with pure heat, headed straight for the kid, who stood at the free-throw line, his back toward me. I broke into a run and cut the distance between us to about thirty feet, the rage inside me building.

Then I sprinted.

Twenty feet away.

I heard a voice behind me: "Andrew!"

Fifteen feet.

"Andrew!"

Ten feet.

I started to swing the bat. The kid turned. He saw the fury in my face. He saw the bat. His eyes widened in sheer terror.

Wham!

Mr. Harper hit me from the side with his shoulder, locking his arms around my knees in a textbook tackle. I grunted as I went down, the bat flying out of my hands, cartwheeling and clanging on the gleaming gym floor.

"You all right?" Mr. Harper said to me.

I grunted again, the wind knocked out of me, and looked up.

The kid's entire face was dripping with fear.

"I'm okay," I said.

"I was waiting for this," Mr. Harper said. "Your mother called the school."

"She did?"

"Yeah. She knew one day you'd go after him."

I exhaled, and when I did, two thoughts escaped with my breath.

First, thank God for my mother. If she hadn't called the school, the entire course of my life could have been completely different.

Second, as that kid now knew, you don't fuck with me.

THE MAIN EVENT

DESPITE GETTING MY head split open, things weren't all bad. I actually had a couple of dates back then with cute chicks. I even went to Pips, the first comedy club in the country, right there on Emmons Avenue in Brooklyn's own Sheepshead Bay. That night was special, 'cause Rodney Dangerfield, already a legend, made a surprise appearance, causing a commotion with his "I can't get no respect" jokes. I laughed my ass off but had no idea—how could I?—that one day this guy would change my life.

As a sixteen-year-old, my life got better when I hitched up with my first girlfriend, Cheryl. She lived in Sea Gate, a gated neighborhood at the end of Coney Island.

We met at a dance on Nostrand Avenue. Cheryl's sister, Bonnie, was tight with my sister, Natalie, so we knew people in common. That helped us skip a lot of the usual awkward bullshit small talk. We soon found ourselves just talking casually and laughing easily. We danced to a couple of fast songs, and then toward the end of the night the DJ played Chicago's "Colour My World," a beautiful slow song. As soon as the instrumental part that kicked off the song started, Cheryl and I both looked away, staring in opposite directions. Then, somehow, I got the guts to lean in and ask her to dance.

We started stiffly, my hands barely touching her waist, her arms lightly on my back. As soon as Terry Kath started singing "As time goes on . . ." we looked into each other's eyes and smiled simultaneously, and I pulled her closer and Cheryl put her arms around my neck. We stayed that way, our eyes closed, our bodies swaying, hardly moving. I felt so . . . comfortable, so natural. And when Terry Kath sang "Color my world with hope of loving you . . ." we opened our eyes at the same time and we kissed.

My first real kiss.

Man.

The room blurred. Time stopped. My whole body felt warm, from my haircut to my feet. Every fiber of my being felt like it was glowing. We held the kiss for what seemed forever, and then as the song ended, we pulled our lips apart, slowly, gently, sweetly, and we both smiled.

Coney Island, the scene of our first date, should have been a romantic backdrop. It was great getting hot dogs and crinkly fries at Nathan's. It was great riding the spinning Ferris wheel. But ten minutes later, as we walked down the boardwalk, it wasn't so great watching Cheryl lean over the railing and throw her guts up into the sand. That wasn't the only stumbling block. After Cheryl cleaned herself up and we were back on our way, holding hands and enjoying the ocean breeze, I saw this big kid coming toward us. His hand was wrapped in a bloody towel and he was holding a knife. He stopped us cold and told me to give him a half a dollar. What should I do?

I figured I could probably kick the knife out of his hand and take the prick down. I wasn't afraid of him or his knife. But I knew Brooklyn. I knew Coney. I heard the rumblings of his friends under the boardwalk right beneath us. There were probably six or seven of 'em waiting to attack. I wanted to keep those guys happy, so I said, "A half buck's not enough. How about five bucks?" That disarmed him. After taking the money he went away, and I walked Cheryl to her house in Sea Gate. Fortunately her parents and her brother weren't home, so we got in about fifteen minutes of heavy petting.

It never went further than my sweaty hands up her shirt. Cheryl was sweet and I was sweet and neither one of us was ready to do the deed. During our months of courtship, in fact, my main memory doesn't have to do with sex. It has to do with Frank Sinatra.

My parents had tickets to see Sinatra in the Main Event, his big splashy concert at Madison Square Garden. I was at Cheryl's in Sea Gate when the live show came on TV. We were sitting with Cheryl's parents, along with her brother and 110-year-old grandmother. No one wanted to miss Sinatra.

I can still hear the nasal voice of Brooklyn's own Howard Cosell doing the introduction. Normally Cosell was talking about some sporting event that I didn't give a shit about. But this was different. This was Howard saying, "Tonight from the Garden, the most enduring champion of them all, Frank Sinatra, comes to the entire Western Hemisphere live with the Main Event: Frank Sinatra in concert!"

The Chairman of the Board was kicking ass. He was singing "The Lady Is a Tramp" and "You Make Me Feel So Young" and "I've Got You Under My Skin." I was doubly excited to see him because my parents were there. My parents were his biggest fans. They told me about how, in the 1950s, he was down and out until he came back with an Academy Award–winning role in *From Here to Eternity,* how he was always coming back, how he always got back in the ring and brought the action. I needed to be right up next to the action. It made no sense that I was in Sea Gate when Frank was in the Garden taking over the world. I wanted to take over the world like Frank. I wanted to command that kind of crowd, that kind of energy. I wanted to take over the Garden.

TEN BUCKS

I ALSO STILL wanted to get laid. But there I was, a horny teenager working on weekends at the Jeanery, one of the first all-denim stores in New York, with my friend Larry Katz, who spelled it out to me.

"If you wanna get laid," he said, "they gotta get paid."

"Who's *they*?" I asked.

"The hookers, schmuck. Who else? They're the only ones who's gonna give you what you want."

"How much?"

"Ten bucks."

I could afford ten bucks. I'd been saving money since I started taking odd jobs. The first one was working with my sister for Stanley Kaplan, a super-smart guy whose business on Kings Highway provided preparatory materials to students taking the SAT and other tests. My sister was a brain, so she fit right in. But being a smart aleck, I'd hand out the wrong tapes or I'd rip pages out of the student guides just to make the kids a little crazy. I didn't last long in the job.

I was better suited for work at the Jeanery, also located on Kings Highway. I wasn't a half-bad salesman, especially when it came to telling the female customers that the jeans made their ass cheeks look great. A couple of them liked my approach and let me take them to the candy store for a chocolate egg cream, but that was it. I still wasn't getting inside their panties—which was why I decided to follow Larry's advice and buy ten bucks' worth of pussy.

"Okay, Larry," I said. "Where do we go to pay for the lay?"

"Where else?" said Larry. "Times Square."

This was the 1970s Times Square of raunchy porn and peep shows. This was XXX-rated funky junky New York City at its downest and dirtiest.

Ground zero was Forty-Second Street, our destination. Larry said he knew just the spot. He led me to a run-down building. We walked up to the fourth floor and knocked on a door. The madam looked like Bela Lugosi in drag. A long cigarillo dangled from her mouth.

"Wait over there," she said.

We waited on a broken-down couch that smelled of cat piss. A scrawny white cat leapt up and landed in my lap. Not the pussy I'd been dreaming of. There were magazines on a half-collapsed coffee table. Incredibly I remember the whole fucking strange collection—*Argosy, Gun World,* and *Good Housekeeping.* Other guys—older men—were also waiting. It was like we were waiting for the dentist, except this time we were the ones who wanted to do the drilling.

I got to pick out the girl, a hot Puerto Rican with big tits and a plump ass. Before we entered her bedroom, though, she frisked me—not in a sexy way, but in a way where she expected to find a hard weapon on me. My built-in weapon couldn't even think about getting hard, not when she brought me into a tiny room the size of a closet. It was like a doctor's examining room. She put me on a bed that looked like an operating table. She then examined my dick to make sure I didn't have cooties. When she touched it, it recoiled. Rather than stand up and proudly present itself, my cock crawled back into my body cavity and went into hiding.

"Look," I said, "keep my ten bucks. I'm outta here."

And that was it. Larry and I left without saying a word to each other. In a hurry, we walked through the neon night, eager for the safety and security of our Brooklyn homes.

I silently vowed never to go to a professional again—and I never have. Then and there I decided that the sex has to be real. The woman has to really want me.

UNDERCOVER COP ON THE MOD SQUAD

AS A TEENAGER, I was an early shaver with a thick growth. I decided to grow a beard like Al Pacino in *Serpico*. I also decided to wear a dashiki, the same kind that Pacino wore in the film. I grew my hair long and bought a pair of extra-dark, extra-cool sunglasses. I became unrecognizable to the point that one teacher, whose class I'd taken the year before, summoned me over to him in the hallway.

"Who are you?" he asked.

"Security," I said in a deadpan Pacino voice. "Undercover officer investigating reports of drugs in the classroom by students and teachers. I'm afraid that everyone is a suspect."

When I told him to put his hands against the wall and spread 'em so I could frisk him, he didn't argue. He actually thanked me.

During May of that same year—1973—I gave a performance that changed my life. I was a junior at James Madison High playing in two bands—the orchestra and the dance band. At the spring concert, I had a featured spot in our closing number, "The *Mod Squad* Theme." It almost never happened.

A few months before the concert, Mr. Musiker, the band teacher, handed out our assignments. I knew the kick-ass drum solo in "The *Mod Squad* Theme" would come down to either me or my friend Larry Schwartz. We were both good drummers, but Mr. Musiker liked Larry better. He was an A student, captain of the basketball team, and an all-around good citizen. I was the class clown. I especially liked to torment Mr. Musiker. I'd make snide comments in class and get everybody laughing, or throw my drumsticks in the air and try to make them stick in the ceiling, or bang a timpani drum in the middle of a ballad. I tortured the poor guy. I guess I shouldn't have been shocked when he chose Larry to do the *"Mod Squad"* solo, but I was.

I was not only shocked, I was crushed. Larry was a fine drummer, but he played by the numbers. He didn't have my showmanship, and that's what the drum solo called for—a performance. You had to blow the audience away. I knew Larry didn't have that in him. Larry knew it, too. He tried, gave it his best shot, and then after the second or third rehearsal, he went up to Mr. Musiker after band practice and told him that I should be the one to play that drum solo, not him. What a class move. Mr. Musiker said he'd think about it, and then the next day he told me, reluctantly, that Larry had gra-ciously given up the *Mod Squad* solo and that it was now mine.

I was thrilled, but I still wanted to mess with Mr. Musiker's head. During practice, I'd flub certain sections of the song on purpose and pretend like I was lost. I made Mr. Musiker a nervous wreck. He begged me to go home and rehearse more. I did just that. I rehearsed like crazy. But the next day at school I'd pretend I was lost again. I'm sure Mr. Musiker second-guessed himself, wondering if he'd made a huge mistake by giving me the solo. I just wanted to keep everyone's expectations way down and build up the drama. No one was prepared for what I was about to do. Everyone thought I'd flub it.

But I wasn't about to flub it. I was up onstage, sitting tall and proud be-hind my drum kit. I looked out into the audience, and in addition to every kid and teacher in the school, my parents and sister were right there in the front row. The Originals were in the house. I was ready.

Time for "The *Mod Squad* Theme."

I kicked it off, the band blasted the melody, and I was deep in the pocket when it was time for my solo. That's when I went nuts. I went into a zone. I became a whole 'nother person. I turned the drumsticks into magic wands. I was a natural wonder. All my preparation paid off. All those months of care-fully studying and combining bits and pieces of Ginger Baker's Blind Faith riffs with the funk of Sly and the Family Stone's drummer, Greg Errico—man, it came together like gangbusters. And if that wasn't enough, on top of the white rock and black soul, I gave 'em a taste of Buddy Rich's *West Side Story* remake: putting on the brakes to where it sounded like I was playing in slow motion—one agonizingly slow beat after another until you think the train has come to a halt—and then the explosion! The colossal rolls! Bombs bursting everywhere! I was going crazy! It looked like I had four arms, all in motion at once. I was bringing back the beat and rocking out so hard that the train was roaring down the track at a hundred miles an hour, and every kid and teacher in my school was up and cheering and giving me a standing ovation.

"You wiseass," Mr. Musiker said afterward. "All the grief you put me through—and all the time you knew just what you were doing, didn't you?"

I just smiled.

The drumming continued. After that performance, I started playing in wedding and bar mitzvah bands. I was determined to be the next Buddy Rich, another Brooklyn boy. My dad was always supportive. He'd drive me to the gigs and drive me home. But he was always realistic.

"I know that you're great at this, Andrew, but there's only one Buddy Rich," he said.

"I'm gonna keep practicing."

"And you should. But Johnny Carson, he keeps practicing too. Johnny can play the drums. But when he has Buddy Rich on his show, Johnny doesn't even try. You understand what I'm saying, sonny boy?"

I did. I was a good showman, but no one can rival Buddy. Besides, the days when a drummer could lead a big band were long gone. Buddy was the last of that breed. For me drumming was about rock, funk, and disco. In that world there were few, if any, real solo stars. You were stuck being a sideman.

Senior year, Artie Blau took over for Mr. Musiker. He heard the energy I brought and put me out front. For the senior concert he placed me at center stage and set up the band around me. I was really feeling my oats. If I'd been good during my junior year, my senior year was off the charts.

My grades, though, were also off the charts—in the downward direction. I failed math, and it looked like I wouldn't be graduating. But then Mrs. Cohen, my math teacher, surprised me by saying, "Andrew, I was going to fail you because your grades are unacceptable. But after watching you perform at the senior concert, I can see you have a talent and a future. Everyone in this school can see that. With that in mind, I'm going to pass you and let you graduate. I'd like to recommend that you attend summer school, but what's the point? You'd never show up."

SUMMER OF LOVE

I'D JUST GRADUATED high school and didn't know what I was gonna do. My odd jobs were getting me nowhere. My drumming gigs were fine, but few and far between. I'd broken up with Cheryl from Sea Gate and was dying to know what it was like to actually fuck a female.

When I answered the phone I was surprised to hear it was Larry Schwartz, the drummer from my high school. He wasn't happy. In fact he was pissed off and yelling.

"You want a job playing drums? 'Cause I'm getting the fuck outta here."

"Of course I want a job drumming. Where are you?"

"The Delmar Hotel."

"Where's that?"

"The Catskills. It's the Borscht Belt. You know, between Grossinger's and Brown's. I'm in a trio with our old music teacher's son. I can't stand the guy."

"What's wrong with him?"

"You'll see. Look, either you want the job or you don't."

"I want it. I'm coming."

That same day I packed my bags and drove up to the Catskills.

This was when, for the first of what would be many variations, I changed my name around.

"If I'm gonna be a famous drummer," I said to Dad, "I don't think Andrew Clay Silverstein is the right name."

"You might be right," said Dad, always understanding. "After all, Louie Bellson was originally Luigi Balassoni."

"And Ringo Starr was Richard Starkey."

"How about Andrew Starr?" Dad asked.

"I don't wanna copy no one. I was thinking Clay Silvers."

"Clay Silvers sounds good."

"Clay Silvers it is."

So now Clay Silvers was walking through your typical Catskills hotel, the kind of place where, to get in, you had to have either a heart condition, a history of strokes, or major prostate problems. When people asked where it was located, the answer was on Route 52 halfway between death and disability. The average guest was ninety. The house comic didn't tell jokes; he had to scream jokes, 'cause no one in the audience could hear.

The band was led by Lee Musiker, son of our high school music teacher. Lee was only nineteen. He was a musical genius who would one day wind up working with Buddy Rich and Tony Bennett. He was a pianist and arranger who could play and write anything. I saw why Larry Schwartz hated Lee, because Lee was a perfectionist. During our first rehearsal I went off on a little drum tangent and Lee started yelling at me to follow the written charts.

"I go by feel," I said.

He stood up from behind his piano, grabbed his schlong, and said, "Feel this."

The whole band broke up laughing, me included. Lee and I became great friends that summer because we dug each other's musical talent and sense of humor. Being close in age helped too.

Next to Lee in the band was Wally Rosen, the sixty-five-year-old tenor saxophone player. There was also Lee Lawrence, a really good singer in his thirties. Lee Lawrence became a big booster of mine. In fact, I wound up calling him Uncle Lee.

"Kid," said Uncle Lee, "you have more talent in your left pinky than most drummers have in both hands."

To keep the old Jews happy, we'd play shit from the forties. To keep the sprinkling of younger couples happy, we'd play a disco version of "The Summer Knows," the theme song from the movie *Summer of '42*. And I sang a lot of the disco songs myself. Of course we were also playing "Feelings" and "Love Will Keep Us Together" and "Laughter in the Rain." Lee Musiker knew how to cover the Average White Band's "Pick Up the Pieces" and I could pick up the funky drum groove right away, but our sax man was lost. That was okay, because most of the dancers were lost.

My parents came up for a weekend that summer to hear us play. They sat in the front row and for our entire set held hands like a couple of newlyweds. At one point we went into "On a Clear Day You Can See Forever" and I took over the vocals. My father beamed, and my mother leaned her head on my dad's shoulder and started crying, dabbing her eyes with her handkerchief. She loved when I sang. She always got choked up.

After the weekend, my dad went back to the city for work, and my mother stayed on for a few more days. One morning after breakfast she said, "Let's go sit by the pool at Brown's."

Brown's was a big fancy resort next to the Delmar.

"They won't let us in," I said.

"Why not?"

"You have to be a guest. They're really strict. They check you."

"So, that's it? You're gonna give up? You're not even gonna try?"

She shook her head, rummaged through her huge beach bag, found some lipstick, applied a fresh coat, puckered her lips, gathered up her bag, stood up, and strolled toward the poolside entrance of Brown's. She oozed confidence. Trying to act nonchalant, I caught up to her as she walked right up to a beefy security guard. He looked like a no-nonsense former cop. He wore an ID badge with his name: Ralph Paulino.

"Good morning, Officer Ralph," my mother said, knocking him back with her dazzling smile. "It's going to be a hot one today. Too bad you can't get out of that sweaty uniform and into a bathing suit."

"I wish," Ralph said, laughing, his face turning sunburn red.

"Well," my mother said, "stay cool."

We started to walk past him.

"I'm sorry," he said. "What was your name?"

She whirled back on him. "Oh, Officer Ralph, shame on you. I'm Mrs. Silverstein. We went through this yesterday. You forgot me already?"

"Oh, no, not at all, I apologize," Ralph said.

In a blink, Mom and I were set up ringside at the pool, wearing sunglasses, slathered in sunscreen, soaking up rays and sipping drinks with tiny umbrellas, lazing in our lounge chairs.

"I can't believe we got past Officer Ralph," I said.

"Sometimes you just do things first and ask questions later," my mother said.

I took those words in.

I would live by them.

FINALLY!

THIS IS THE summer when I met Laurie, the daughter of the Delmar's house singer. The house singer happened to be in love with the Delmar's house comic. But the Delmar's owner, Max Jacobs, was also in love with the singer. Turned out that the singer was fucking both guys—the comic 'cause he made her laugh and the owner 'cause he gave her money. Meanwhile, I sneaked off with Laurie for what would be the sweetest gift a woman can give a man.

At that point I was starting to seriously doubt whether I would ever have sex with something that wasn't fur-lined and 60 percent cotton, 40 percent polyester, never mind with a real girl and someone as sexy as Laurie. She had long blond hair, a killer body, and heart-shaped, succulent lips. I had become a major make-out artist, and while I was far from Casanova—hell, I was still a freaking virgin—girls always told me I was a terrific kisser. Great. So I could hit a solid single. I wanted to round the bases and slide into home.

So, a couple of weeks into the summer, Laurie and I were lying on my bed in my little room in the back of the hotel, as usual making out like crazy. But that night the kissing seemed hotter and the petting went further. I put my hand under her shirt, and this time she didn't stop me. In fact, she unhooked her bra. And then she started to gently take over. Our kissing became slower, more intense and even hotter, and then with gorgeous, generous, luscious Laurie guiding me each incredible step of the way, I suddenly felt as if I'd fallen completely inside her, but not just her body, her entire being. I felt spirited away, lost, like I was on some kind of drug trip. Then I felt locked inside her, literally, and I exploded. I saw stars. Planets. Constellations. It was like my head blew off. I don't know how long I was gone, probably seconds, but then I opened my eyes and saw that her eyes were open, too, and we started laughing, like two happy drunks. I knew it wasn't her first time, but I didn't care. I felt grateful. Laurie was kind and gentle and special. I'm not sure, but I think I whispered, "Wow," and then, "Thank you."

Laurie had a beautiful free spirit. It didn't feel like we were using each other— just enjoying each other. Whether fooling around in the pool, walking in the woods at night, or hanging out in my room or hers, we loved the touching and the friendly feeling, but mostly we loved the fucking.

Between playing with Lee Musiker on the bandstand and playing with Laurie in bed, it was the best time ever. It got even better when Larry Winocor, my friend from Brooklyn, came up to visit. Just as a goof, he brought me a big gas-charged BB gun complete with a shoulder holster. I put it on and paraded around the pool. Max Jacobs, the owner, yelled that I was scaring the eighty-year-old swimmers. But I kept parading anyway.

I wasn't exclusive to Laurie that summer. Lee Musiker set us up with older girls, telling them we were twenty-one. One date didn't go so smoothly. Driving down the highway, he had to swerve the car to avoid a deer. We all got bruised and wound up at the ER, where—here came another embarrassment—in answering the doctor's question about my age, I had to admit, "I'm seventeen."

Before the summer was over, my sister, Natalie, checked into the nearby Raleigh Hotel, where she watched me do a belly flop off the high diving board.

I heard some of the Catskill comics that summer—notably one guy named Sal Richards, who somehow got an audience to give him a standing ovation with one good joke. The guy was a great showman, and I was happy to run into him years later in L.A., but I can't say he influenced me. I can't say any comic really influenced me back then, 'cause I was thinking in terms of music, not comedy. And even when I did start fooling with comedy, it wasn't other comics that I modeled myself on; it was rock-and-rollers like Elvis.

WELCOME BACK TO BROOKLYN

BACK IN BROOKLYN, I started college on a Monday and ended it on a Friday. But I held on to my odd jobs—working at clothing stores, playing in dance bands. In the coming months I'd fall in love—along with the rest of America—with Gabe Kotter, Arnold Horshack, Juan the Puerto Rican Jew, and, of course, Vinnie Barbarino in *Welcome Back, Kotter.* John Travolta as Vinnie took over the show. He had the charisma. He had the happy-go-lucky attitude. He had the confidence. He had the look. And he had the voice. Early on I saw that I could imitate that voice perfectly. With *Saturday Night Fever* and *Grease,* Travolta would soon become the biggest star in the country. Along with Stallone's Rocky, Travolta's characters would inspire me to do things I never thought possible.

But first there was a wrong number.

It was a girl looking for someone who wasn't me.

"But who are *you*?" she asked.

"Andrew."

"Tell me about yourself, darling."

A wrong number—and she was calling me "darling." This was interesting. I told her about myself. She was interested.

"How old are you?" she asked in a sultry, sexy voice.

"Just turned eighteen. How about you?"

"Seventeen. You have something against young girls, darling?"

"No."

"Then can I see you Saturday night?"

"Yes."

Come Saturday, I liked what I saw. Her name was Dolores. She was short, stacked, a little thick in the middle, but sexy as hell. Her sexiness—and eagerness to fuck—blinded me to her true nature. She was the ultimate Jewish American princess, a girl from Georgetown—a Brooklyn neighborhood bordering Mill Basin and Canarsie—who'd been spoiled by a doting mother and father. She was a ballbreaker, but because my balls were soon slamming against her beefy thighs, I overlooked that fact. Our first fuck happened right there at 3202 Nostrand, apartment 4A, on my parents' bed. *Her* parents took such a liking to me that her dad got me a job at Seidman's, a clothing store on Canal Street in Manhattan, where I worked for a small commission.

Seidman's was managed by two characters—Bill Trotsky and Marcel Goldfarb. They bought suits for $20 and sold them for $500, calling them three-piece vested Swedish knits. The suits we sold were made a little better than papier-mâché. One time a guy brought back a suit I sold him because the sleeves had fallen off.

"On purpose," I said, repeating the line that had been given to me by Marcel, a wisecracking Brooklyn street tough. "The sleeves come off for summer to give you better ventilation."

In winter we'd sell buckskin jackets with fake fur. I'd explain that the fur was actually carpeting. "These are Allen Carpet coats," I'd say. "You don't get any warmer than that."

I took whatever little money I made at Seidman's and went on dates with Dolores, who loved shopping as much as fucking. I was so crazy about her body, I put up with her crazy jealous mind. If we were walking around Kings Plaza mall and I just happened to glance at another girl, she'd go nuts. On the other hand, she never hesitated to tell me how much she loved looking over those Italian boys in their tight jeans. "They're just my type," she loved to say.

One snowy Brooklyn night Dolores accompanied me to an audition for Sy Kogan, another orchestra leader big in the wedding/bar mitzvah party circuit. He liked what he heard and said he'd use me in one of his bands. I couldn't have been happier, but Dolores couldn't have been more miserable.

With snowflakes coming down like feathers, we were walking by the park on Flatlands Avenue when I asked her what was wrong.

"The girls," she said. "When you play those weddings, the girls will be all over you. They'll see you up there on the bandstand—a handsome guy beating the drums—and they'll come after you."

"You don't gotta worry about that," I said. "You can come to the weddings with me. You can come to every gig and be my date."

"I'll be bored."

"No, you won't. You'll be looking at me. And I'll be playing just for you."

I thought my words had calmed her down, but when we got into the car and were driving across Ralph Avenue, she started up all over again.

"Enough with this stupid goddamn jealousy!" I said.

Next thing I knew, Dolores opened the door to the car and tried to jump out. Because of the snow, I wasn't going that fast, but I grabbed her and stopped her anyway. I knew it was all part of her princess high drama, but it got me upset. No one wants to see his girlfriend jump out of a fuckin' car.

Our first breakup didn't happen over jealousy, though; it happened over money. Dolores insisted that for New Year's Eve I take her to some fancy Manhattan nightclub for dinner and dancing that would cost over three hundred dollars. I just wanted to go to the local disco in downtown Brooklyn, where admission was five bucks. But Dolores wanted what Dolores wanted, and when I refused she threw a fuckin' fit. Far as I was concerned, we were through.

"She's driving me crazy," I told my man Marcel that Saturday at Seidman's.

"She's driving you crazy," said Marcel, "because you're crazy about her."

Marcel was right. "It's gonna be a lonely New Year's Eve without her," I had to admit.

"You see how we always got replacement inventory here at Seidman's? When one line of suit doesn't sell, we bring out another. It's the same with broads. I can't believe a good-looking guy like you doesn't have replacement inventory."

"Well, there's Lorraine."

"Who's Lorraine?"

"I met her at a disco. She even gave me a number. Only one problem."

"What's that?"

"She's eight years older than me—she's twenty-six—plus she's divorced and she has a baby."

"She doesn't sound like a problem, Andrew. She sounds like a party."

I followed Marcel's advice and asked her out that same New Year's Eve. I turned it into a triple date.

By then the long-standing members of what I affectionately called the Nostrand Avenue Schmucks—Larry, Jan, and Neil, famous for hiding behind his long dark hair—had been my closest friends for years. Jan and Neil didn't have New Year's dates, and I asked Lorraine if she could fix them up. She did. Neil's date was a looker. But we wound up calling Jan's date the Man because she looked more like a he than a she. I'm not sure how the evening wound up for Neil and Jan, but I had a happy New Year's fucking Lorraine on the floor next to the crib where her baby was fast asleep.

SALAMI

BY THE SUMMER of 1976, I was back in the Catskills and back with Dolores. It wasn't as much fun as the previous summer with Laurie. Lee Musiker was no longer at Delmar's, and Dolores was always trouble. First she licked my balls, then she broke my balls.

One night after we'd fucked I was still breathing heavy when she said, "I got something to confess, Andrew."

"What?"

"When we were broken up, I went out with someone else."

"No big surprise," I said.

"Except he really had a big surprise."

"What are you talking about?"

"He was Italian. And he was big. Really big."

I didn't need to know how big, but Dolores took her hands and showed me just how big.

"I can't help it," she had to add. "I like it big."

I was a confident young man. I knew how to please a woman—or at least I thought I knew. But when a woman starts talking about abnormally big cocks, a normal man can feel insecure. I was haunted by what Dolores had said—that for months she'd been getting plugged by some salami-sized Italian, and loving it.

After an afternoon of arguing, she and I took a ride down Loch Sheldrake Road to cool off. It was all sweet until she started up again. She was so upset that she was gonna throw herself out of the car. Only this time when she opened the door, I didn't try to stop her.

"You don't have to throw yourself out," I said. " 'Cause I'm gonna push you out."

I took my feet and did just that. Like a basketball, she went rolling down the hill toward the lake. I drove a quarter mile up the road, parked the car, sat on the hood, and smoked a Marlboro 100 while I waited for her to climb the hill. It didn't take long. There she came, trudging up the hill, cursing my name while waving her fist in the air.

Good times, my friends, good times.

Somehow we survived the summer. Hot sex can get couples through all kinds of shit. But hot sex can't make the big issues go away.

That fall we were back in Brooklyn driving around Flatbush when she saw this young Italian stud walking out of a corner candy store.

"Imagine the package he's carrying around," she said.

"I got no interest in imagining that. But if you do, I don't wanna hear about it."

"Oh, men can have fantasies but women can't. Is that it?"

"I told you this before and I'm telling you again—keep your fuckin' fantasies to yourself."

"If that's how you feel, why are you going out with me?"

"If it wasn't for the sex, I probably wouldn't."

"What sex?" she said. "You've never even made me come. Not once."

"You're just saying that to be mean."

"I'm saying it 'cause it's true. You don't know how to satisfy a woman. You don't know what gets us excited; you don't even know how to kiss. You don't know the first thing about foreplay. You just grab for it. I bet anything you've never made *any* woman come. And you sure as hell didn't make me."

By then, I was parked in front of her apartment building. She got out of the car and slammed the door behind her, and I figured this was it. I'd said it before, but this time I meant it. I was through. Except I wasn't.

I kept going back because . . . well, who the fuck knows? Was I in love? Maybe. Was I in lust? No doubt. Was I young and stupid? For sure.

One night I was feeling so many fuckin' feelings for Dolores that, up in her apartment, I asked her to marry me. She said yes. But then she started describing the kind of engagement ring I had to get her. She wanted a big diamond. I couldn't even afford a little diamond. The more she demanded, the angrier I got. Ten minutes after the engagement was on, the engagement was off. Then I was running outta there, and she wrapped her arms around me, trying to stop me from leaving.

"Get your daughter off me!" I yelled at her father, who couldn't get her to budge.

Everyone calmed down. Her father went back to watching TV, and her mother returned to reading her book. Dolores changed into her robe and walked me out into the hallway. She opened her robe so I could see she was naked underneath.

From inside the house I hear heard her mother saying, "How long are you gonna tell him good-bye, Dolores?"

But Dolores wasn't interested in answering her mom. She was interested in letting me finger her dripping vagina. She wanted it right there and then.

Who was I to argue? I fucked her pussy inside and out. When I finally left, she had a belly full of sticky paste.

Time went by. We dated, we fought, we fucked, we broke up, we made up, and it all started over again.

In the meantime, I switched from selling at Seidman's on Canal Street to another clothing store on Church Avenue in a rough black neighborhood in Brooklyn. Since I got along good with the brothers, I had no problems.

"Andrew," the manager said to me one Saturday afternoon. "You got a call."

It was Dolores. She had two words for me: "I'm pregnant."

I didn't say anything. I just stayed in shock. That night I called her from my parents' bedroom phone. She told me that her mother knew but her father didn't. What did I wanna do?

What could I do? Nice Jewish boys are raised to marry the women they get pregnant. But this nice Jewish boy wasn't even making $200 a week. The last thing he needed was a child and a wife who could put him in a mental institution.

"Lemme just think about this," I told Dolores before hanging up.

When I walked into the living room, my mother was sitting there. She took a puff of her cigarette, exhaled slowly, and looked into my eyes. No one could read me like my mother.

"She's pregnant, isn't she?"

"How do you know?"

"Your face. I see it in your face."

"What am I going to do?"

For five or six seconds, Mom didn't answer. Then she asked only one question.

"What's her phone number?"

"Why—you gonna call?"

"Just give me the number. When I call, don't say a word. Leave this to me."

I gave the number, and Mom dialed. When Dolores's mother answered, Jackie Silverstein took charge.

"I'm calling because of the situation with your daughter and my son," she said. I couldn't hear what Dolores's mom was saying, but I could guess from my mother's response. "Oh, please. You have to know what your daughter was doing up there in the Catskills with my son. It takes two to tango. You're not gonna blame all this on my son. If you think your daughter's gonna wreck my Andrew's life, you got another think coming, lady."

By the time the conversation concluded, Jackie Silverstein had prevailed. She hung up and told me, "Tomorrow morning you're going to pick up Dolores and her mother and go to the hospital. You'll wait there until it's over."

I always listened to my mother.

Next day I took Dolores and her mom to the hospital. Hardly anyone said a word. While Dolores went off to the operating room to have the abortion, I was sitting next to her mother. I was feeling like shit.

After fifteen minutes of silence, she turned to me and said, "Don't ever hurt my daughter again."

"I won't," I said.

Ninety minutes later, Dolores appeared. I couldn't believe the way she looked. She'd changed into a sexy dress and put on major makeup. She was ready to go out dancing.

Outside it was freezing cold. Snow had started to fall. I slowly drove mother and daughter back to their apartment building. When we arrived, the mother got out first, leaving me and Dolores alone.

"Wanna come up for a hot chocolate?" asked Dolores, as if nothing had happened.

"Get out of my car," I said.

"Why are you so touchy?" she asked.

"Just get out."

When I got home, I told my mother everything that happened and everything that Dolores had said.

"It's over," I said.

"No it's not," said Mom.

"What are you talking about?"

"She'll come back after you. I know the type. She'll keep coming after you until you do one thing."

"What's that, Mom?"

"Wait a few days. Then call her and tell her you've been seeing a psychiatrist. Tell her the psychiatrist is worried that you might get violent with her. Tell her that, and you'll never hear from her again."

I listened to my mother. I told Dolores, and never heard from her again.

I'M JOEY TRAVOLTA

REMEMBER HOW TRAVOLTA as Tony Manero prunes and grooms himself before heading for the disco in *Saturday Night Fever*? That was me the night I went with my sister and one of her friends to Studio 54. I stood before the mirror, blowing out my hair, then working on the waves until every strand was in perfect fuckin' place. I put on my tight blue polyester shirt, tight blue polyester pants, and black pointy Italian boots and headed out into the night. I was Tony Manero.

Studio 54 was the place where everyone from Diana Ross to Liza Minnelli to Andy Warhol to Michael Jackson to Mick Jagger to Donna Summer to Sly Stallone and Susan Anton was boogying and bumpin' their butt off. I wanted to be inside the ropes of the midtown Manhattan disco where the all the beautiful people came to be seen and get high on coke. Though the booze and coke didn't interest me. Now and then I might smoke a little joint up in my bedroom and go off on a jerk-a-thon, but that was it.

When we arrived at Studio 54 I went up to the muscleman doorman and, in my best Vinnie Barbarino voice, said, "I'm here."

"So what?"

"It's me. Let me the fuck in."

"Who's you?"

"Are you fuckin' kidding me? It's me. Travolta."

The muscleman snickered. "Nice try, kid. The real Travolta walked in an hour ago. Now get lost."

In her usual sweet manner, my sister said, "One day soon my brother's gonna be a big star. Can't you just let him in for a while?"

"Not a chance in hell."

Did that take me down a notch? Sure it did. But did it ruin my evening? Hell no. Me, my sister, and her friend headed back to Brooklyn. What would Vinnie do at a time like this? He'd go to the neighborhood pizza joint for a hot slice.

Sitting in a booth, I was still in my Travolta head, doing a Vinnie Barbarino monologue about how much I was loving the cheese pizza, when two chicks sitting at the next booth overheard me.

"You sound just like John Travolta," said one.

"You look just like him," said the other.

"I'm not John, I'm Joey, his brother."

"You're kidding," they said.

"No, I ain't. I'm his kid brother. Matter of fact, I was just over there at Studio 54. We was over there with all the stars until I got a little bored."

So I carried on the conversation, and before long the two girls were over at our booth. Natalie, who is extra-cool, saw that I might be getting some action, so she and her friend left me to the women.

As I carried on with my routine, the girls were hanging on my every word. I was telling them how I'd just come from Hollywood, where I was racing cars with Paul Newman and hanging out with Olivia Newton-John. I was so deep into character I was believing this shit myself.

Turned out that one of the girls—a redheaded Irish beauty—lived only a couple of blocks away from 3202 Nostrand. She invited me over to her finished basement for a couple of beers. When we got to her place, she handed me a black Magic Marker and asked me to sign the wall. In giant letters I wrote, JOEY TRAVOLTA WAS HERE.

The two of us were laughing so loud we woke up the mother, who opened the door at the top of the stairs and shouted down, "What's going on down there?"

"Nothing, Mom," said the Irish girl.

The mother walked down a couple of steps and looked at the wall.

"Who the fuck wrote on my wall?" she screamed as she spotted me standing next to her daughter. "And who the fuck is he?"

"It's Joey Travolta, John's brother."

"I don't give a shit who you are," she said. "Get the fuck outta my house."

I ran out. But the next day I was back. The mother was gone, and the daughter was happy to see me. Now sober, she didn't care that I was only Andrew and not John. We went for a walk and ended up in the stairwell in my building, where she gave me a masterful blow job. Later that same week, when I fucked her in my parents' bed, she might have been fantasizing that I was Travolta. But I didn't care, 'cause I had fantasies of my own. When it comes to sex, I never run out of fantasies.

THE ACT

WHEN *GREASE* CAME out in the summer of 1978, I ran to see it with my pal Neil at the Oceana movie theater in Brighton Beach. I loved every scene.

Driving home, I had a vision.

"I got it!" I yelled.

"Got what?" asked Neil.

"Something I can actually perform."

"What are you talking about, Andrew?"

"You know how I can do Jerry Lewis in *The Nutty Professor*? You know how I can imitate him as a nerd before he turns into the lizard lounge singer Buddy Love?"

"You do him perfectly."

"Well, what happens if after drinking the magic potion, the professor doesn't turn into Buddy Love but into John Travolta? But I gotta do more than that. I can't just talk like him and look like him. I gotta sing like him and dance like him."

Practice became my obsession. I became a man on a mission, a man who finally saw his future staring him in the face. If this act worked, the world was mine. But first I had to find a way to get it down so good that everyone would have to love it. I needed a place to practice.

I booked rehearsal time at the Fly Studios, Brooklyn's finest, on Kings Highway, run by two recording nerds named Skinny Neal and Four-Eyes Bob.

"You got a band?" asked Bob.

"No."

"Then why do you need a studio?" asked Neal.

"You'll see. One day you'll be putting up a historical marker that says, 'It all started here.' "

Before my first day at the studio, though, I went back to see *Grease*, this time taking careful notes. I decided that the scene I wanted to do was Travolta's sexiest moment—when he breaks into "Greased Lightning." I had to figure out names and descriptions for all Travolta's dance moves—the windmill, the finger point, the bump and grind. In those ancient days before YouTube, I had to sit through three showings of the film to get all my markings straight.

If I did the act right, every girl in the audience would feel like Travolta was her date. That meant I had to look just like him. Before that, though, I had to look like Jerry as the nutty prof.

So I ran over to Kings Plaza and found the biggest ruffled shirt in the tuxedo store. The thing came down to my knees. Then I was off to JC Penney, where I bought a fake leather jacket that was really made out of vinyl for twenty bucks. I already had the polyester pants that I had been wearing to the discos.

With my props in hand, I locked myself in a room at the studio, where no one—not even Skinny Neal or his partner, Bob—could see me. I had my boom box with the music, I had my costumes, I had my hair grease, I had everything I needed.

After spending two long weeks in my rehearsal cave, I was ready to give a limited audience a taste of my genius. I decided to start out with the Fly boys. Having watched me disappear into their back room for countless hours on end, Skinny Neal and Four-Eyes Bob were dying of curiosity. I invited them, along with Natalie and her friend Nancy, to watch my act in the band room of the Fly Studios. They were all behind the glass in the control room. Neal and Bob were gonna work the music.

I came out onto the studio floor dressed as the nutty prof, my hair pushed forward, those little glasses on the tip of my nose, the giant tuxedo shirt hanging off me down to my bare knees. My pants were rolled up so all you could see were black boots. Natalie and the guys were laughing even before I opened my mouth.

"Actually I'm a human pity," I said in my perfectly attuned Jerry Lewis super-nerd voice. "In this glass I've concocted a magic formula that can turn me into the kind of man I want to be."

I took a sip and started to shudder. I cued Neal and Bob to shut off the lights, and in the dark I threw off my shirt, rolled down my pants, slicked my hair back in DA style with the big curl in front, and threw on my vinyl jacket. As the lights came up and the music kicked in, I picked up the collar on my jacket and turned to face my audience like Danny Zuko turned to face his buddies in the "Greased Lightning" dance sequence.

I gave that famous Travolta-ish laugh and said, "So you thought it couldn't be done, huh?"

I looked up and saw that Skinny Neal and Four-Eyes Bob had invited some girls into the control booth. I couldn't hear them, but I saw they were laughing. Natalie and Nancy were all smiles. Everyone was digging me.

As Travolta, I said, "Let me tell ya what happened that day in the garage." I paused, nodded for the music to start up, and, right on time, broke into it:

"This car could be systematic, hydromatic, ultramatic. Why, it could be . . . greased lightning!"

I did the singing, I did the dancing, I did the moves, I did the leaping and loving, I did everything perfectly. I was not imitating Travolta. I *was* Travolta, just the way Travolta wasn't imitating Elvis. He *was* Elvis, Elvis as born-again Jersey-born Travolta, who was born again as Brooklyn-born Andrew Clay, my new name and new lease on life.

"What do you think, Natalie?" I asked my sister.

"I think it's terrific, Andrew. I really do. I think you're about to turn your dream into a reality."

Hers was an opinion I took seriously. Natalie was a serious person. She also knew comedy. She'd been to all the edgy clubs in New York, like the Improv and Catch A Rising Star. She knew what was lame and what was hip, what was fake and what was real.

"You have real talent," she said. "Wait till Mom and Dad see what you've put together," she added.

"I don't want them to see it. Not yet."

"Why not? You can do it for them tonight in the living room."

"I've been doing shtick in the living room since I was a little kid," I said. "I don't want them to see it in the living room. I want them to see me perform it in a club."

PIPS
SEPTEMBER 13, 1978

LEAVE IT TO me to pick the toughest comedy room in the country. But what choice did I have? It was the one nearest to where I lived. Pips held no more than a hundred. If the customers didn't think you were funny, they'd drown you out by screaming, "Get the fuck off the stage before we fuckin' throw you off!" It was the place where comics like David Brenner and Rodney Dangerfield blew up. In fact, it was George Schultz, Pips's owner, who gave Rodney his signature line, "I don't get no respect."

Two weeks before I got up onstage at Pips I went to check out the comedy clubs in Manhattan. I'd arrive at nine P.M. and not leave till three in the morning. I would just sit there, watching comic after comic. Most were awful, some were great. And then there was Joe Piscopo from *Saturday Night Live,* who impressed the hell out of me. But nobody had an act nearly as impressive as the one I was preparing to unleash on an audience.

Because I'd be appearing at Pips on a Wednesday Amateur Night, I went there the week before with my friend Neil to see what the other amateurs looked like. A couple had a few funny lines, but mostly they were lame.

Every day leading up to the big night I was rehearsing and honing the act to a fine point. I was training like Rocky. Pumped up, I was about to get in the ring and do some serious damage.

On September 13, I arrived at Pips early to make sure there were reserved seats for my family. Then I stood on line to get one of the audition numbers given out by Seth Schultz. He and his brother Marty, both sons of George, were now running the place.

Seth looked at me and said, "Hey, you look a little like Travolta. What's your act?"

"It can't miss," is all I said.

I went into the kitchen, where I changed into my nutty prof outfit and waited my turn while the cook grilled burgers and fried fries. I listened to the other comics who went on ahead of me. None of them were funny. It was a tough audience, and no one was laughing. I could feel the crowd's impatience. The crowd wanted something good.

Seth wandered into the kitchen and jumped back the second he saw me in my costume.

"Who the hell are you?"

"The guy you said looked like Travolta."

"So why in hell did you put on this getup?"

"You'll see. Just make sure you don't mess up my music cues."

When I walked to the stage, my heart was beating fast. I could see my entire extended family sitting at four tables close to the stage. I started in with my Jerry Lewis nasal-voice thing. The crowd wasn't impressed. They started heckling and booing. I could see that my parents were puzzled. They had been watching me do this bit for the past ten years. It was not so special. It was old hat. As I rattled on, the crowd was getting angrier, and I could feel my family freaking. I was making a fool of myself. But that was the point. I needed to establish the fool. The nutty prof was the fool. I welcomed these boos, because booing the nerd was part of the setup. It was the fuckin' foreplay. I was ready to stick it in.

After going through the bit about drinking the magic potion, the music came up—the Trammps' "Disco Inferno" from *Saturday Night Fever*—the room went dark, and a taped announcement said, "Ladies and gentlemen, I'd like to introduce you to someone new, someone exciting, someone guaranteed to blow your mind—Andrew Clay!"

The lights came up and there I was, posed as Danny Zuko in *Grease*. I was combing my hair back just like Travolta did in the movie. I stuck a cigarette in my mouth, pushed up my collar, gave that little Travolta chuckle, and said, "And you thought it couldn't be done."

I went into some Vinnie Barbarino patter, then *boom!* I broke out into "Greased Lightning," and the place went fuckin' nuts. The joint exploded. They were shouting and hollering. They were turning over tables. They loved me so much they didn't know what to do. I saw my parents beaming. I saw Grandma Shirley cheering me on. Natalie had tears running down her cheeks. It was absolute bedlam. As I finally finished the number, I fell to one knee, and with my right arm outstretched, I embraced the crowd, taking in the love. The standing ovation went on for five full fuckin' minutes.

On the way out, Seth Schultz and his brother Marty grabbed me.

"Where else are you performing?" Seth asked.

The answer was *nowhere,* but I was too excited to say a word.

"We wanna book you for the weekend," said Marty. "We want you to headline."

"Well, I really don't have that much material," I said. "All I got is what you saw tonight."

"That's enough," said Seth. "So, it's fifty bucks . . . for the whole weekend."

I didn't hesitate. "I don't care how much it is. I just wanna get back up on that stage."

After that first performance, women came up to me, willing women eager to go off with me right then and there. Some were my age, some younger, some older. This was my first encounter with groupies. Naturally I was flattered. I wanted to go off with all of them. But that isn't what I did. On that night of nights I wanted to be with my family. So after the show we all went to the Sheepshead Bay Diner, where we got a big table in the back.

At first no one knew what to say. My relatives just sat there, reading the menu, ordering cheesecake and Danish and sweet noodle kugel. They were still stunned by the frenzy in the club. Before that evening, I was just Andrew, a good drummer but a guy without a future. There was always the question—*what the hell's gonna become of Andrew?* Now we had the answer.

That night I couldn't fall asleep. In my mind, I kept running one riff after another: Rocky telling Adrian that he isn't just another bum from the neighborhood, Tony Manero fighting to become more than a guy working in a paint store, Danny Zuko and his dream girl Sandy flying off in the Greased Lightning car, me taking over the world.

ROYAL PROCESS AGENCY

AS SOON AS I got my start at Pips, I realized I'd need a job that would give me time to pursue my show business career. The best gig I could think of— the one with the most understanding boss—was with my dad. He'd built up his business of serving summonses to where he could afford to hire me part-time. The office was at 16 Court Street in downtown Brooklyn, right by the big courthouse and law offices.

I wasn't the best employee. I was supposed to get up early and open the office, but that usually didn't happen. When I would finally arrive, Dad would already be there.

"Where you been, big shot?"

"I was up late," I'd say. "Went to Pips."

"That's good, just keep going up onstage, and just like with the drums, you're only going to get better."

I explained to my father how I was studying all the other comics, like Paul Reiser and Larry Miller, who for my money turned out to be one the funniest comics of his generation. (Years later he was hilarious as a salesman in *Pretty Woman* and the principal in Eddie Murphy's remake of *The Nutty Professor.*)

"Every time I go and see a new comic," I told Dad, "I learn something new."

Dad was quick to forgive me and quick to ask whether I was hungry. Always. The two of us would go downstairs to the little deli-diner in the building, where I would have my usual—a bagel with butter and bacon. A good Jewish breakfast. For the next hour, we'd discuss my career. Dad had great ideas about booking me in places other than comedy clubs, like discos.

By late morning, I'd be ready to work. I would be running around Court Street, making friends with the guy without legs who rolled around downtown Brooklyn on a board with wheels and flirting with all the secretaries.

My job was picking up summonses from different attorneys to bring back to the office. One attorney was a former city marshal, a guy in his seventies. The marshal was tall and skinny with a face like the caved-in side of a mountain, all creases and crevices. Not a pretty sight. His personality was no better than his looks. He was short-tempered and cranky. But being the charmer that I was, I had to get on his good side. When I noticed his suit, I put a hand on his shoulder and said, "Swedish knit. Very nice, very impressive."

"How do you know it's Swedish wool, kid?" he asked.

"I know my way around fine suits," I said. "I've worked in clothing stores."

"How long you been working for Silverstein?"

"I'm his son."

"Well, if you're Freddie's kid, you better tell the old man to pull his head out of his ass."

"What are you talking about?"

"He fucked up two of my summonses last week."

"My father doesn't fuck up anything."

"That's what you think. You tell your old man if he fucks up again, I'm putting him out of business."

When I heard my father being threatened, I lost it. I started yelling at the marshal, *"Who are you to threaten my dad? We don't need your fuckin' business!"*

I turned around and stormed out.

By the time I got back to 16 Court Street, the marshal had called my father to complain. Dad was furious.

"What the hell did you tell the marshal?" he asked.

"He was screaming and threatening to put you out of business. I put him in his place."

"You did, huh?" He gave me a half smile. I could tell he was annoyed but impressed that I stuck up for him. "That guy screams and threatens everyone. As long as he pays his bills, let him scream and threaten all he wants. All right. Now get back to work, sonny boy."

WELCOME TO THE FUNHOUSE

AFTER MY DEBUT at Pips, I was building a local rep and drawing big crowds. One night a couple of older women called me over to their table. When I say older, maybe they were thirty-five. I was twenty-one. I quickly got the idea that they were into me. I was certainly into them, especially the brunette wearing a blouse two sizes too small for her big tits. Her tits were barely being held back by the kind of thin bra that let me see the outline of her nipples. I had no doubt that her tits wanted to be touched. This brunette wasn't much of a talker, but the blonde, who was not as sexy and wearing too much eye shadow, was Chatty Cathy.

"We're both married," she said. "My husband, he works at the navy yard, and April's husband is a bookkeeper at a bank. He's boring. April's bored with her husband, aren't you, April?"

"Very," said April.

"But you aren't boring," the blonde said to me. "You're exciting, you're really something, the way you do those imitations and all. I think you're very talented, and I think April thinks you're very talented, and I think April wouldn't mind going to the Windjammer Motel with you. It's right down the street. Do you know the Windjammer?"

"I know the Windjammer," I said, "but I'm wondering why April wants to go to a motel with me when she's married."

"I told you," said the blonde. "Her husband's a creep. He's Jerry Lewis before Jerry drinks the formula and becomes Travolta."

"And besides," added April, "I can do things with you I can't do with my husband."

I was tempted, but I turned it down. My morals said, *Don't fuck someone else's wife.* Don't get me wrong; I'd already fucked half the secretaries on Court Street, but none of them were married. Many of them were not only sweet, but they were not shy about showing me the ins and outs of pleasing a woman. Ever since Dolores claimed I never made her come, I'd been paying strict attention to what women wanted and needed. In school, I was one of the worst students. In bed, I was one of the best.

My professional life was going as good as my sex life. Everything and everyone was coming together. My dad was both my manager and booking agent. He was terrific at it. Other comics my age were making $50 a night at little clubs, but Dad had the smarts to go to the discos. Figuring that my *Nutty Professor/Grease* act was perfect for those huge venues where everyone was dancing their asses off, he booked me into the Electric Circus and the Funhouse.

The Funhouse was really wild. When I turned into the Travolta character, the owner wanted me to share the stage with naked porn stars, including Mark "Ten Inch" Stevens. Naked girls were rubbing their twats all over me. I was digging it, but the distraction made singing difficult.

"Don't worry about singing," said the owner. "Do the whole thing in pantomime."

So for $800 a night, I did my act silently.

There were two discos in Brooklyn—one right on Nostrand and another on Ralph—where I was also making $800 a night. When I turned into Travolta, the girls got so crazy that Dad and Uncle Ernie had to pull them off me. I felt like Elvis.

Dad didn't stop at the Brooklyn discos. One time he booked me three weeks in advance into a disco on Staten Island, his old stomping grounds. The club was inside the Lincoln Motel, known to everyone as a mob-run joint. It was a two-night gig at $1,000 a night, unbelievable money for an unknown like me.

"One thing to keep in mind," said Dad. "If the guys decide not to pay you at the end of the night, don't argue."

"What do you mean don't argue?" I asked. "The whole point is to get paid."

"The whole point is to build your reputation. These are guys you do not want to antagonize."

Fine. I listened to Dad.

Before the gig came up, I was also trying to listen to Mom. It was a Sunday, and she and I were at the pool at the Golden Gate Motor Inn on Shore Parkway. The Golden Gate had been a big part of the Silverstein family for years. It was not exactly the French Riviera, but for Brooklyn, it was nice. There was a restaurant too where we had a thousand family meals. For a brief time when my parents broke up—I never knew why, I never asked why, I never wanted to know why—my dad went to live at the Golden Gate. That happened when I was back in high school. After I got my act together at Pips, the Golden Gate became a regular summer hangout.

"A woman over there is staring at you," Mom said as I got out of the pool. "An older woman. She's been looking at you like you're a piece of meat."

Naturally I glanced over and saw a lady in her forties. She was wearing a one-piece black bathing suit. Long dirty-blond hair. Good complexion. A pretty, I'm-available smile that reminded me of Dyan Cannon. Strong, long legs. Perky tits. Great ass.

"Don't look so long, Andrew," my mother warned me. "She goes with tough guys."

I stopped looking but kept taking peeks 'cause I felt Dyan peeking at me.

"You're staring," said Ma.

"No, I'm not."

"Ignore her. She's poison."

"How do you know that?"

"She's too old. She's on the hunt for someone young. Leave her alone,

Andrew. Stick with your own age. You wouldn't know what to do with the aggravation."

Maybe, I thought to myself, *but I sure as hell would know what to do with the pussy.*

More than once, Dyan strolled back and forth in front of me and Mom so I could see what I was missing.

"Disgusting," Mom said under her breath.

I didn't say nothing. I was just wishing Mom wasn't there. But I wasn't gonna disrespect my mother. I left Dyan alone. Didn't say a word.

Next week I was back at work at Royal Process. It was ten A.M., Thursday morning. I had my head on the desk and I was fast asleep when Dad walked in.

"Hard at work, big shot?" he asked, waking me up. He wasn't angry, 'cause he knew as soon as he arrived I'd run out and serve whatever subpoenas he needed. But it was a slow morning without much to do. We started talking about my upcoming gig.

"This Lincoln Motel gig is going to be good," he promised. "These guys know how to promote. You'll do big business out there, and it'll help get your asking price even higher."

I was glad to hear all this, but still didn't like the prospect of not getting paid. On the other hand, it was my father, not me, who knew how to move into this territory.

While we were talking, the radio was on. In between songs I heard a commercial about "the glamorous Lincoln Motel on Staten Island."

Dad and I stopped talking and listened.

"This weekend only," said the announcer, "for one night only—John Travolta, live and in person!"

I was shocked. Dad wasn't.

"Dad," I said. "They can't do that. They can't say Travolta's gonna be there."

"They can say whatever they wanna say."

"But it ain't true."

"Doesn't matter."

"But what's the audience gonna do when they figure out Travolta ain't there?"

"You gotta make them believe Travolta *is* there."

"It's an impression—that's all it is," I said. "They're gonna sue. They're gonna riot when they see they've been duped. You gotta call the guys who run the room and tell 'em to stop the commercial."

"Not a good idea, Andrew. Not good for you, and not good for me."

With that, Dad walked away.

I worried like hell. What had my father gotten me into?

I talked to Mom, who wasn't worried at all. "They're just promoting you, that's all," she said.

"They're not promoting me, they're promoting Travolta."

"Same thing."

Worrying didn't do me any good, so I stopped. I got myself geared up to go to the gig. I rode over to Staten Island with my father. There was a line outside the door going around the corner. People were clamoring to get in. I was nervous. I'd never been pelted with rotten tomatoes. But I had no choice but to go on.

I came out as the nutty professor. As usual, I got some boos.

"Hey," screamed one guy, "where's fuckin' Travolta?"

I hurried through the Jerry Lewis bit, drank the formula, went to black, and emerged as Travolta. As soon as I started speaking as Travolta, I could see that half the people in there actually believed I was him. The other half didn't care. I didn't get one complaint. Dad was right. They loved me.

Afterward, Dad said, "Let's go to Junior's to celebrate."

Junior's is a big diner in downtown Brooklyn.

"Actually, Dad, some friends of mine came to the show, and I'm gonna hang out with them."

"Do that, sonny boy. You deserve to have a little fun. You were great tonight. And we even got paid."

I told Dad good-bye and headed to the bar. During the show I'd seen her sitting there alone. It was the Dyan Cannon lookalike. She'd been crossing and recrossing those long legs of hers all night.

"Hi," I said.

"Hi. You wanna get out of here?"

I loved how she was so direct.

I said, "The only problem is that I don't have a car."

She said, "I do."

We drove to her place in Bay Ridge, where Dyan and I went at it like a couple of porn stars. I never saw her again, but, man, we had ourselves a fuck fest.

You gotta understand: I'm a sex enthusiast. That was my turn-on, how I got high. I didn't drink or do drugs. I'd take an occasional hit off a joint because I found out that pot's a great aphrodisiac. If I was with a girl and she lit up a joint? Beautiful. Because twenty minutes later, she'd be sucking on my joint.

SYLVIA

SYLVIA WAS A blond, blue-eyed Jewish girl with a great body. My pal Neil and I had been watching her wiggle that sweet ass of hers for years all around Brooklyn. One night she was at Pips, calling me over to join her for a drink.

"Why don't you come over to our apartment and say hello to my mom and dad?" she said. "I've been telling them all about you. Everyone in the neighborhood has been talking about you."

The Cohens reminded me of the Silversteins. They loved show business. They liked to stay up late and watch TV. Her mother was in the kitchen smoking cigarettes and drinking coffee. Her dad watched Johnny Carson. Her brother did exercises on the floor. I was comfortable with them, and they were comfortable with me. We spent a nice evening together. I kissed Sylvia good-bye and we agreed to get together again real soon.

Next day I called Neil, who was living alone in an apartment on Ocean Parkway. He was still hiding behind his long hippie hair.

"Guess who invited me home to meet her parents?" I asked Neil.

"Who?"

"Sylvia Cohen."

"Wow. You gonna start dating her?"

"Maybe. She acts like she really likes me."

She did really like me. She invited me back to have dinner with her family, and I asked her out to have dinner with mine. Unlike Dolores, she was not a princess. She had a good job working behind the pharmacy counter at a drugstore on Nostrand Avenue.

On our third or fourth date Neil asked us over to his place. He had gotten some strong weed and urged us to get stoned. I turned down the joint, but Neil and Sylvia smoked and Neil passed out in his bed. The pot went straight to Sylvia's pussy. She was so hot she let me bang her on the floor in Neil's tile bathroom. It was a beautiful fuck that climaxed with my pulling out and spilling my sack syrup all over her thighs.

"You know, Andrew," she said "you're the first guy who ever pulled out."

I thought to myself, *That's an impressive statement; this is an honest broad. And so fucking romantic. Plus the pussy is fantastic.*

Mom was a little less impressed with Sylvia than I was—but then again, when it came to women, Mom was always protective of me. Mom, Dad, Sylvia, and I were at the Golden Gate Motor Inn, watching a great musical duo, Sticks and Fingers, playing in the lounge. They were friends of mine, black guys I knew from my suit-selling job on Church Avenue. When they asked me to sit in on drums, I jumped up there. While I was playing, I saw Sylvia get up from my parents' table and go to the bar, where she sat and ordered a drink.

After I played a couple of songs with Sticks and Fingers, I came back to the table. Sylvia arrived a minute or two after me. That's when Mom let her have it.

"Don't ever do that again," Mom told Sylvia.

"Don't do what, Mrs. Silverstein?" asked Sylvia.

"Don't ever get up when my son is performing. It bothers him. It distracts him. Besides, this place is filled with men looking to pick up women. If you're sitting at the bar, you're saying that you wanna be picked up. You either came here to be with Andrew or you came here to get picked up. You can't have it both ways."

Sylvia knew better than to argue, so she kept quiet.

Next day when Mom and I were alone, Mom had more to say.

"She's not a nice girl, Andrew. Be careful of this one."

I couldn't say what was on my mind—*But, Mom, the pussy is too sweet to pass up*—so I also kept quiet.

When we went to comedy clubs Sylvia downed Jack Daniel's like it was water. She could drink any six men under the table. I didn't mind, because the more she drank, the more she wanted to ball.

I thought about Mom's warning when I learned that Sylvia was doing more than working the cash register at the pharmacy. She was stealing and selling prescription drugs behind the pharmacist's back, making an extra four or five thou a week.

But the sex was so sensational I wasn't thinking straight. How could I think straight when one time at her apartment—with her parents and brother in the living room—she took me in the bedroom that she shared with her brother and said, "Stand on the bed. I'm gonna suck your dick until your knees buckle."

"There's no lock on the door, Sylvia," I said. "Anyone can walk in."

"Don't worry about it. It won't take long."

It didn't. With my pants around my ankles, with my cock in her mouth and her big beautiful blue eyes looking up at me, telling me how sweet I tasted, I blew a load that actually made my knees buckle.

The more I went with Sylvia, the more I got the idea that fucking one guy wasn't enough for her. I couldn't prove it, but I felt it.

One winter night, for instance, I asked her and Neil to go with me to Dangerfield's comedy club in the city. They both declined. This was unusual. But what the hell—I would just go alone. I was about to leave when I saw that it was starting to snow. Besides, I had this gut feeling that told me I should take a walk in the neighborhood. Following the feeling, I put on my parka and started walking over to Sylvia's building. I was hoping I was wrong, but something told me I wasn't. I'd been waiting in the stairwell by her lobby for an hour or so when I saw them walking through the front door. I waited till they got close before stepping out of the shadows and saying, "So this is how it is."

Neil started defending himself. "Nothing happened. We just smoked a little dope and talked. That's all. I swear."

"Just go home, Neil," I said. "Just get outta here."

I was about to lay into Sylvia when she said, "I gotta go upstairs. Wait here. I'll be back in a second."

She came back holding a big container of chocolate Whoppers. Still stoned, she started popping them in her mouth, one after another. She had a bad case of the munchies. As far as my catching her with Neil, she couldn't have cared less.

"Have a Whopper," is all she said.

"Fuck you," is what I said. "I'm building a career, and you got no part of it. You and me, we're through."

I walked home in the snow.

In the following weeks a big freeze set in between me and Neil. That hurt me. I'd gone out with Sylvia for months, but I'd been friends with Neil for years. Because he was shy with women, I was the one who set him up with most of his dates. Then this happened.

A month after I caught him with Sylvia, he drove by 3202 Nostrand one evening when I was leaving for Pips. Neil knew my schedule, so it was no accident he was driving by. He asked me if I wanted a lift.

"Sure," I said. It was hard to stay mad at Neil.

In the car he started asking about Sylvia.

"Andrew," he said, "did you ever have sex with her?"

I wanted to say, *Are you fuckin' kidding? All we did was have sex. Sylvia uses sex to weave a web like a fuckin' black widow. She's poison.*

But Neil was so nerdy and innocent I didn't have the heart to bust his chops. So all I said was, "I never kiss and tell."

He dropped me off at the club, and that was it. Except it wasn't. Not many nights later Sylvia showed up at Pips looking for me. Soon we were back to making out and fucking in all the hidden corners of Brooklyn. If she wanted to give up the pussy, I was not turning it down.

This went on until one night when I was up in my bedroom in apartment

4A, alone and fast asleep. I got awoken by screams from the street. I looked out and saw Neil and Sylvia standing toe-to-toe.

"If you want him," Neil was yelling, "go up there and ring his bell. Go up there and get him."

I couldn't help but enjoy the moment. Sylvia didn't come up, but she did call me a few days later, wanting to get together.

"If you ever call me again," I said, "I'll tell Neil exactly who you are."

"And who is that?"

"A scumbag," I said, and hung up.

That was finally the end of me and Sylvia, but not the end of Sylvia and Neil. He started dating her again. This time they got even more serious. Eventually they got married.

The whole thing was devastating and, for the first time, made me wanna get out of Brooklyn.

SONNY BOY IS READY

BEYOND THE MESS with Sylvia and Neil, I had other reasons to get out of Brooklyn. Career-wise, I wanted more than Brooklyn had to offer. I wanted to be written about and featured. I wanted Johnny Carson calling me up. For all Dad's expertise, he didn't have great hooks into publicity. No one I knew did. I realized I'd have to make my own contacts.

But how?

One night I was watching this talk show hosted by Joe Franklin, New York's local answer to Johnny Carson, and it came to me in a flash: *I gotta get on there with Joe.* It turned out that Joe had begun this whole TV talk show thing back in the early fifties—before Steve Allen or Jack Paar or any of 'em—but had never gone national.

Joe was only five foot three but a giant in New York show business. He always had big stars on his show. Everyone knew Joe Franklin. And soon Joe would know me. If I could get on his show, maybe someone like Stallone would be watching and put me in one of his movies.

I got the address of Franklin's office on Forty-Second Street, not far from the sleazy whorehouse that had turned me off a few years before. I was surprised that Joe wasn't located somewhere snazzier, like Park Avenue. I guess he just wanted to be close to the theater district. My idea was to go in there dressed in my nutty prof costume and introduce myself in my Jerry Lewis voice before turning into Travolta and blowing his mind.

The office wasn't anything like I'd expected. It was in a dilapidated old building. There wasn't even a receptionist. You just opened the door that said JOE FRANKLIN ENTERPRISES and walked into this room filled with metal file cabinets. It was a mess. Half the drawers were open. Papers and pictures were spilling out and piled up everywhere. The walls were covered with eight-by-ten glossies of every star you can imagine, from old-timers like Martha Raye, Sophie Tucker, and Phil Silvers to current stars like Diane Keaton, Robert De Niro, and Christopher Reeve. This was exciting stuff.

Beyond this area was a private office with the door closed. I heard men's voices. One of those voices belonged to Joe Franklin. I waited a few minutes and then knocked on the door. When a guy opened the door and looked at me in my tuxedo-shirt costume, he was startled. I got a glimpse of little Joe sitting behind his desk. Joe also looked startled. The two of them got even more startled when, with my hair pushed down over my forehead, I opened up my mouth and started talking in my nerdy Jerry voice.

"Oh, Mr. Franklin, you just gotta let me on your show, 'cause I got this magic formula I gotta tell the world about," I said as I moved toward the talk show host.

The other guy quickly moved between me and Joe. He was worried I was some pervert who'd wandered off sleazy Forty-Second Street.

"Get outta here, kid," he said.

He got even more alarmed when I turned my back and reached into my shirt. Maybe he was scared I was reaching for a gun. But before he could grab me I had already recombed my hair into the Danny Zuko style, put on my leather jacket, hit the play button on my boom box and was singing the first explosive notes of "Greased Lightning." I sang the song right in Joe's face.

Joe loved it. He knew talent when he saw it.

"So how can I help you, kid?"

"Put me on your TV show, Mr. Franklin."

"It's a little soon for that, isn't it?"

"Not really. I think it's right on time."

Joe laughed. "I like your confidence, but this is something you gotta earn. If you wanna earn it, here's what you can do. There's a place out in Queens called Fireside Lounge. On dead nights during the week different acts compete against each other. If you win the first night, you get to go to the grand finale. If you win the grand finale, you get to be the opening act for Tiny Tim. Tim's gonna headline two weekends at the Fireside. Plus you get to come on my show. How does that sound?"

"Sounds great, Mr. Franklin. Sounds like I'll be on your show in a month."

I was.

The club out in Queens held four hundred people. One of the contestants was actually Ron Jeremy, the future porn star, trying to be a comic. He wasn't too funny. Lucky for him that later on he started using his head—the one at the end of his foot-and-a-half-long dick.

Lucky for me, during the early show before the big finale I met a sexy little Broadway dancer named Bright who volunteered to help me improve my moves. She asked me up to her apartment, where she wore a half-top T-shirt and teeny-tiny red short shorts. She turned out to be a great teacher, wrapping her dancer's legs around my back as we stood on her balcony twenty-eight floors above a lit-up Times Square while I thought, *What a view*.

With Bright's help, my "Greased Lightning" was better than ever. I blew the doors off of the Fireside Lounge in Queens. I won the contest and got to open for Tiny Tim, who was a huge star, with his ukulele and his tiptoeing around the tulips and his marriage to Miss Vicki live on Johnny Carson that garnered the biggest ratings in TV history. Soon after I made my first TV appearance.

Joe Franklin was a sweetheart. He practically fell down laughing as I went through my characters, which now included killer versions of Stallone and Pacino. He predicted I'd wind up in Hollywood. He was right, but I had to go in through the back door.

THE COAST

CALIFORNIA KEPT COMING up in conversation.

Mitchell Walters, a comedian from L.A., had come back to Brooklyn to visit Pips, where he used to play. After seeing me onstage, he came over to my dad and told him that I had to get out to L.A. and meet the owner of the Comedy Store, Mitzi Shore.

"Mitzi," Mitchell told Dad, "would love your kid."

This was something I had to think about. I'd built up a reputation in the great borough of Brooklyn and conquered Pips. I'd gotten myself on TV with Joe Franklin, and everyone in the neighborhood thought I was the greatest. But that was the thing. I hadn't ever left the neighborhood. That was good, 'cause I loved the neighborhood, but that was bad, because the neighborhood might have been holding me back. The neighborhood wasn't the world. I wanted to conquer the world. When I talked to my parents, they were thinking the same way. Great minds think alike.

The tipping point came when Mitchell Walters kept calling my father from L.A., insisting that I needed to be out there. On one of those calls he mentioned Sandy Hackett, son of the great comic Buddy Hackett, who was running a comedy showcase in Tahoe. Mitchell said that Sandy was willing to put me on.

It was a gray winter day when my parents drove me to Kennedy airport. All three of us were sharing the same feelings: we were happy, we were sad, we were excited. And we all agreed on one thing: I had to go.

• • •

Tahoe was cold and snowy. Pine trees everywhere. I was all worked up and ready to kill. I was in my nutty prof getup when I first met Sandy Hackett. But since no one had told him about my act, he was confused. He saw me in the oversized tux shirt and thought I was some crazy guy off the street. He tried to kick me off the stage. In my Jerry voice, I kept saying, "No, I'm supposed to be here, I'm the guy, I'm really the guy." It wasn't until I turned into Travolta that he got it. By then "Greased Lightning" was blasting and the audience was howling, and I was the big hit of the night.

Next day I flew into Vegas, where my sister and her husband drove in from San Diego and picked me up at the airport. I couldn't believe the place. In 1979, Vegas was still wide open spaces and Sinatra and Tom Jones and Sammy Davis and Wayne Newton. I loved the boiling sun, the dry desert, the neon craziness, the action, the throngs of people who came from everywhere but mostly seemed to come from New York. To me, Vegas spoke with a New York accent. It felt like my town. I looked at Vegas as a suburb of Brooklyn.

I hit the Sahara, sat down at a slot machine, dropped in a couple of quarters, and yanked the one-armed bandit. *Ka-ching.* Lights flashed, and a flood of coins clanged into the tray. I'd won $400. What better omen? Actually, that would turn out to be the most expensive win of my life—but we'll get to gambling later. Then, I didn't have time for gambling. I had to focus on playing a showcase at the Sahara, also run by Sandy Hackett. The focus worked. My act went over. Standing ovation.

I went back to San Diego with my sister, who was telling me that in Southern California the comedy club craze was everywhere. It was through the clubs that huge comedians like Robin Williams and Jay Leno were breaking out. There was even a Comedy Store in La Jolla, a well-to-do suburb of San Diego that was run by Sandi Shore, the daughter of Mitzi, who owned the big clubs in L.A.

We drove up the coast in early afternoon. I was gazing out at the ocean and thinking this was fuckin' paradise. I saw there was an open mic that night at the La Jolla Comedy Store and I told the man at the bar I wanted to perform. He said to talk to Sandi Shore. I knocked on the door of her office.

"What do you want?" asked a voice that sounded tough as nails.

"I wanna make you laugh."

She opened the door and looked me over. I did the same. She had a nice-Jewish-girl look. Black curly hair. Big boobs. Nice ass.

"Where are you from?" she asked.

"Brooklyn."

She liked that. She said, "You can put your name on the list, but there's no guarantee you'll get on."

"I *gotta* get on."

"You *gotta*? Why do you *gotta*?"

" 'Cause I got the greatest fuckin' act in the world—that's why."

"What's it like?"

"Put me on and you'll see."

"And if it's not funny?"

"That's not even remotely possible."

I saw she liked me, and I was sure she was gonna put me on the bill. But she didn't say so.

"Come back at eight and I'll see what I can do."

I showed up at eight, went on at nine, and by nine thirty I owned La Jolla. Sandi Shore was laughing harder than anyone in the club.

After the show I whispered to Natalie, "Drive on back to San Diego. I think I'll stay out here tonight."

Natalie, who knew me as well as anyone, kissed me on the cheek and said, "I'm proud to be your sister."

Sandi saw me hanging around the club.

"What are you waiting for?" she asked.

"You."

Another laugh. A couple of drinks, and twenty minutes later I was riding shotgun in Sandi's big Riviera. She told me how she, her brother, and her mom each had their own condo on the ocean. We were going to Sandi's place, where, I'm happy to say, my life in California started off with a helluva bang.

MOTHER MITZI

BEFORE I COULD get to the Comedy Store and meet Mitzi Shore, I had to find a place to crash. My friend Jan Barrie, one of my original Nostrand Avenue boys, came through. Jan had moved to the coast a couple years earlier. Married to a nice Mexican gal, he lived in Alhambra, a town outside L.A., in a small one-bedroom apartment. He set me up on the couch.

"Hey, Andrew," said Jan's wife. "How'd you like a date?"

"I'd love a date," I said.

"Let me call my girlfriend."

I heard her telling her girlfriend how she had this good-looking guy from Brooklyn staying over. I couldn't hear the other side of the conversation, but I was getting the idea that the girlfriend might be hesitant, so I said, "Tell her I'll cook dinner for everyone."

The invitation worked. I ran out to get some London broil and baked potatoes. I fixed up a beautiful salad and cooked the meat to perfection, just like Mom had taught me.

My date was chubby, but I like chubby. She had a pretty face and long black curly hair. She liked to smile and laugh and told me I was a great cook. All-around good time. We all watched an old horror flick on TV and, feeling tired, Jan and his wife went to bed.

Not more than fifteen minutes later I had my date's ass just slammin' into me on the couch on the other side of their bedroom wall. Next thing you know we were flipped over and she was on top of me and we were sixty-nining, her big brown tits flopping on my stomach, and then she started screaming. But she wasn't your normal screamer. She screamed the play-by-play like she was Vin Scully announcing a Dodgers game: "Up the middle! Deep to right! Oh, no—you're out!"

The next morning Jan told me that he and his wife had heard the whole thing and that his wife was upset.

I was surprised. I thought his wife liked baseball.

A few days later, thanks to Mitchell Walters, who arranged it, I got invited to audition at Mitzi's Comedy Store on Sunset. When I got to the club, I introduced myself to the emcee, who told me I had to limit my set to three minutes. He gave me my time slot, and I went into the bathroom to change. While I was putting on my costume, a guy came in. He looked me over and then said, "You know, you're awfully cute."

"Sorry, pal," I said. "That's not what I do."

"Me either," he said. "I'm just messing with you. Just don't go over four minutes. They're very tight."

"I'm Andrew Clay," I said, extending my freshly washed hand.

"I'm Garry Shandling," he said. "Good luck."

I didn't need luck, but I did need more than four minutes. So I took twenty-eight. I knew it was twenty-eight because the comic who was the emcee had timed me. He came up to me afterward and said, "No one comes in this club and does a twenty-eight-minute audition."

"I just did," I said, "and I left the audience screaming for more."

"That's not the point."

"I thought that's the whole fuckin' point—to please the fuckin' audience."

"There's protocol."

"Well, it looks like I just broke it."

The next day I got a call from Steve Moore, one of Mitzi's assistants. Word about my set had spread. Mitzi wanted me to come over and sign a contract. This had to be a good thing, right? Nothing felt certain, because I still hadn't met her. I raced over to the Comedy Store, and as I parked my car I saw Henry

Mancini—the legendary composer of a million hits like "Moon River" and the theme from *The Pink Panther* and *Peter Gunn*—walking into the club to film a commercial side by side with Kirk Douglas. Fucking Spartacus! I admit it, I gawked like a tourist. I snapped out of it, got my shit together, and found Steve, who pulled out the paperwork for me to sign. It was official. Mitzi wanted me to start performing that night at the Westwood Comedy Store.

Right after I finished the Westwood gig, I got the word I was waiting for: Mitzi wanted to meet me. I was beyond excited. This was the woman who held the key to the kingdom. In the world of comedy, she was a queen bee. I hustled into my car and headed up to Sunset.

I found Mitzi in the back parking lot of the Comedy Store with a bunch of comics, her favorites, I would learn later: Argus Hamilton, Ollie Joe Prater, Alan Stephens, and Mitchell Walters. I stepped out of the car and started walking across the parking lot toward them.

"Hey, Mitzi," said Mitchell, spotting me as I came closer. "Here he is. Andrew Clay. Your new star. Have you met him?"

"No," she said. "But my daughter has."

Mitzi said it with a smile. She was a small woman in her midforties, not bad looking but not spectacular. I was taken in by her eyes, tiny lasers that stared right through you. I would learn later that Mitzi was a woman who would say whatever the fuck was on her mind—nasty or nice, it didn't matter.

"Sandi said you were a nice Jewish boy, Andrew. Is that true?"

"Of course I'm nice," I said, "but so is your daughter."

"I'm glad you two are getting along."

I could tell that she approved of our relationship, even if I myself was not interested in anything permanent.

"You interested in working down in La Jolla again?"

"Sure," I said. "But I'm more interested in working here."

"My daughter said you have movie star looks, and I agree. So I'm not going to make you a doorman. Movie stars don't work the door. There's never been a comedian who looks like a movie star. Gangsters have looked like stars. You even look a little like Bugsy Siegel. You're definitely star material."

• • •

Sandi Shore might have fallen for me in a romantic way. She was always happy when Mitzi sent me down to La Jolla to work her club. But, at least in my mind, it wasn't anything serious. On the other hand, I believe that Mitzi fell for me in a motherly way. Although Mitzi was hardly a prude—she wasn't above fucking certain comics she took a fancy to—our relationship was always above the table. I became one of Mitzi's favorites because she saw I was sincere about working my ass off to get to the top. She also saw that, unlike the other typical comics, I wasn't a schlub. I didn't wear corduroy sport jackets or khaki pants. I didn't belong to the Woody Allen tradition of the poor Jewish nerd who can't get laid. Fact is, my act—going from the nerdy prof to Travolta—was about turning that tradition on its fuckin' head. In short, Mitzi saw that I had nothing to do with the past and everything to do with the future. That got her excited. It also got her to take me under her wing. Early in our relationship she said to me, "You got the stuff—the talent and the looks—to be more than a comic. You got the stuff to be a movie star."

CRESTHILL

CRESTHILL WAS THE street, just up the hill from the Sunset Strip Comedy Club, where Mitzi owned a big Spanish-style house. Her favorite comics got to live there. Just weeks after I met Mitzi, she let me know I could live there too.

Granted, I was put in the maid's room, but I was still plenty excited. The maid's room was right off the kitchen. From floor to ceiling the maid's room was painted red, the color of the Comedy Store. The ceiling was red, the carpet, the walls, even the furniture. And not just a mild red, but fuckin' fire-engine red. I liked this. I thought it was hot. And so did the girls I took there. But before I get into sex scenes in the Red Room, let me describe the cast of characters who were also living in the house.

First there was Yakov Smirnoff. Yakov was a great guy. He might have been a little scared of me 'cause I was so Brooklyn. I'm not sure he'd encountered my kind of bold Brooklyn before. Early on, though, I put him at ease and let him know that I wanted to make friends. He was much further along in his career than me. Maybe 'cause he was Russian and had to be smart to survive in the Soviet Union, he was careful with his money and had more cash than the rest of us. His big line was "What a country!" He had jokes like "I come to New York and see a big sign, 'America loves Smirnoff.' What a country!" Or "I read want ad in paper for 'Part-Time Woman Wanted' and think, *Even transvestites work here.* What a country!" Yakov was also a good wheeler-dealer. He'd take off for a few days and fly to Germany to buy a couple of Benzes cheap. He'd sell one and with the profits keep the other.

When Mitzi found out that the comics using the phone at Cresthill had made $10,000 worth of calls, she yanked out the line. Only Yakov had enough money to put a phone in his bedroom. Yakov was shrewd and funny and knew how to charm the right people. He won over Johnny Carson, which, in those days, was like getting blessed by the Pope.

Bill Hicks and Argus Hamilton were also living at Cresthill. Because Argus was Mitzi's boyfriend, he got the big bedroom. He was a smart political satirist from Oklahoma who idolized Johnny Carson. When Johnny had him on, Argus nearly collapsed from happiness. He also nearly collapsed from partying. This was a time—the late seventies—when Cresthill was headquarters for beer drinking, wild sex, and drugs. Of all those things, I didn't give a shit about any except the sex.

Argus was also a guy who used the word "brilliant" a lot. Every comedy show was "brilliant." Every comic was "brilliant." This guy's got a "brilliant" future, and that guy's a "brilliant" writer. Mitzi also liked saying "brilliant." I figured this was Hollywood talk. In Brooklyn you'd use the word "okay." In Hollywood, "okay" wasn't good enough. You had to be "brilliant."

I'd been living at Cresthill for only a few days. I was off to myself in the Red Room and hadn't even met all the other guys sharing the house. The idea was that we all had kitchen privileges, but I was the only one who cooked. One night I was broiling a chicken. I put on all the right seasonings so it was smelling great. In walked this guy who must have weighed 350 pounds, wearing nothing but a white wifebeater and his underwear. Face covered with a beard. Big cowboy hat on his head. Talked in a super-kicked-back slurry Midwestern accent.

"How you doin'?" he asked.

"I'm all right. How 'bout you?"

"Hungry."

"Me too."

"You that guy from Brooklyn?" he asked.

"That's me."

"I hear that you're fucking Sandi Shore."

"I can't argue with that."

"I hear that's how you got in the house."

"No, I got into the house because of my talent, and I got into Sandi 'cause I'm good-looking."

"I like that. So you're looking to be a star."

"I'm looking to get done cooking this fuckin' chicken."

"You seem like a good guy. You wanna be buddies?"

"Sure. I could use a friend out here."

"And I could use some chicken. Give me some of that paprika chicken and we'll be buddies."

"I'll give you a wing."

"How about two?"

"He's only got two."

"A wing and a thigh."

"Okay, man, I'll give you a wing and thigh."

"And the breast. The breast is the best part."

"This ain't no negotiation," I said.

"Hey, we're buddies, remember?"

That night he wound up eating the better part of the chicken, but I didn't care because I really did have a new buddy: Ollie Joe Prater.

There are a lot of great comics you never heard of, and Ollie Joe is one of them. He died of a stroke about twenty years ago, still a very young man. He never led a healthy life, but he was one funny motherfucker. This was a guy who'd work the main room of the Comedy Store by coming out and tipping back his cowboy hat, taking a beer bottle, popping the top with his teeth, and spitting it out. He'd slip the bottle into a holster strapped around his fat stomach and say, "That's everything I learned in college." He called himself the Last Renegade White Man. Sometimes he'd come out and not say nothing, just yawn, wait a few minutes and then say, "I'm exhausted. I got up today at three." Then he'd break into his routine:

"They asked me to make an announcement. There's a brown Pinto out front, Alabama license plates. You ain't doing nothing illegal, but you're making the club look real shitty. Move that hunk of shit. I think anyone who owns a Pinto should be forced to go with someone who owns a Pacer."

Ollie had great flow, slow and funky. His thing was laziness, sloth, and drugs. He was a big party animal. Loved coke and booze. Chicks dug him. Strangely enough, little chicks dug him. He always got pussy and he always got laughs. He also stole everyone else's material. He got away with it 'cause the other comics were too scared to confront him. He'd beat the shit out of you, and besides, he delivered your material better than you did. I loved the guy. He actually inspired me. If I was following him, he'd come off and say, "I didn't leave nothing for you. I took it all." But when I went on before him, he'd say, "Take it all. Don't leave nothing for me." His thing was, go for broke every time you go out there. Once Ollie Joe went out there stark naked. He was so fuckin' coked up he left Cresthill wearing nothing but his cowboy hat and holster. That was a lot of blubber to behold. He didn't give a shit. He walked onstage and did his beer-opening routine like he always did. The audience howled. Mitzi had to intervene because she was scared of getting busted for having a big fat naked comic onstage.

THE STORE

THE COMEDY STORE had great history. It used to be Ciro's, once the most glamorous club on the Strip. Sinatra came to Ciro's looking for Ava Gardner. Martin and Lewis performed there. So did Sammy Davis. You had Clark Gable and Tyrone Power coming by for a nightcap and Bette Davis getting drunk at the bar. The vibes were still there.

Mitzi secured the comedy club as part of her divorce settlement. She built it up into the premier comedy spot in the country and ran it with an iron fist. She knew comedy was a contact sport. If the fans didn't fall down laughing, the comics weren't worth a shit. She'd kick your unfunny ass out in a New York minute.

The Store was really three rooms—the original one sat about 175. That was my favorite. Very stark. Just a black curtain behind you and pin spots in your face. At three A.M., when there were only twenty people in there, it was the place for perfecting new material. On a Saturday night, when it was packed, the energy was explosive. If you killed, you were high all week. If you bombed, you wanted to run in front of a bus on Sunset.

The Belly Room—named, I supposed, 'cause it's where you went for the belly laughs—was a small space upstairs with room for no more than seventy. That was used as a holding room for the customers looking to get into the main room, where, if you were lucky, you got to see Robin Williams or Richard Pryor. The main room held 450. The ultimate was to get on the lineup for the main room. Sometimes during the day I'd walk into that empty room and picture myself onstage. All of Hollywood would be in the audience. It would be the night that Johnny Carson would break his usual habit of going home after *The Tonight Show* and instead come to the Store to check out this new comic from Brooklyn.

In fact, one night the man who booked the Carson show, Jim McCawley, showed up and caught my act. I thought Johnny would love to see me go from Jerry Lewis to John Travolta. McCawley didn't agree.

"Johnny likes monologists," he said.

"Yeah, but Johnny also has guys who do impressions."

"Not your kind," said McCawley.

To this day, I'm convinced that if Johnny had seen my routine, he would have dug it. But it wasn't meant to be.

FORGET SCHOOL

AS GREAT AS that routine was, I needed something more than the nutty prof turns into *Grease*. Like everyone else out in Hollywood, I was doing what I had to do to get by. Comedy was fine, but I figured that to be the big star I was born to be, I needed to become an actor.

I knew about the acting schools—Lee Strasberg and all the rest. I read about method acting, where you gotta go back and find some bad shit that happened in your childhood and apply that to the character you're playing. It made sense, but it also seemed like something I could do on my own. Besides, I never liked school as a kid, and I had no reason to like school as a grown-up. The idea of hanging around a classroom with a bunch of wannabes was not appealing. Of course I couldn't deny that I was also a wannabe. But I was a wannabe who figured I could do it on my own without handing over my hard-earned money to some schmuck teacher with a spiel about finding the fuckin' "inner core" of a character.

At the same time, I was practical. When I met the lady casting director for *Taxi* who ran an acting class and suggested that I attend, I went to check it out. What I saw was a bunch of actors running through scenes who didn't have a clue. She started talking to them in her teaching bullshit—how to "make this choice" or "articulate that feeling"—when she should have just said, "You're talentless. Get the fuck out of my class." If this was what she called teaching, I didn't need it. I got up and split.

That same week I decided to call Bob Marcucci, a teacher/guru/manager

I did admire. Marcucci was the guy behind Fabian and Frankie Avalon. Back in Brooklyn with my family, I'd seen *The Idolmaker*, the movie about his life. When I learned he was living in L.A. I made it my business to seek him out. He lived with his son in a little house in Westwood.

"What can I do for you?" he asked.

"What you did for Fabian and Frankie Avalon."

"I don't manage anymore, but I like your chutzpah."

"Then you'll come see me at the Comedy Store?"

"Name the night."

As it turned out, the night that Marcucci came, the lady from *Taxi* also showed up. After my show, Marcucci was beside himself. "Look, kid," he said, "if I was still managing, I'd be handing you papers to sign. You got it. You really fuckin' got everything it takes."

As he was singing my praises, the *Taxi* lady came by.

"You do pretty good impressions," she said in a matter-of-fact voice.

Her backhanded compliment ticked me off. I reacted the way my mother reacted when she encountered bullshit. I got enraged.

"Is that all you see in me?" I asked. "Because if that's the case, you can't see real talent. And you should give the money back to those talentless students you're robbing blind."

I never got a job on *Taxi*.

ROLLIN' WITH DICE

THE HOLIDAYS WERE coming, and I was feeling like I needed to go back home to the family. See some friendly faces and assess my situation. The Originals hunkered down over the Christmas and Hanukkah holidays as I told them what little I had so far figured out about Hollywood.

Natalie was home too, and one night after dinner we started going through old photos. Natalie grabbed hold of the album with my bar mitzvah pictures from nine years ago. There I was, looking handsome as the devil and enjoying being the center of attention. There were all the relatives. And there were all my buddies from Hudde Junior High. Everyone was smiling. Everyone was having a great time. I spotted my pal Jimmy D. Maria, the big redheaded Irish kid. It hit me then like a bolt of lightning.

"Natalie, I got it! I got the name. *Dice*. Andrew Dice Clay."

"It is a good name," she said.

"You don't understand. Even if people forget my full name, they will remember the name Dice."

I went to bed that night in my old room, whispering to the ceiling, "Ladies and gentlemen, Caesars Palace in Las Vegas is proud to introduce the man you've been hearing about. The man you've been waiting for. The one. The only. Andrew. Dice. Clay."

When I got back to L.A. I tried out the name on the pros. Everyone liked it. With encouragement from comics like Mitchell Walters and Ollie Joe Prater,

I also moved away from the nutty prof transition bit and developed a new kind of stand-up.

The first question was an obvious one: *What is Andrew Dice Clay gonna wear?*

There was no way in the world I was gonna look like the Paul Reisers, the Jerry Seinfelds, the Garry Shandlings, and the other good Jewish boys in their neat Ivy League sports coats. That look bored me to death. Besides, that wasn't Andrew Silverstein or Clay Silvers or Andrew Clay. And it sure as shit wasn't Andrew Dice Clay.

Andrew Dice Clay—soon to be known as the Diceman—wore leather. It would all begin with a leather jacket. Marlon Brando wore leather in *The Wild Ones*. James Dean was a leather guy. Elvis was all about leather.

Before I could afford leather, though, vinyl had to do. But when I got the call to do Don Kirshner's TV show *Rock Concert,* I knew I couldn't fuck around. Everyone from Leno to Letterman to George Carlin to Steve Martin had done stand-up for Kirshner. He was a rock-and-roll legend. When I did his show and he told me, "Dice, you're a rock-and-roll comic," that meant the world to me. I threw out my vinyl jacket and called my folks for a favor: loan me the money for a real leather jacket. They did me one better. They sent me a beauty from Wilson's House of Leather in Brooklyn. It felt great to have Brooklyn on my back. I ended up hitting a home run on Kirshner, doing the longest spot in the show's history, almost thirteen minutes.

Back at the Comedy Store, I had moved into this new creation, Diceman. I had an attitude that was fresh and unique. I'd come out onstage, I'd flick open my Zippo, I'd light my cig, I'd inhale, I'd exhale, I'd inhale again, I'd exhale again, I'd stalk the stage—all the time saying nothing. Looking up at this handsome dude in a leather jacket with a greased-back ducktail hair-cut, the audience didn't know what to think. I'd smile. I'd wait a few more beats. And finally, when they were dying to know what the hell was happening, I'd say, "You know, I been up here for what? Three, four minutes? I haven't done shit. Haven't told a single joke. Just smoking this cigarette. And the reason I can do all this, the reason I can command your attention, ladies and gentlemen, is *because I'm just that fuckin' good."*

Because I'm just that fuckin' good became my mantra.

When I became the Diceman and turned myself into a balls-in-your-chin Brooklyn street comic, Mitzi was sure that I was making a mistake.

"It's not gonna work, Andrew," she said. "That character is too tough. Too hard-core."

I respected Mitzi because, when it came to stand-up, Mitzi was an old pro. But I respected my own instincts even more.

"You're wrong," I told her.

"I don't think so, Andrew, but at least you got attitude."

True. Onstage I did jokes like "I know what you're thinking. Cute comic, but he's got an attitude. So, fuck you. The second I was born, the doctor smacked me on the ass. I said, 'Doc, you got a problem?' I remember in school the teacher would say, 'Dice'—we were on a first-name basis—'Dice, what's the difference between two-eighths and three-eighths?' I said, 'Teacher, you're right, what's the fucking difference.' Ohhh! 'Now get me a cup of coffee.' "

THE RED ROOM

MY NEW DICE persona not only helped my comedy, it also helped my chick-scoring abilities. Soon after I started gaining traction at the Store, I was at a party and saw this woman I'll call the Widow Kelsey checking me out. I call her that because she was seventeen years older than me. But her body was slamming. She was wearing this sexy dress, tight on top, revealing a lot of cleavage, and flared out below, showing me her great ass. It was one of those summer dresses made of thin, nearly transparent material. You could practically make out the lines of her thong. She was unbelievably sexy without even trying.

When I saw her looking at me I saw her salivating. I saw her eating me up with her eyes. When I asked her to dance, she was all over me. I was dry-humping her to "That's the Way (I Like It)" by KC and the Sunshine Band. That was all it took. She told me that she was recently divorced, and I told her I was recently a rising star at the Comedy Store. "As long as you keep rising," she said. I assured her that I would. Next thing I knew we're heading back to the Red Room. Before anything happened in the Red Room, though, I went for my mix tapes. I gotta have music with sex and sex with music. They go together like pussy and dick. The late seventies was disco time, and I fuckin' love disco. I like all music styles, but disco really works with the hump-and-bump because the four-on-the-floor groove is a fuckin' unrelenting beat, and as a drummer I know how to keep the beat. So I was mixing "Ring My Bell" with "Shake Your Groove Thing" with "I Love the Nightlife" with "Boogie Oogie Oogie" with "Bad Girls" with "Don't Stop 'Til You Get Enough." I was turning the Red Room into a disco, and the Widow Kelsey was digging it. It wasn't long after we were dancing hot and heavy that she started slipping out of her dress. Her thong showed me that her pussy hair was the same blond color as the hair on her head. I dig blond pubes. Before we fucked, though, she said she wanted to blow me. Well, okay, honey, if you must. She insisted on doing it with me sitting catty-corner on the edge of the bed while she went to her knees. By her moves, I could tell this chick was advanced. I estimate she'd blown at least a thousand guys. And the whole time she was sucking my dick, she was staring me in the eyes. That's a turn-on. Another turn-on was that deep guttural sound she made in her throat. When I was about to blow, she stopped sucking and said, "Let it go in my mouth." This is another distinct pleasure. I exploded like a volcano.

"Any chance you can go again?" she asked me after I came. "A good chance," I said. And I did. With her knees pressed against her gorgeous standout tits, I rammed her so hard she was screaming loud enough to wake up people in Pasadena.

The Widow Kelsey was the proverbial fuck machine. She didn't want wine or roses or small talk or sweet-smelling candles. She wanted dick. She wanted to suck, fuck, and then go home. Every man's dream. Even better were the words she spoke when she left.

"What I can bring you when I come over next time?"

"A carton of Marlboro 100s and a six-pack of Dr Pepper."

So the pattern was set. Twice or three times a month the Widow Kelsey and I got it on hard and heavy. I had enough cartons of Marlboros to last me years.

One time the Widow Kelsey invited me out to her home in the Valley. This was a first. She said she wanted the thrill of my fucking her in her own bed. But when I knocked on the door, her teenage son opened it. This felt a little weird, since I was closer to his age than his mom's.

"Your mom home?" I asked.

"She's back in her bedroom."

I went back, and she was wearing this purple velvet jumpsuit zippered down the front. The crotch was so tight I could see her pussy lips.

"Hey," I said, "I don't want to be fucking you when your kid's around. That feels creepy."

"He'll be asleep in a half hour. He won't hear a thing. He sleeps like a baby."

"Still," I said, "it don't feel right."

"Feel this," she said, taking my hand and pressing it against the hard nipples of those break-your-neck tits.

That did it. We fell into our usual routine. A blow job first with her swallowing my load, followed by an 8.0-earthquake fuck. In the middle of the earthquake, I heard banging on the door. It was her kid.

"Hold it down in there!" he was screaming.

"Go to sleep!" she screamed back.

"This is awful," I said, "you're ruining the kid's life."

"You're ruining my orgasm," she told me as she grabbed my ass with both her hands and shoved me deep into her steaming-hot twat.

The Widow Kelsey would not be denied.

There was this one time that she outdid herself. Ollie Joe Prater threw a Halloween party at Cresthill. No surprise that Ollie Joe dressed up as a pirate with an eye patch, an earring, and a fake parrot on his shoulder. I didn't need no costume 'cause I was already the Diceman doing the last show at the Comedy Store in Westwood. I drove back to Hollywood and saw that the party was so big that Ollie Joe had valet parking and a security guard at the door. Not everyone could get in. I had to convince the guard that I actually lived there. The house was wild that night. People snorting up coke like it was going outta style. Weed and whiskey everywhere you looked. Ollie Joe had rounded up the hottest comedy groupies in L.A. He invited far more women than men; there were at least four wet pussies for every stiff dick. The drinking and drugging didn't interest me none, but the loose pussy was beautiful. Girls were taking me in the closet to jerk me off and coax me to fuck 'em standing up. I didn't need coaxing. This went on for hours. Had to be three in the morning when I went to my room to fall into the bed. I was almost asleep when I heard a banging at my window.

It was the Widow Kelsey dressed as Barbara Eden in *I Dream of Jeannie*, with the long ponytail, the harem pants, the bare midriff, the whole bit. I got out of bed, stark naked, and walked over to the window.

"They won't let me in the front door," she said. "Open this window."

"I can't," I said. "It's got these bars over it."

"Unlock the bars."

"They don't unlock."

"Then push your dresser in front of the window."

I pushed the dresser in front of the window and said, "Now what?"

"Stand on the dresser."

I stood on the dresser. "Now what?"

"Push your hips against the bars so I can get to you."

"You gonna blow me through the bars?"

"You ask too many goddamn questions. Just stand there."

After what I'd been through earlier that evening I wasn't sure I could even get it up. But within ten seconds the Widow Kelsey, being the pro that she was, had me up and in her fuckin' mouth.

"What if someone sees what you're doing?" I asked her. "What if someone's looking?"

"Let 'em look. That only gets me hotter."

I don't want all these stories to get you thinking that I don't have a sensitive side. I do. I'm an extremely sensitive guy. If you think about it, all the guys I admired and started imitating had sensitive sides. Starting with Brando and James Dean and going through Elvis and Travolta and Pacino and Stallone, these were macho guys with soft hearts.

But a couple of things changed when I got to L.A. First, the women were wilder than any women I'd ever known. Compared to L.A., Brooklyn chicks were very fuckin' conservative. L.A. women—especially the army of actresses on the make—were so eager to give up the pussy that even I, a lover of pussy, didn't always know how to handle it. When the pussy comes too easily, a man can miss the pursuit. The pursuit is part of the fun. Perfecting the pursuit is part of the mating game. But when you live in a city where the pussy is pursuing you, the script gets flipped.

Then here comes the Diceman, this guy I invented. I dreamed him up like Jerry Lewis dreamed up Buddy Love, but he was also me. I had to *make* him me. Dice was now part of my name, part of my mind. When I got onstage, I was Dice. And the more Dicelike I got—cocky and rude and ready to say anything to anyone—the funnier I became. When I got offstage and called Mom and Dad back on Nostrand Avenue to tell them how great I was doing, I was sonny boy. I was Andrew. But they also understood that I was becoming Dice.

So sometimes, in spite of my sensitive side, it was Dice who went out on the dates. It was Dice who liked to hang out at Ben Frank's coffee shop in Hollywood and eat at the counter, where one day I saw a woman who I was sure was Tanya Roberts from *Charlie's Angels*. She had the light blue eyes and the blond hair and the great tits. She was sitting at a booth by herself.

In Dice mode, I went over and asked her, "You that girl on TV?"

"I wanna be on TV."

"Oh, I thought you were Tanya Roberts."

"A lot of people say that," she said as she looked over my black leather jacket and snug black jeans. "You live around here?"

"I live in a house just up the street from where I work, at the Comedy Store."

"That's cool. Let's hang out over there."

Just like that she invited herself to the Red Room. When we got there, she reacted the way most chicks did.

She said, "This is a sexy bedroom."

I said, "Yeah, I know."

She said, "Well, what are you going to do now?"

In most situations, even sex situations, I'm a gentleman. I never force myself. I aim to please. But in some situations, like this situation, the Diceman, rather than Andrew, takes over. And in this situation, the Diceman was gonna play it cool. The Diceman was gonna make this Tanya Roberts lookalike beg for it. The Diceman was gonna sit on the bed and lean back against the wall and smile.

"What do you wanna do?" asked the Diceman.

"You know what I wanna do, or I wouldn't be up here," said Tanya.

"Well, I need to hear you say it."

She looked at my crotch and saw that I was up. In that area, I have nothing out of the ordinary. I have the standard equipment carried by Jewish boys from Brooklyn. I'm not packing fifteen inches, but I was showing very stiff interest. She liked that.

"I see you're ready," she said.

"But I gotta hear exactly what it is that *you're* ready for."

"You. I want you to make love to me."

"You want me to make love to you or to fuck you?"

I could see my question had gotten her hot. "I want you to fuck me," she answered honestly.

Now I wanted more honesty. "You want me to fuck you nice and gentle or you want me to fuck you like a fuckin' animal?"

"I want you to fuck me like a fuckin' animal."

"Okay, but before I do that, I gotta make sure you know how to kiss. If I like the way you kiss, maybe I'll fuck you like a fuckin' animal. If I don't, maybe I'll have to look for someone else."

She came over and stuck her tongue in my mouth like her life was on the line. Her tongue was going wild. She was showing me just how much she wanted it.

"Is that good, baby?" she asked. "Is that good enough?"

"It's a decent start. But now I want you to tongue my cock the way you tongued my mouth. If you don't know how to suck dick, you ain't gonna get dick."

That was all she needed to hear. She went downtown, where her mouth turned into a supercharged Hoover. She sucked great dick.

"You ready now?" she asked.

"Maybe," I said. "But first I wanna watch you touch yourself. I wanna watch you play with that pretty clit of yours."

She played with her pussy for a few seconds. The thing was dripping wet.

"Now are you ready?" she asked.

"Beg."

"Please, I'm begging you, please . . ."

"Lemme watch for another minute. I'll count down from sixty seconds."

I did a long countdown, slowing down as I got to the last numbers. Finally I got to 10 . . . 9 . . . 8 . . . 7 . . . 6 . . . 5 . . . 4 . . . 3 . . . 2 . . . 1 . . . and gave her what she wanted. She exploded the second my cock filled her twat. By the time we were through, we'd nearly busted both the box spring and her box.

THE FUCKINATOR

IF ARNOLD WAS the Terminator, I was the Fuckinator. I had all the other comics who lived in the house shaking their heads. They were amazed at how much ass I got. So amazed they wanted to challenge me.

One day, I was about to fly down to San Diego to do a show the following night at the La Jolla Comedy Store, see my sister, and spend some time with Sandi, Mitzi's daughter. Sandi and I had a kind of loose thing going on, in my mind a little like the Stephen Stills song "Love the One You're With." As I was about to start packing for my flight out of Burbank, Dan Frischman, a comic who lived in the house, said, "I got a proposition for you. I bet you a hundred bucks you can't bang three different chicks before you leave. Has to be here and has to be three chicks you never slept with."

I checked my watch. I only had a few hours before my flight. And three chicks I'd never slept with? First, I had to find three chicks, and then I had to fuck them, factoring in at least a minimum amount of recovery time in between. I'd be an idiot to take that bet.

"You're on," I said.

I rushed over to Schwab's Pharmacy down the hill from where we lived. I knew a cute waitress there who was into me. I sat at the counter and turned on the charm, sweet-talking her back to the house as soon as her shift ended.

Within minutes I had the Schwab's waitress out of her uniform and sitting on top of my dresser. We started going at it. I wasn't even in yet when she whispered the four sweetest words I ever heard: "I come really quick."

She went off, shivering, shaking, convulsing with a roar that rattled the walls of the Red Room. Dan, along with everybody else in Hollywood, had to have heard her. Then we started kissing and she apologized for coming so fast and I told her it was great, I loved it, and I hated to rush her out but I had to pack for my trip.

Next I called a chick I knew who worked at the Improv. I've forgotten her name, so I'll call her Big Tits. I do remember those. Big Tits showed up wearing a sexy cut-off T-shirt and extremely short shorts. She was playing coy, which was making me nuts both because she was unbelievably hot and because the clock was ticking. She wanted to hang out on our porch and check out the view. On a clear day you could see all the way to the ocean. She leaned her elbows on the porch, giving me a clear view all the way to her ass. Then the comics started coming outside one at a time—Yakov, Dan, and Carl Edwards. They all knew about the bet. They started bullshitting, I think to delay my move and take time off the clock. Finally, I convinced Big Tits to get off the porch and check out my room.

Ten minutes later she was on her hands and knees and I was fucking her from behind, Big Tits's big tits jiggling like crazy. I knew the guys were all listening, so I encouraged her to scream, which she did. I decided the only way I could win the bet and dutifully bang Sandi once I got to La Jolla was if I didn't come, so I got Big Tits up on my bed and started sucking and kissing her swollen pussy lips until she lost it and came like a waterfall, and we both collapsed.

After she left, I sat around with Dan, Carl, and Yakov. I was fucking exhausted, not to mention that my balls were bloated to the size of basketballs. I was tempted to forfeit, but I needed the hundred. Plus I had my pride and my reputation to consider. Before I knew it I was down on Sunset shopping for pussy number three.

I found her in the front of a used-car lot. She looked like a starlet out of a 1950s movie. She wore a long black skirt with white gloves up to her elbows, and had a full figure and full lips. We talked cars. She complimented my Brooklyn accent. I complimented her style. We clicked. I invited her to the house. I winked at the other comics as I paraded her past them and into my room.

She wanted it and she wanted it slow. Once I got her out of her stylish outfit and naked on my bed, I discovered that she had skills. The woman was advanced. At a certain point, I think when I was teasing her pussy with my tongue and she started to come, squirting and soaking my bed, I realized I was never gonna make my flight.

Later, after she left, I called Sandi, who broke up with me on the phone. She said she didn't think I was serious about our relationship. I started to object, but then I looked in the living room and saw five comedians, all nude, stoned, dancing in a line, kicking like the Rockettes, while some girl was blowing another comedian in the corner.

"Maybe you're right," I told Sandi.

As for the bet, I did bang three chicks I'd never met—but according to Dan, not before I actually left for La Jolla, since I missed my flight.

We called it a push.

DOLLFACE

I'D BEEN IN L.A. a couple of years and slowly started building up a rep at the Comedy Store. The other comics thought I was crazy because of my attitude. If I was playing the last set of the night in front of ten people, I was still excited, still rarin' to go.

Looking out at the empty club one night, another comic said to me, "It's a shame that you gotta work such a bad crowd."

"Are you kidding?" I said. "I'm gonna go out there and stop traffic. A year from now these people will be paying fifty bucks a ticket to sit in the front row to see me at the Forum."

"You're nuts, Dice."

"Just wait and see."

There was no way to explain my confidence. I didn't have a big-time manager or agent. If someone offered me work outside the Comedy Store, I'd call my dad, always my main consultant, and get him to cut the deal. Little by little I had some calls to read for parts. One of those calls resulted in my first movie, a film called *Wacko*. I was cast in the role of a Travolta-like character called Tony Schlongini—the name being a combination of "schlong," the Yiddish slang word for "dick," and "linguini," the Italian pasta. The flick was a comic spoof of a horror flick and was especially attractive to me because it starred Stella Stevens, who played Jerry Lewis's love interest in *The Nutty Professor.* Just like Jerry was the nerd who turned into Buddy Love, Stella was the innocent girl who turned into a sexy vamp. That was easy for

Stella to do, 'cause she'd just been chosen as a Playmate of the Month. Jerry Lewis liked her so much that he kept her name—"Stella"—as the character's and opened *The Nutty Professor* with the song "Stella by Starlight." Stella was hot.

That was 1963. This was 1982. Nineteen years later, as far as I was concerned, Stella was still hot. I told her all about my love for that movie and what an honor it was to work with her in this, my first film. She was tremendous. The cast also included George Kennedy, who'd won an Academy Award as Best Supporting Actor for *Cool Hand Luke* with Paul Newman. I also knew Kennedy from those *Airport* disaster movies.

It was a silly movie, but I had no problem playing the part. I needed any and all exposure. During the shoot one of the extras, a fan of mine, said he had this chick Cathy he wanted me to meet. I said sure. I love meeting new chicks. Have her come to the Comedy Store to dig my act.

During my set, I looked out into the room and saw this very pretty blue-eyed, long-haired blonde wearing blue-and-white striped overalls. She had a face like a doll. She was adorable. She looked like she'd been head cheerleader and homecoming queen for her high school. I saw that she was smiling and laughing all through my act. Clearly, she was digging me.

I went over and said, "Are you Cathy?"

"I am."

"You're a doll face. Mind if I call you Dollface?"

"Not at all. I didn't know you're from Brooklyn."

"You couldn't tell by the way I fuckin' talk?" I asked, exaggerating my accent.

"Well, I'm from Iowa, and I'm not too good at figuring out accents."

"What are you doing out here in L.A., Dollface?"

"I work for a real estate company."

"That's nice."

"But I really want to be an actress."

"You and every other chick in this room."

"I'm serious about it," she said.

"Well, if you're really serious, don't get too serious about me."

"Why?"

" 'Cause I'm the wrong guy for a girl who wants to be an actress. A couple comprised of two struggling actors ain't no good. It's bad enough for one person to have to deal with the rejection. When two people are going through it at the same time, they'll drive each other nuts."

"I have my real estate job. I'm a practical girl."

"I'm not sure I'm a practical guy. I'm more of a crazy guy who believes, no matter what, that I'm gonna be one of the biggest stars in the world."

Even with my hesitations I have to say that it was a pretty great first date. Dollface asked lots of questions, and I don't gotta tell you that I like talking about myself. Fact is, I'm my favorite subject.

Things heated up on our second date. Dollface was eager to see the Red Room, where I discovered that, underneath her striped overalls, she had a killer body and was almost as horny as me. After some heavy-duty rock-and-rolling, we were both enjoying the afterglow when, on the other side of my closed door, we heard this loud sound from the kitchen—a *snap!* Next we heard the voice of Yakov and a couple of the other comics.

"What are we gonna do?"

"Kill it."

"I'm not touching it."

"Me either."

Me and Dollface threw on some clothes, opened the door, and saw four panic-stricken comics looking at this rat writhing in a trap. The spring hadn't functioned right. It missed his head but caught the lower half of his body, so the thing was thrashing around like crazy.

Everyone was freaking out except Dollface. She grabbed a broom, hauled back, and smashed the rat with the wooden handle. The rat's brain splattered all over the place. The comics were horrified. I was laughing and thinking, *This is what happens when you date a farm girl.*

Back in the Red Room, we were relaxing when I heard a knock on the window. It was a chick I'll call Polly, a waitress from the Comedy Store in Westwood who'd had a crush on me for weeks. Polly was a little loaded.

I went to the window and told her, "I'm busy."

"I gotta talk to you," said Polly.

"Not now."

"It's important," Polly insisted.

Dollface was annoyed.

"You better go see what she wants," said Dollface.

"I'll be right back," I told Dollface.

"Don't hurry," said Dollface. "I gotta be at work anyway. I'm leaving."

"Meet me by the front door," I told Polly.

Dollface got dressed and left.

I got dressed and met Polly at the front door. She was crying her eyes out. She said she was lonely for me. I said I was about to get into a relationship with Dollface. Polly said that didn't matter. She didn't want much. "Just hold me," she said. "Just show me you care. Show me you're my friend." I held her. I showed her I cared. She showed me that she was wearing a thong under her short skirt. And that's how two friends wound up fucking.

In spite of this little detour, I started dating Dollface, and she started introducing me to her friends as her "boyfriend." I wasn't quite that serious, but I didn't mind. Call me whatever you like.

RONNY DOWNTOWN

THE RELATIONSHIP WITH Dollface had been going on for several months when I realized I'd been away from Brooklyn for too long. I missed Mom and Dad and wanted go home for a few days. I invited Dollface home to meet the folks. Mom took one look at her and said she was gorgeous. From the airport they took us out to a place they liked in Bay Ridge. It was a gambling hall, a well-lit, busy place with respectable Brooklynites playing very illegal poker, blackjack, and roulette. Mom wanted me to meet someone there.

"He's a nice guy and good to know," said Mom.

"How?"

"He can watch your back."

"Why do I need my back watched?"

"Maybe not now. Maybe later. When you get really famous."

The guy turned out to be someone they called Ronny Downtown. We met him only a few minutes after the four of us walked in. Maybe five or six years older than me, Ronny Downtown spoke Italian-Brooklynese—that's the same as Jewish-Brooklynese except he used his hands more and his grammar was a little more fucked-up than mine, which is saying a lot.

"Finally get to meet you," he said. "Your mother, she's always talkin' about you, and then we see you on that Don Kirshner TV show. You's funny, ya heah?"

"Thanks."

"I got all kinds of friends who are working as comics. Making good money."

"That's good."

"I heah you's got a good future out dere."

"I hope so."

"I heah you been to the mansion."

"What mansion?"

"I heah there's only one mansion out dere that count. The Playboy Mansion."

"Haven't been."

"I got a friend who might be able to get you invited."

Ronny looked the way a Brooklyn bookie should look: lean build, dark hair with too much hair grease, thin mustache, blue silk suit with more polyester than silk. He was all over me 'cause he saw me as a rising star. Naturally I liked the flattery, and I actually liked him. Like Mom said, he was a nice guy. It was only his name that gave me problems.

"Ronny Downtown," I told him, "ain't the right name."

"What you mean?" he asked. "It's been my name for years."

"You got your fuckin' name backward. If someone says, 'Here comes Ronny Downtown,' I'm thinking that Ronny is on his way downtown."

"Ya heah, I ain't had no problems with no misunderstanding."

"But that don't mean you won't. All I'm telling you is to flip the script. Ronny Downtown don't make no sense. But Downtown Ronny does."

Whether Downtown Ronny heard me or not didn't make any difference, 'cause I kept calling him Downtown Ronny, and having heard me, everyone followed suit. This was far from the last time I'd see Downtown Ronny, and later on when Dicemania really took off he was part of the group of guys who would travel with me. All characters.

The other thing I remember about that night was borrowing $50 from my dad to play blackjack. I lost it all, but something about the game kept me glued to the table. At the time I thought, *No big deal.* Without knowing it, the seeds of a very serious fuckin' addiction had been planted.

KINISON

BACK IN HOLLYWOOD, me and Dollface continued to date. It wasn't that the Red Room didn't continue to attract chicks other than Dollface, but little by little I was starting to settle down. At least a bit.

Every week I was meeting new comics while working Mitzi's circuit. One of the guys I liked the most was Sam Kinison, a crazy motherfucker—and the most insecure cat in the history of comedy—whose brand of insanity I found funny as hell. Sam and I became fast friends. As the last two acts at the Comedy Store practically every night, we hung out all the time. There might have been only fifteen people in the club—assholes too drunk to get up and leave—but Sam would carry on like there were fifteen hundred. I was the same way. Those times when we shared the stage were magical. Dice, the wiseass from Brooklyn, and Kinison, the preacher from the Midwest, were hysterical together. We broke each other up. And, as a matter of fact, I helped Sam get his timing down.

Kinison had a great opening line but didn't know how to set it up. I showed him. I said, "Sam, I love your act. But you gotta put more theater into it. You gotta get out and play with your glasses. Put 'em on. Take 'em off. Then you light your cigarette. You take your time. You suck the audience in. You say, 'How you doin' out there?' You wait for them to yell, 'Great. We're doing great.' Then you say with a smile, 'I bet you saw a lot of acts tonight that you liked. I bet you liked them enough to come back here. I bet you've had a great time.' Now this is when your smile turns to scorn.

This when you say, 'Well, all I can promise you is one thing. My name is Sam Kinison and . . . ,' big pause here . . . big fuckin' pause . . . before you blow your stack and hit 'em with, '*And you're gonna wish to God you'd never seen me!!!*' "

It was a killer opening that Sam used for most of his career. What made it great was not only Sam's explosive raging fuckin' anger but the originality of his material. As a onetime minister, he could invent shit about what it would be like if Jesus had to come home to a nagging wife who wants to know why he's been gone so long. Only Sam could get Jesus to say something like, "Leave me alone, you fuckin' bitch, I was busy with a little something called the resurrection."

In this beginning period when we were still struggling comics riding down to La Jolla or out to Westwood, Sam and I had our own little two-man support group. Other people might have thought that I was too far-out, too outrageous or disrespectful, but not Sam. I backed up his balls-out nuttiness 100 percent, and he backed up mine. Many were the nights when we'd go to Ralph's grocery store together, steal a bunch of pork chops, and head back to Cresthill, where we'd cook 'em on the grill. After dinner we'd do routines for each other. We wouldn't mince words. When I thought he should push it further, I said so. And the same for Sam.

On one of those nights—this was when Sam was just getting into his ear-shattering scream—he yelled so loud that Yakov Smirnoff woke up out of a dead sleep and came running down the stairs, thinking some violent crime had been committed.

He took one look at crazy Sam, whose scream hadn't stopped, and said to me, "What is this guy doing?"

"He's killing me," I said in all sincerity. "He's absolutely killing me."

Sam and I would watch the big stars run in and out of the Comedy Store. Those were the days when, on any given night, Steve Martin, Robin Williams, or Eddie Murphy might show up to try out new material. Eddie was an early fan of mine. Like me, he's an Elvis freak and saw me as the Elvis comic.

Eddie was always supportive. With his movie career taking off, though, going back to stand-up could make him nervous. A couple of times I found myself standing next to him and saying, "You're the fuckin' greatest. You're Eddie Murphy. You got nothing to be nervous about." He'd look over at me, smile, and say, "Thanks, man, I needed to hear that."

Sam was an ass-kisser. He'd butter up anyone, including and especially Mitzi, to get ahead. I was too proud and sure of myself to ass-kiss anyone. For instance, when Robin Williams came into the club I never tried to get close to him. I left him alone. He was a superstar, and superstars need their space. One night I went onstage after him in the main room and was flattered that he stayed around to hear me. Afterward, Kinison, who was buttering him up, took him to a party at Cresthill. Robin came over to me and said, "Man, you buried me."

"Believe me, Robin," I said, "that wasn't my intention. You're where I wanna be one day. I give you nothing but respect."

WHO WOULD HAVE THUNK?

I GOT MARRIED.

Yes. You heard me right.

I got fuckin' married in the eighties when I was twenty-six. I got married in the middle of my Red Room crazy days. I got married when marriage was the last thing on my mind. I got married when I was out of my mind. I got married when I should have gotten a brain transplant. I got married because . . . well . . .

Dollface called me when I was home in Brooklyn. When I called her back, I was actually in a phone booth on Nostrand Avenue. She said two words that I wasn't exactly waiting for: "I'm pregnant."

My response was quick. "Then we'll get married."

I'd always wanted a family anyway, and besides, I'd been dating Dollface, I'd been loving on Dollface, and, according to my code of honor, if a girl you've been dating and loving says she's pregnant, you marry her.

"You'll come to Brooklyn," I said. "We'll get married here."

No arguments. Dollface would have married me anywhere. I didn't want no fancy ceremony, and neither did Dollface. My dad knew a hundred judges and picked the one he liked the best. So with my family around us, we went to the judge's chambers for a civil ceremony. I caught it all on a cassette tape recorder.

That night we went to the Golden Gate Motor Inn on Knapp Street. I spent the extra ten bucks for the vibrating bed. We fucked liked bunnies and the next day drove out to Governor's comedy club on Long Island, where I had a gig. Two days later we flew back to the coast.

When the cab pulled up to Dollface's apartment on Havenhurst we both got out, but I told the driver to wait.

"I'll help you with the bags," I say. "Then I'm going back to Cresthill."

"The Red Room?"

"Yeah."

"Why?"

"I wanna see the guys and maybe go down to the Comedy Store and see if I can get on tonight. I wanna see if Ollie Joe and Kinison are around."

"So you're not coming in?" she asked.

"I just said I'm not coming in. I'm going to Cresthill."

"And what about later? You're coming back here tonight, aren't you?"

"Depends. If I get to talking with the boys, it could be late—four or five in the morning. You gotta be up by seven to go to work." Dollface still had her job as a receptionist for a Realtor.

All this time we're out on the street, with the cab driver waiting.

"Let me get this straight," she said. "You don't intend on moving in with me, do you?"

"Well, to be honest, everything happened so fast—with this marriage and all—we haven't really discussed it."

"You don't expect me to move into that awful house with that awful bunch of horny comedians, do you?"

"Of course not. I'd never ask you to do that."

"Then you *will* move here."

"I'm not so sure about that."

When she heard that, she threw down her purse. "I can't *fuckin'* believe this. We're married, and you don't want to live with me."

"The marriage is something between us. Right now it's nothing I want to broadcast."

"What are you talking about?"

"My career. I got a certain image to protect. My comedy depends on the audience looking at me in a certain way—a guy on the loose."

"I'm not believing this."

"You'll like the arrangement," I said. "You'll get used to it. It's romantic. I'll come to your place, you'll come to mine. We got two different places where we can hang out. I see it as the perfect way to start a marriage."

It wasn't. I didn't like staying at Dollface's apartment. She'd go to sleep early and I'd get bored. I missed hanging out with the other comics at Cresthill, where something was always going on. It wasn't that I was cheating on Dollface. I wasn't. I just didn't want to live there in a place that didn't seem too exciting. Then came the night when I heard something I hadn't heard before.

First it was crickets. There seemed to be a bunch of them chattering with each other. Couldn't tell whether they were under our bed or out in the yard. Dollface had already fallen asleep, and all I could do was listen to these fuckin' crickets.

A few minutes later I heard her neighbor—this short, stacked blond bombshell I'd seen around the complex—talking to some guy. They were outside and, because they were probably a little drunk, they were talking loud.

"Mind if I come in?" he asked her.

"I want you to come in," she said.

Now my interest was up. Soon my dick would be up. By the sound of her voice I figured she had every intention of giving him pussy. My only prayer was that her bedroom and our bedroom shared a wall.

Their voices were distant but soon they got closer.

"Do you like doing that kind of thing?" I heard him asking her.

"I love doing that kind of thing," I heard her respond.

My prayer was answered. Her bedroom did share a wall with ours. And even better, the walls were paper thin. Those cheap apartments were made outta tissue paper and glue. The way the couple was sounding, they might as well have been in the same room as us.

Not only did I hear their voices, I started hearing her making those sucking sounds that I know and love so well. Holy shit! With audio clearer than a fuckin' Bose speaker, I heard her sucking on his cock like it was a lollipop. I heard him breathing heavy and I heard her moaning. I imagined her pussy was soaking wet. I looked over at the bed and saw that Dollface was turned over on her belly with her long blond hair flowing down her back and her panties riding high up into that plump corn-fed ass of hers. Dollface was looking good, while the couple on the other side of the wall had changed positions.

"Do me," I heard Blondie telling the cat.

"I'll do you good," he said.

So I imagined him spreading her out and licking that clit until she went from moaning to screaming. The screaming woke up Dollface, who saw that I was out of bed, standing up straight, my dick standing up straight, a big smile on my face. I pointed to the wall.

"Listen," I told Dollface.

She liked what she heard. The sound of Blondie getting sucked by the guy got her hot. She started licking my cock, and grabbing it, and sticking the whole head in her mouth. With Blondie providing the soundtrack, this was one of Dollface's better blow jobs.

Meanwhile Blondie was screaming for dick, and boyfriend was about to bone her. The second the bone slipped in, we heard about it. Blondie was screaming, "Feel that pussy grab your cock! Fuck that tight pussy!"

Their headboard started banging and the wall started shaking and, looking down at my wife, I saw her pussy juice flowing like it had never fuckin' flowed before. She wanted me to fuck her, and naturally I wanted to oblige, but I also wanted her to join in the screaming.

"Let 'em hear you scream," I told her. "I want you to out-scream Blondie."

Well, that had to be pretty fuckin' loud, 'cause Blondie was hysterical and the walls were shaking, but the second I slammed into Dollface she matched Blondie scream for scream, my balls slapping her thighs, her hands grabbing my ass to make sure I was thrusting the full cock deep into her box.

She was lifting up, swaying side to side, but mainly she was screaming her head off about how good the dick was, and Blondie was screaming the same thing. Naturally the two women were hearing each other and were getting off on each other's screams, and we were banging our headboard every bit as hard as they were banging theirs, and we wanted to keep banging 'cause we wanted to win this fuckin' banging contest about who could bang and fuck the longest. I didn't have a stopwatch on me so I can't tell you exactly, but it had to be a good ten or fifteen minutes of solid rock cock-slamming fucking before—and this is the part that floors me—both of these chicks scream, "Oh shit, oh God, I'm coming!" at the exactly the same fuckin' time.

Thinking back, this was the night that I fell in love with my wife.

The next afternoon, on my way out, I happened to run into Blondie in the parking lot. She was dressed in a prim-and-proper pantsuit as she unlocked the door of her Toyota Corolla.

"Good afternoon," I said to her.

"Good afternoon," she said to me. No smile, no nod, no wink—nothing to let me know that she knew that I knew that last night her boyfriend—and, by extension, I—had fucked her brains out.

DRUNK DICE

THAT WAS PROBABLY the happiest moment of my marriage. As it turned out, the sad moments outweighed the happy ones. One of those moments came early when Dollface said she had her period—a big surprise—so she wasn't really pregnant after all. That made me stop and wonder.

By this time I'd made up with my old friend Neil, one of the original Nostrand Avenue Schmucks. On a trip back to Brooklyn, I happened to be revisiting Pips when I noticed Neil walking into Captain Walter's, a big log-cabin bar in the middle of Sheepshead Bay. By then I knew that he and Sylvia were divorced; they'd been splitsville for years. I didn't have hard feelings. I just felt bad that Neil had to learn about Sylvia the hard way. So I went in and had a drink with Neil. It was just like old times. He was happy to hear about all my success and said he'd love to visit me in California and meet Dollface. Wasn't long after that he made the trip to L.A. That's when he said it looked to him like me and Dollface were really in love.

Well, if we were, the love didn't last. The love hit a big speed bump that I didn't see coming. While I was out working the comedy club circuit, Dollface was out fucking someone else. I can't say that I didn't deserve it. The guy she was fucking probably didn't even know she was married, because we kept that fact to ourselves. My fault. But strange as it may be, even though this was an unconventional marriage and even though I'm an unconventional guy, I really had fallen for Dollface and started getting crazy when I realized she was cheating. Ironically, that's because it happened at a time when I was being loyal.

One night I left the Red Room at Cresthill and went to her apartment, only to discover she'd gone out. Like a nut, I went looking for her. I found her at Barney's Beanery on Santa Monica Boulevard, where she was at the bar with her girlfriend whore—they always got a girlfriend whore—and had some guy leaning over her.

"Hey, pal," I said to the guy. "I'm gonna assume she didn't tell you that she's married."

"You assumed right."

The guy, seeing that my eyes weren't right, wisely moved away.

"Don't make a scene," said Dollface.

"I ain't gonna make no scene," I said. "I'm just gonna drink."

I went to the end of the bar and downed four shots of Jack Daniel's on an empty stomach. This was one of the only times in my life when I drowned my sorrow in booze. I got plastered.

I got up and, ignoring Dollface and her girlfriend whore, went to the Comedy Store, where I walked into the lobby of the main room. Mitzi was standing right there talking to some people. I lurched a little and leaned on her shoulder.

"You're drunk," she said. "I can smell it. That's not like you, Andrew. You're no drinker."

"I need to talk to you. Let's go outside."

We went to a quiet spot in the parking lot.

"Why do you think I want to make it?" I asked her.

"Money," she said. "Everyone wants the money."

"No, I wanna make it for my family. I wanna make it for my mom and dad back in Brooklyn—that's who I wanna make it for."

"Fine," she said, trying to placate me.

"No, it ain't fine. It won't be fine until I make it. Which is why I got to know the truth. Why do you have a problem with me, Mitzi?"

"I don't."

"You do. Or you wouldn't put me on at one thirty in the fuckin' morning in front of nobody."

"I do that because the other comics complain that they don't wanna follow you."

"I gotta be punished for that?"

"It's no punishment. Do you know how many other comics would give their last nut to have that late-night spot?"

"Lemme tell you something, Mitzi, and remember I told it to you. I'm gonna be the biggest stand-up who ever walked through the doors of your club. Now, maybe you can slow that down a little, but I'll find my audience. I fuckin' promise that I will find my people."

Tired of talking to a drunk Dice, Mitzi just walked away. That was fine with me, 'cause I needed to sit down. My head was spinning. I was feeling sick. I walked to the front of the club, where there was a little porch and a couple of stairs. I sat down, put my head on a table, and threw up all over myself. As if on cue, Dollface came driving up in the 1970 green Caddy convertible I'd just bought her.

"Get in," she said.

I don't remember what happened after that. I just remember waking up the next morning alone. Dollface had gone off to work.

KAMIKAZE COMIC

THINGS KEPT MOVING along. No big breaks, but steady progress. In 1984, I was cast in *Making the Grade*, starring Judd Nelson. I was able to convince the director to name my character Dice. I had a plan: even though I was only getting bit parts, using the Dice name could be a way to build up some recognition for my comic character.

A year later I appeared in *Private Resort*, which was filmed in Key Largo. During the shoot, the producer, an Israeli named Ben Efraim, took three of us actors aside and said, "I don't know how big this movie will be, but I know that all three of you guys are gonna be superstars."

The other two were Rob Morrow, who went on to star in *Northern Exposure* and *Quiz Show*, and Johnny Depp, who went on to become Johnny Depp.

Back in L.A., when my audience didn't come to me, I came to them. And I don't mean small audiences. I mean big ones.

I was crazy enough to go to the giant movie theaters in Westwood, the suburb of L.A. by UCLA, and jump onstage before the film started and go right into my shtick. I'd be up there having the audience howling for at least three or four minutes before the manager came to pull me offstage. By then the crowd was loving me and hating to see me go.

I remember that during one run of *Prizzi's Honor*, I was so fuckin' on at this huge Westwood theater that the manager actually asked me to come back. I was happy to—free of charge. My thinking was that maybe some big-time producer or his kids were in the audience. You never know.

I was so outrageous that one of the local papers sent a reporter around as I ran out on the stages of the movie palaces all over L.A., fearless about facing audiences who—until I started talking—hadn't planned on listening to some crazy comic. The writer called me a "Kamikaze Comic."

One night, late, I was at Ben Frank's, trying to convince a young William Morris agent to represent me. I could tell he was impressed by my confidence and ambition, and he promised to check me out at the Comedy Store. But one thing I know for sure—never let a waiter or an agent leave your table, or you'll never see them again. I looked around the restaurant—it was three A.M. and the customers were your basic late-night coalition of pimps, hookers, punk rockers, and out-of-work actors. My kind of people. I decided to go all Kamikaze Comic on them.

"Watch this," I told the agent. I grabbed a cig—you could smoke in restaurants in those days—lit it up, and stood up on the soft cushion seat of the booth. "Hey, everybody, how you doin'?" I said, loud. The customers stopped eating and talking and looked over at me.

I went into about five minutes of my material, turning Ben Frank's into a comedy club. The customers went berserk. I did a few jokes and then I started heckling this couple the way I do in my act. "So, what's your name, honey?" I said to this guy's date. "Any idea?"

The whole place went nuts. But then the manager of the restaurant, a nervous little fuck with a bad comb-over, came over and told me to cut it out and sit down. I took a little bow and sat down to insane cheering. A few minutes later, thanks to the douche-bag manager calling 911, six cops showed up. No lie. Six fucking *cops*. With the customers booing and shouting *"Attica!"* I left Ben Frank's on my own recognizance. Outside the cops told me I was banned from Ben Frank's for life and then went off to solve a real crime, and the young agent from the Morris office, convulsing with laughter, said he'd sign me.

I still worked the crowd in other restaurants. One was Larry Parker's, a fifties-type diner done up retro style on South Beverly Drive. I knew Larry, the owner, who let me get on the loudspeaker at one A.M., where I'd blast everything from Roy Orbison to Kool and the Gang before doing my thing. It got around town that the Diceman was performing at the diner, and soon I had a cult following.

One night I was at Larry's cracking 'em up when who should come up to me but Tommy Lee.

"I dig your comedy, man," he said. "You're very rock and roll."

That's all I needed to hear—this compliment coming out of the mouth of the drummer of Mötley Crüe. I was flying. I was telling him that I played drums too, and he said, "I can tell by the way you lay down the beat."

"Listen, Tommy," I said, "if you ever think of having a comic open for you guys, it would be the honor of my life." I almost said, *I'll pay you,* but I didn't.

"How can I get in touch with you?" he asked.

"Easy," I said. I gave him a card and wrote my dad's phone number on the back. "My dad's back in Brooklyn and he's booking my big gigs. Call my dad."

My dad never heard from Tommy, but I didn't get mad. Tommy was a busy guy, and besides, to have him say that I was very rock and roll was enough to keep me happy for another six months.

The Kamikaze Comic kept rolling, and after a while the Morris office came through, getting me to play myself, or at least a version of the Dice character, in a couple of movies. One was *Night Patrol,* a cop drama parody, with Linda Blair and Pat Paulsen. I also got cast as a bouncer in a John Hughes movie, *Pretty in Pink,* with Molly Ringwald and Harry Dean Stanton. All this was fine. But in terms of big-time showbiz, I hadn't broken through. I needed to go further. I needed better material. I needed to go where no comic had ever gone before.

HICKORY DICKORY DOCK

THE LIMERICK BIT began in a small way. Howie Mandel used to play the Comedy Store around the same time as me. He had this rhyme thing that he used to do. Like if a girl in the audience had a birthday, he'd say, "Roses are red, violets are blue, today's the day that you became you." Of course this wasn't original with Howie, but it was part of his act. I changed it around and said, "Roses are red, violets are blue, I'm a schizophrenic, and so am I." That got a laugh, but not from Howie. Howie got pissed that I was stealing his shit. Well, I liked Howie, so I apologized and forgot about it until I realized that no one has a copyright on rhymes. People have been rhyming since fuckin' Mother Goose. And that got me to thinking.

I thought of Little Miss Muffet sitting on a tuffet eating her curds and whey. Along came a spider who sat down beside her and said, "Hey, what's in the bowl, bitch?" That got a big laugh—something as simple as that—so I bought the Mother Goose nursery rhyme book to see what else I could turn upside down.

The guy who helped me string together the jokes was Neil. I had started calling him Hot Tub Johnny. The name really didn't mean a thing. It was just something I picked up from Elvis. Elvis had his Memphis Mafia. I had my Brooklyn Buddies, all guys I used to be pals with from the neighborhood. One night me and Hot Tub Johnny were drinking a few beers, and I broke out the Mother Goose book. We started riffing together. I'd say, "Little Bo Peep." He'd say, "Fucked her sheep." I'd say, "Blew her horse." Hot Tub would say,

"Licked his feet." I'd say, "She ate his ass so very nice." He'd say, "Tongued his balls not once but twice."

By the end of the evening, we must have put together twenty rhymes. You know, "Jack and Jill went up the hill both with a buck and a quarter, Jill came down with two fifty . . . fuckin' whore!" Or "Old Mother Hubbard went to her cupboard to get her old dog a bone. When she bent over, Rover took over . . . and she got a bone of her own."

The other big piece I added to the Dice act that ended up bringing me a lot of laughs and even more heat came to me when I was jogging. It happened during Halloween. I threw on my jogging shorts and tank top and went out for a run. When I run, I clear my mind and get all kinds of ideas. Running is a very fuckin' creative thing for me. When I'm running I think of shit that wouldn't ordinarily occur to me. I think of situations or, seeing funny people, come up with funny lines. So there I was, running down Santa Monica Boulevard, when I saw this horde of people coming toward me. They were way off in the distance so I couldn't make them out at first. They looked like an invading army. The closer they came, the more I could see they *were* an invading army—an army of queers. It was the West Hollywood boys out on a Halloween run dressed up in tutus and skirts and short shorts and makeup. There were queens in leotards and musclemen with handlebar mustaches and fruits and fairies and every variety of rectal pioneer known to man. That's where I got the idea that gays come from their own planet—Fagotron. It was funny, and it was a perfect thing for Dice to latch on to. It pushed me to the edge.

DIRTY, DIRTY JOKES

I WAS PLAYING the Laugh Factory on Sunset, working out my new material. In between sets I would walk next door to Greenblatt's Deli to get my bagel with butter and bacon. One day I was sitting with my pal Mark Carducci, a screenwriter, when this guy came up to me. He had long scraggly hair, a big bushy beard, and baggy sweatpants. He looked like a homeless guy. He gave me the idea that he wanted to sit and talk. I was about to give him a few bucks and send him on his way when Mark whispered to me, "Do you know who this is?" I didn't. "He's Rick Rubin," said Mark. "He's the guy who invented rap." Turned out Rubin was the producer of Run-D.M.C. and the Beastie Boys.

"Just wanna tell you that I'm your biggest fan," said Rick. "I saw your first set, and I'm going back to catch the second. One day I'd love to make a record with you."

"Cool," is all I said.

Redd Foxx always worked on the edge. He was one of the first guys to work blue—and didn't give a shit. He knew dirty was funny, and unlike prudes like Cosby, he didn't have a snobby attitude about what's correct. I also admired Redd for how he made the transition to the mainstream with *Sanford and Son*. So when he asked me to be one of the comics on his *Dirty Dirty Jokes* video, which came out during the mideighties VHS rage, I jumped at the chance.

It was shot at Foxx's comedy club in L.A. and included other people, like Bob Schimmel. Bob was one of those rare comics who never judged his fellow comic. He didn't operate on jealousy. He was his own man, and he worked as blue as me. He'd open by saying, "The other day I heard you could make money donating sperm to a sperm bank. Well, that aggravated me, because I realized that in the last year alone I let five or six hundred dollars slip through my fingers."

Unlike me, Bob dressed conservatively, in a sports coat and button-down shirt. But unlike the conservative comics, he wasn't scared of telling pussy and dick jokes, even if he did look like a young professor teaching freshman English. He had a deadpan, dry-and-wry delivery and came out of the tradition of Lenny Bruce and Mort Sahl, smart-ass Jewish boys who saw the world in their own twisted way. The fact that I came out of a whole 'nother tradition—rock and roll and Elvis—didn't faze Bob. He respected the differences between us.

There were some similarities. Schimmel also saw humor in queer jokes. He was the first guy I heard who asked the question "When do people decide they're gay? Do you happen to be walking down the street one day and say, 'I think I want a dick up my ass'?" Schimmel wasn't scared of bathroom humor. He'd say, "You ever take a shit and look at the turd and realize that it looks like someone you know?" Then he'd ask, "Then did you ever tell that person, 'Hey, you look like the turd I just shit out'?"

I saw Schimmel as a brother in arms. He had the guts to make fun of everyone and everything. He encouraged me. He'd say, "Fuck those people who say you're disrespectful. Disrespect is the essence of good comedy. Let the rest of the world live by those goody-goody rules. The only rule of comedy is make 'em laugh. If you're afraid of bad taste, don't be a comic. Be a rabbi or be a priest. Priests say, 'Excuse me,' after they fart. Wouldn't it be better if they said, 'Look out,' before they did it?"

Schimmel was something of a nerd, but he never made you feel dumber than him. He just had your number. He knew us men are worried about the size of our dicks, so he made dick jokes. "Ever see John Holmes's cock? It doesn't look like a cock. It looks like a ride at Magic Mountain." He knew women like to come, so he made come jokes. He talked about buying a giant vibrator for his wife that took twenty D-cell batteries so powerful that when she came he used her to jump-start his car.

Schimmel had a rough life. He got bad cancer and had to go through hellish chemotherapy. He beat it and wrote a great book called *Cancer on $5 a Day*. Just when he got well, though, he was riding in a car with his kids when the car flipped over. His kids survived, but he didn't. He died at sixty, way too young. Bob helped me to understand that I had to keep fighting—no matter what. And when I got my big break in 1986, Schimmel was the first guy to congratulate me. I'll never forget him.

BUSTING UP, BUSTING OUT

I KNEW DOLLFACE was still banging someone else, but I didn't wanna admit it. By then we had made a couple of moves. We tried living together at Cresthill, but Mitzi found out and nixed it. Mitzi didn't want her comics shacked up with broads. So me and Dollface found a cool apartment on Laurel Canyon just above Sunset to try to work it out. But every time I went out of town and called home, no one answered or the line was busy. There was only one reason why I couldn't get hold of Dollface. And that's 'cause she had gotten hold of someone else.

I was in Texas when I realized I had to stop bullshitting myself. I had a New Year's Eve gig at a comedy club in San Antonio, a converted old movie theater, and I wanted Dollface there to ring in New Year's Eve. I'm romantic that way. We had it all planned. But then the came the call. It was December 30.

"Sorry, but it doesn't look like I'm gonna be able to make it there by New Year's Eve. But I can get there the next day."

"The next day!" I exploded. "The whole goddamn point is for us to spend New Year's Eve together."

"Well, the people where I work—"

"Fuck the people where you work. You're my wife."

"But it's my job."

"Quit your job."

"I can't."

"You gotta."

"Okay. I'll try and be there for New Year's. I really will."

For whatever stupid reasons, I got my hopes up. I really fooled my-self into thinking that Dollface was gonna get there in time for my New Year's gig.

All day I kept waiting for the phone to ring in my hotel room. But it never did. And there I was at eight, standing in the lobby and looking around to see if Dollface might be running through the door in time to catch my act.

That's when this chick—I'll call her Jane—came up to me and said, "Ex-cuse me, Andrew. May I call you Andrew?"

The way Jane looked, she could call me anything she wanted.

"I want to thank you for mentioning me in your interview," she said.

"What interview?" I asked.

"The one in the newspaper today where you talked about the nice fan letter you got. Well, I'm the fan who wrote it."

"Oh, so you're the nice lady who's been writing me?"

"I sure am."

"Wow! That's beautiful. And you're coming to the show, right?"

"I am."

"Where's your date, Jane?"

"I came alone."

"Then you'll meet me after the show?"

"I'd love that."

After the show she was right there.

Back in my hotel room, two very horny people fucked each other till they were delirious. The pussy wasn't just good. The pussy was spectacular. She was giving it up not only willingly but sweetly. Some pussy is tight and ter-rific but fishy. Some pussy is sour. Her pussy was sweet. Jane was sweet. Blowing me and kissing me and riding me until we both hit the jackpot together. This was the era when women were talking about G-spots. Well, every spot on Jane's beautiful luscious smooth-skinned curvaceous body had a *G* written all over it—her earlobes, her fingers, her creamy soft thighs, her hips, her hot little ass.

Round 'bout midnight, just after we had gone around the merry-go-round for the second time and both grabbed the brass ring, the phone rang.

It was Dollface.

"Andy," she said. "Just calling to say happy New Year."

"Hold on," I said, handing the phone to Jane. "Just say 'Happy New Year,' " I told Jane.

"Who is it?" Jane asked.

"Doesn't matter," I said.

And in the sexiest I'm-so-satisfied-because-I've-just-been-fucked-so-good voice I've ever heard, Jane took the phone and told Dollface, "Happy New Year."

When I got back to L.A., me and Dollface were barely able to talk to each other. She kept up the lie that there wasn't someone else. Now she wanted to talk about being an actress. If I had seen she had any talent, I would have encouraged her. I always encourage people with talent. But I couldn't bullshit her. And that made her resent me more.

I started off looking to get laid because I wanted to get even, but then some of the women I met became legit girlfriends. There was a hot cocktail waitress in Vegas named Mable, who to this day is close to me and my sons. And Sue, a chick in New York who owned a boutique leather shop off Columbus Circle.

"Maybe you can try one more time," my dad urged me when I was back in New York visiting my parents. "I'm not saying it'll work, but it's worth an effort."

So I called Dollface in L.A. to say I was coming home and maybe we could talk. But, just like before, the fuckin' phone was always busy. I'm sure she took it off the hook—either to aggravate me or to avoid disturbing the hot fuck she was getting from her boyfriend.

On the spur of the moment, I decided to head back right then and there. I ran out to the airport and caught the early morning flight that landed at LAX at eight A.M. A pal picked me up and drove me to the Laurel Canyon apartment. First thing I noticed was that my '70 Caddy convertible wasn't there.

Neither was Dollface. So I went in, made myself a pot of coffee and waited. Half an hour later Dollface came strolling in carrying a little overnight bag.

"What are you doing here?"

"I live here, remember?"

She was all flustered. She didn't know what to say. "I just . . . I just had to run out to get a few groceries."

"I don't see no groceries. I just see your overnight bag."

"I had to see a sick friend last night."

"The only one who's sick around here is me, for believing these lies for so long."

"Who are you to talk that way to me? You have girlfriends. You've even thrown them up in my face."

"Only after I found out about you. But look, it doesn't matter. Once a cunt, always a cunt. I'm out."

I went to the bedroom, threw my shit in a couple of suitcases, and got the fuck out. I drove the Caddy directly to the offices of Jacoby and Meyers and got a $350 divorce.

Dollface didn't like that. She was saying she deserved something. I was saying she didn't deserve shit. A smart friend said, "Look, you're gonna be a big star. You know it and I know it. So rather than have her come after you when you're making big money, give her a settlement. Keep her happy so she'll go away."

Made sense. I offered her 4Gs down and a G a month for the next eighteen months. She took it and went away, for the moment.

But with the bad comes the good. Around that time, John Hughes cast me in *Pretty in Pink* with Molly Ringwald. To keep up the plan of increasing my name recognition, I asked him if I could call my character Dice. "No problem," he said. I got only one scene, but I made so much of it that Hughes turned it into two. That was where I wrapped my arm around my head to light my cigarette. This gesture turned me into a cult favorite of comedy film fans and became one of my most beloved signature moves.

CRIME STORY

I WAS BACK in New York when I got a call that Michael Mann, the famous producer-director who did *Miami Vice*, was doing another big TV series called *Crime Story*. I was called in to read for a casting director, who told me I'd done a good job. Looking into the camera, though, I couldn't help but say, "Hey, Michael, how come you ain't here? You too much of a big shot to come to my audition?" Probably not a good idea, but since my chances of landing a role on a network TV series were less than great, why not take a chance and say something he'd remember?

I promptly forgot about the audition, and for months afterward I didn't hear a word. Besides, my comedy club career was moving ahead. I got a gig at Rascals, a club in West Orange, New Jersey, where I'd developed something of a following. It was a 425-seat club owned by a guy who became a big supporter and loyal promoter.

I got to New York on a Wednesday to open at Rascals on Friday. That Thursday I was at my folks' apartment in Brooklyn when I got a call from an agent back in L.A.

"Fantastic news," she said. "You've been cast in *Blind Date*, the new Blake Edwards film with Bruce Willis."

"Great. When are they shooting?"

"This weekend. They need you for about a week."

"Where?"

"L.A. I've booked you on the red-eye that leaves New York first thing tomorrow."

"Unbook me."

"What are you talking about?"

"I'm at Rascals all weekend."

"Fuck Rascals. This is Blake Edwards, the man who did *Breakfast at Tiffany's* and *The Pink Panther*. Kim Basinger is costarring. It's a big film."

"But it's a big weekend for Rascals. They're sold out Friday and Saturday. I can't let the owner down. It'll cost him a fortune."

"You'll make it up to him one day."

"Listen, I can't do it."

"Misplaced loyalty has you confused."

"I'm not confused. I'm playing Rascals."

"It's a juicy part. You get to do your Travolta thing in a disco."

"I've done the Travolta thing before."

"Not on the big screen like this."

"Sorry, my mind's made up."

"You're making a mistake," she said.

"Maybe, but it won't be the last."

On Friday I was fast asleep in my boyhood bedroom when my mother came in to wake me up. I was groggy; my mind was in a fog. For a second, I thought I was back in grammar school.

"I don't wanna go to school today, Ma."

"An agent is on the line."

"Tell her I don't wanna go to school. I don't wanna to talk to her."

"She's calling from California."

"Tell her I'm not talking. I'm not doing that movie."

Mom told her.

At noon I was at the kitchen table, where Mom was fixing me a bialy with butter and bacon, my favorite. The phone rang. Ma answered. Her look told me that it was the agent. I signaled *No, I ain't talking.*

"He's out," Mom said.

An hour later, the agent called again. I saw that I was just gonna have to tell her myself.

I picked up the phone and said, "I'm not taking the fuckin' movie."

"I'm not calling about that fuckin' movie," said the agent. "I'm calling about a television series. Michael Mann."

"I auditioned for that months ago."

"Apparently the audition went well, 'cause you've been cast. Twenty-five hundred dollars a week. Seven episodes guaranteed per season. The network sees it running for at least five seasons. They start shooting in Chicago on Monday. Can you make it?"

"Sure, I can make it—and only 'cause I turned down that Bruce Willis thing."

"I realize that. Your luck fell into place."

"You call it luck. I call it loyalty."

Michael Mann's *Crime Story* was a big deal. Centered in Chicago and Vegas in the early sixties with a great pop music soundtrack and fantastic fuckin' cast, it set the stage for movies like Scorsese's *Goodfellas* and *Casino* and TV shows like *The Sopranos*. The big criminal was played by Tony Denison and the chief cop was Dennis Farina. The pilot, where my thug character Max Goldman first appeared, was directed by Abel Ferrara, who'd go on to do *King of New York* with Christopher Walken. Everyone from Kevin Spacey to Julia Roberts to Gary Sinise to David Caruso to Stanley Tucci to Deborah Harry to Miles Davis to Michael Madsen acted on the show. Most of the characters were based on real-life people. It was a powerful, hard-hitting drama.

BABY ELEPHANT IN THE RAIN

AFTER THE FIRST weeks in Chicago, I had some drama of my own. Michael Madsen came to town to shoot a couple of episodes. We were both at the Ambassador East Hotel, got friendly, and started hanging out. This was before Madsen got famous for making those Tarantino movies, like *Reservoir Dogs* and *Kill Bill*. In person, he came across the same way he does on screen: a macho tough-talkin' cigarette-smokin' drinkin' fuckin' animal. My kind of guy.

"Chicago's all about drinking," he said. "All about bars."

"I'm not that crazy about drinking," I said, "and I don't really hang out at bars."

"That's gonna change tonight, Dice," he said.

And it did.

We hit the corner bar, which, according to Madsen, had been there for a hundred years and served up some famous cocktails. It only took two to get me plastered. There were a couple of cute chicks at the end of the bar who seemed friendly. We bought 'em some drinks and started chatting 'em up. I figured this evening was gonna end up beautifully for both Michael and me. So the four of us left the bar together and were walking along the street and I was closing in on my girl for a little kiss and a little feel and she was willing. She was going along with the program just like Michael's girl was grooving with him, then *bam*—there was a cloudburst and the rain started coming down in buckets. Rather than add to the sexiness of the situation, the rain got the girls giddy. They started running down the street, heading back to the bar.

"What are you gals doin'?" I asked. "Let's go to the hotel."

But by then they had made their way back to the bar. Michael and I both figured they were too much trouble. We let 'em go, and now it was really fuckin' raining—I mean it was a deluge—and him and me were running back to the hotel, no umbrellas, no coats, getting soaked. It was then that we saw this whale of a woman dancing in the middle of the street with her shirt off and her dress pulled up to her waist. When I say a whale of a woman, I'm talkin' somewhere between three hundred and three hundred fifty pounds. She had her mouth open, drinking in the rain. She was crazy drunk and singing at the top of her lungs. She had a pretty face and big brown smiling eyes, and the way she was twirling around she looked like a dancing baby elephant. Because I was tanked up myself, I went over and started dancing with her. This made her happy. She encouraged me in this sloppy rain dance to the point where she was grabbing my ass so she could grind up on me. It became a sports event. It became an athletic challenge, and neither of us backed down. Madsen couldn't believe his eyes. Neither could several other passersby, but me and my plus-size honey, we didn't give a shit. We were into it.

I can't lie and tell you that I wasn't excited to see that each of her tits was bigger than my head. I was plenty fuckin' excited as, dancing and grinding like fools, we kept moving closer to the hotel.

"You're crazy, Dice," was all Madsen kept saying. "You really aren't gonna do this, are you?"

"Fuck yes, I'm doing it!" I said.

"Fuck yes, he's doing it," said Baby Elephant.

Shaking his head in wonder at the madness of the Diceman, Madsen went off to his room while me and Baby Elephant, who was practically out of her clothes already, couldn't wait to get to mine. The second I closed the door behind us she threw me on the bed, ripped off my pants, and climbed on top. At first I was scared that this house of a woman would suffocate me.

I was scared that back in Brooklyn Jackie and Fred Silverstein would have to read the news about their son being literally fucked to death in some Chicago hotel room. I was also worried that the healthy, normal-sized, circumcised Jewish schlong belonging to me wouldn't be up for the job. Or wouldn't be adequate for the job. On both counts, though, there was nothing to worry about, because Baby Elephant liked what she was getting and knew how to position herself to get more. I liked how her freak-sized tits were slapping me in the face. I liked how her nipples were so fuckin' enormous I couldn't even get my mouth around 'em. I liked how her mouth was so fuckin' enormous that when she finally got off me to suck me, she was able to get my cock *and* my balls in her mouth all at once. I wasn't worried that she was going to bite 'em off, because I knew she wanted dick too bad to do anything to hurt my chances of banging her even harder.

Act 2 turned into something of a wrestling match. She actually threw me off the bed and went after me on the floor. At this point I would not be outdone. I would not be snuffed out. When she came at me, I grabbed her, flipped her on back and went in for the kill. I threw myself between her thighs, which were big as fuckin' oak trees. I was bouncing up and down like she was a human waterbed or a trampoline made up of nothing but pussy. I could feel myself—I mean *all of myself,* cock, ass, legs, chest, head—falling into that pussy. I liked falling into that feeling. But now it was time for Act 3.

Act 3 took place in the bathroom. Don't ask me why, but Baby Elephant climbed up on the marble counter and situated herself so her oak-tree thighs were spread apart and her dripping pussy was pushed out in my direction. I was scared her weight would bring the counter down. But at this point, who gave a shit if we brought the whole fuckin' hotel down? I still had the energy and she still had the desire for me to keep slamming her with my overworked but still stiff dick, my sweaty balls slapping her sweaty thighs, until she squirt-came like a fuckin' fire hose.

"Is that enough?" I asked, proud of myself for having climbed Mount Everest.

"For now," she answered.

• • •

Next morning, I was on the van with Michael Madsen and Dennis Farina.

"Dice wound up with a date last night," said Madsen. "Didn't you, Dice?"

I had a hangover from hell. Even worse, every bone in my body was sore from my massive wrestling match with Baby Elephant. I didn't bother answering.

"What's wrong, Dice?" asked Michael. "Didn't that lovely young thing last night show you a good time?"

I still had nothing to say to Madsen. But to the driver I said, "Pull over."

That's when I got out of the van and puked my guts out.

I don't want you to think that I regret my sexual encounter with Baby Elephant. It was the drinking part that got to me. The booze part was still another reminder of how drinking fucks up my digestion. No matter; on the set that day I still acted my ass off and got high marks from the director.

I felt that *Crime Story,* which aired for two seasons, would send my acting career into orbit. Maybe if it had been picked up for another two or three seasons, that would have happened. Who knows? All I do know, though, was that while I was in Chicago shooting the series two other things happened that changed my life.

The first had to do with a woman named Trini.

The second had to do with a comic named Rodney.

TRINI

ON MY SECOND trip to Chicago—this was after my wrestling match with Baby Elephant—it was summertime. I checked back into the Ambassador East and immediately went out for lunch. I was starving. I was walking past this storefront with the windows blacked out when I heard a *tap tap tap*. Some guy was trying to get my attention. I thought nothing of it and kept walking until another *tap tap tap*. I still didn't stop until this guy came running out of the door and said, "Ain't you Andrew Dice Clay?"

"Yeah."

"I seen you on that Redd Foxx *Dirty Dirty Jokes* tape. You're hysterical."

"Thanks."

"You gotta come in and meet my friends."

"I'd love to, pal, but I'm starving."

"We'll get you a burger. Come on in."

I went in and saw it was a bar/restaurant joint that hadn't opened yet. This guy and a friend were playing pinball. They made a big fuss over me—they were both fans—but even with the flattery and the promise of a burger I was about to leave, since I had nothing much to say to these guys. The reason I didn't leave, though, was because a great-looking chick was walking toward the pool table. Without saying a word, the chick convinced me to stay. She had that girl-next-door look: blond, blue eyes, sweet face, gorgeous smile, gorgeous body.

"Go ahead," I told my two fans. "Order the burger."

While we were waiting, we started chatting. They wanted to know about the comedy game. I wanted to know about the blonde, but the blonde wasn't talking.

"Who are you, the mysterious silent type?" I asked her.

"Who are you, some guy out of Brooklyn?"

"I am. And wherever you're from, it can't be far from Brooklyn."

"Jersey."

Her voice reminded me of Cathy Moriarty in *Raging Bull*. It had that gravelly, sexy quality that made me want to get to know her.

"What's your name?" I asked.

"Kathleen."

Strange, I thought, *that was the name of my first wife. Oh well . . .*

"But," she said, "they call me Trini."

"Would you like to have lunch with me, Trini?"

"I already ate. I'm off for a walk to the river."

"That sounds all right to me."

"Hey," said the guy who had tapped on the window, "what about your burger? You said you were starving."

"I just lost my appetite," I said, and then left with Trini.

She was happy to have me for company. She gave off this super-friendly vibe, and she had a beautiful spirit.

"What were you doing back in that joint?" I asked.

"There's an employment agency upstairs. I'd just given my application and was passing through. I just got here from Jersey and I'm looking for a job. You live in Chicago?"

I explained who I was and what I did. She was intrigued by *Crime Story*, but I'm not sure she believed that I was really an actor.

"To prove it," I said, "come back to my hotel and see the script I got to memorize. You can help me learn my lines."

Trini was not quite ready for that, but I could see she was liking my company. I liked how openly she spoke. She told me that she came to Chicago to live with her boyfriend. I didn't like hearing that. But I did like hearing that she and the guy broke up. Now she was living with her ex-boyfriend's mother.

"I haven't heard of that arrangement before," I said.

"The mother and I got close," said Trini. "Turns out she's a lot nicer than her son."

"Well, you'll see that I'm also a lot nicer than her son. I think you should help me with my lines."

I didn't push it, because I felt like she was moving in my direction. We found a little neighborhood place, the old-fashioned kind with the red checked tablecloths and the travel posters of Venice on the walls. The more we were together, the easier the conversation. She wanted to know if I was involved. I told her about Dollface and how that was over. Trini listened like she cared. She let me tell my story without interrupting. She laughed at my stupid little jokes and didn't hurry through dinner. She let those good feelings linger.

After dinner we walked around for an hour or so, and I led her back to the Ambassador East.

"Come on up," I said. "Absolutely no fooling around. Just work. I got to learn this script or I'm in big trouble."

We hung out in my room and she even stayed the night, but all we did was make out. We hung tight for the next few days until I had to leave for California. Soon as I was back in L.A., I called her. Her ex's mother answered and said she wasn't there.

"Just tell her that Andrew called and to call me back, please."

"Will do."

I expected to hear from her that night, but I didn't. I figured she was probably busy. Probably had a new job. No problem. So I called the next day, and the day after that, and the day after that. It was always the ex's mom. She was always polite and said she'd be sure and let Trini know. But Trini was in no hurry to call me back.

This went on for over a week. I was devastated. I was thinking, *Here's a chick I really dug. This is a chick I had a great connection with. The feeling was real. I could tell she dug me. Not just on the surface, but dug me deep down. But that goes to show what I know about chicks. So all I am is a toy to her? Well, maybe I had it coming. Maybe that's my payback for treating some chicks like they're playthings.*

I tried to forget her. I tried to chalk it up to experience, but I couldn't get her outta my mind. Every moment with Trini lingered. I kept replaying them and trying to see where I'd missed the mark. Where I got the signals fucked up. Where I failed to see that this woman really didn't give a shit about me.

All this was on my mind while I was at the Comedy Store on Sunset, hanging out with Mickey Rourke, the star of *Diner, Body Heat,* and, later, *The Wrestler,* who had become my new best friend. This was a big thrill for me, because when it came to acting, Mickey was up there with Brando. He was so fuckin' good he scared me. He'd seen my act a couple of times and had become a fan. Even better, Mickey had turned out to be a down-to-earth guy, like someone from the neighborhood, a guy I'd known my whole life.

Mickey knew I was a night owl like him, so he'd call me at all hours. "Hey, Dice, wanna smoke a pack of Marlboros and hang out at Fatburger?" So, that's where we would go. Mickey and I, sitting outside Fatburger on La Cienega, smoking and bullshitting until four A.M.

So this night I was at the Comedy Store with Mickey when the doorman came over and said, "Dice, you got a call."

No one called me at the Store. If it was a casting agent or a promoter, they'd call my dad. If it was a friend or a chick, they'd be calling me at home.

"Who's calling me here?" I asked.

"Got no idea, Dice, except to say that it's a female."

"Old or young?"

"It's not your mother, if that's what you mean. She's young."

I went to the phone, not knowing what to expect.

"Hello, Andrew."

It was Trini.

"Where you been?" I asked her.

"That's what I'm about to ask you."

"I've called you a million times."

"You haven't called me once."

"I left word with your ex's mother."

"Well, that explains everything."

"Explains what?"

"Why I never got the messages. She wants me back with her son."

"That nasty . . ."

"She's a nice lady. It's just that she doesn't have a nice son."

"Stay away from her son."

"I told you we broke up. When you are coming back to Chicago?"

"Now that you're calling me, sooner rather than later."

When I got back to Rourke, I was all smiles.

"You got that gleam in your eye, Dice," he said, "like you're about to get laid."

"It's better than that, Mickey. A lot better."

On my next trip to Chicago, Trini ran over to the Ambassador East soon as I arrived. It wasn't even about jumping into bed. It was just about being together. We were happy; we ran out and decided to see a movie. Jeff Goldblum in *The Fly*. It's a horror flick that's funny and scary and a big kick in the head. Trini was squeezing my hand the whole time. Afterward we went shopping together. I had to get some clothes. At Marshall Field's she was posing in front of the mannequins, wearing my sunglasses and trying on men's leather motorcycle jackets. She was doing me. She was cracking me up.

We walked to an outdoor café for an early dinner. At a table across from us there was older couple in their seventies. The old man had his arm around the old lady. He was looking in her eyes like he was a teenager in love.

The words came spilling out of my mouth. "That's us in forty years."

Trini looked surprised.

"You mean that?"

"I don't say nothing I don't mean."

"For a comic, you're getting awfully serious, Andrew."

"When I see what I want, Trini, I get so fuckin' serious it's crazy."

"Now you've got me thinking crazy."

"Good," I said, " 'cause I see us living a crazy life together."

RODNEY

RODNEY CAME CHARGING through the front door of Dangerfield's at Sixty-First and First Avenue like a storm, a fuckin' hurricane. He didn't just enter a room. He blew up the room. His raincoat was flying open and he was still taking it off as he got onstage and, without being introduced, just ripped into it.

"I don't get no respect. My wife, she don't give me no respect. The other night she's up saying sexy things. I looked up, she was on the phone. No respect. I got no respect, I got no sex life. The dog keeps watching me in the bedroom to learn how to beg. I said to the dog, 'Watch my wife and learn how to roll over and play dead.' When my wife does have sex with me, there's always a reason. The other night she used me to time an egg. Even my kids, they don't respect me. I tell my son, 'Someday you'll have kids of your own.' He says, 'So will you.' Doctors, they don't respect me. When I was born the doctor tells my mother, 'We did all we could but he pulled through anyway.' I tell him, 'Doc, my gums are shrinking.' He says, 'Stop brushing your teeth with Preparation H.' My proctologist, you think he gives me any respect? No, he sticks his finger in my mouth. You'd think my mother respected me. Think again. She breast-fed me through a straw. Even the hooker, she don't respect me. She says, 'Not on the first date.'"

This was the great Rodney Dangerfield in his club. He was a big bulky guy who was always puffing on a cigarette or a cigar and tugging at his tie. He had this nervous, sweet manner of someone who couldn't sit still. I loved him and I loved his club. I loved the club not just because it was Rodney's, but because of the legends that were born there—everyone from Roseanne to Seinfeld to Kinison to Jim Carrey to Tim Allen. I also loved it because I became one of the legends who was born there. It took years, though, before that happened.

Before I moved to L.A., I'd gotten up onstage at Dangerfield's to do my Jerry Lewis/Travolta act. That's when I first met Tony Bevacqua, better known as Babe, the character who ran the club for Rodney. Babe had this Beatles haircut and a preoccupation with filing his nails. No matter what was happening in the place, Babe never stopped filing his fuckin' nails. He was a good guy, though, because he'd give young comics a chance. "We'll give you a hamburger, you'll go onstage"—that was Babe's standard line.

During the first time I did my act at Dangerfield's, I was still dressed as Jerry Lewis when I started picking on audience members. To one guy in the back I said, "Holy shit, you look like a disaster. You look like a good argument for mercy killing."

After I was offstage, Babe came over. I thought he was gonna compliment me on all the laughs I got. Instead he said, "Hey, what was the idea of picking on Rodney?"

"What do you mean?" I asked.

"That guy you were shredding—that was Rodney."

"The way the spotlight was blinding me, I couldn't see. All I could see was some guy who wouldn't pull his face outta his food. I had no idea."

"Well, now you got a good idea."

"Should I go over and apologize?"

"No, he's already gone."

My father reassured me, saying, "He's probably not even angry. After all, he's a pro. He had to recognize that you're a great talent on your way up."

Dad's words helped, but I still felt like a schmuck for having gone after the one guy I had no interest in pissing off.

Six or seven years later, after I made some noise in L.A. and got the part in *Crime Story*, I came back to New York because I wanted to get on one of Rodney's *Young Comedians Specials* on HBO, where careers were being launched. Babe had taken a liking to me. He kept saying he'd make sure that Rodney came again to see me when I played the club. That seemed to take forever. Meanwhile, the other guys I started out with—like Seinfeld and Kinison—were featured on the special, and as a result, their careers took off.

Finally my dad got a call from Babe.

"He's coming tonight," he said. "Tell your son I'll put him on while Rodney's here."

I was ready. We drove to the city and, just like he promised, Rodney came storming into the club. Five minutes later Babe had me onstage. I didn't hold back. I fuckin' killed. I had my Elvis energy going. I had everyone in the club howling at the nursery rhymes and the whole Dice deal. After my standing ovation, I came down and looked around for Rodney. He was talking to some chick at the bar. I tried to get his attention, but he didn't even look at me. Not a glance. I figured by now he would come up to me and say something. I figured he had to acknowledge how I'd just leveled his fuckin' club. But nothing.

"This ain't right," I told my dad. "We come all the way in here from Brooklyn just to perform for Rodney and I don't even get a thank-you. I'm going over to say something."

"Leave him alone," said Dad. "He's a busy man."

"I don't care how fuckin' busy he is. He's gonna know I'm here."

"He already knows that, Andrew. Leave him alone."

Ignoring Dad's advice, I marched over to Rodney, who had put on his raincoat and was ready to leave.

"Rodney," I said, "I came in to do this showcase just for you."

Tugging at his tie and giving me his jerky head motions, he said, "You're okay, kid."

"But how come you've haven't put me on your special?"

"I gotta run. Gotta go."

"I know why you haven't picked me," I said, my anger getting the better of my judgment. "It's 'cause I'm better than you and you know it."

"That's funny, kid, that's great. You're better than me. You're better than everyone. You're okay. I like you. I gotta go."

And with that, he was out the door. I wanted to chase after him and give him more hell, but I looked over and saw my dad, who had an expression on his face that said, *Leave him the fuck alone!* So I backed off.

Back in L.A., both my hopes and frustrations mounted when a manager named Barry Josephson told me that he was setting up a meeting with his boss, Sandy Gallin. In the eighties, Gallin was one of the most powerful managers in show business. At one time or another, he had managed Sylvester Stallone, Barbra Streisand, Dolly Parton, Cher, Whoopi Goldberg, Neil Diamond, and Michael Jackson.

"I've been telling him about you for a couple of years now," said Barry, a regular at the Comedy Store. "He's ready to meet you."

"Why don't you have him come to the Comedy Store to see me work?"

"Sorry, Dice. Sandy doesn't come to you. You come to Sandy."

I'd been around long enough to know that Gallin was part of what was known as the Gay Mafia. Along with his close friends David Geffen, whose label put out Guns N' Roses' records, and Barry Diller, who ran the 20th Century Fox movie studio, he was part of an out-of-the-closet Hollywood power-house. Given that, would he hate my brand of comedy?

"Don't be ridiculous," said Barry. "Sandy's a pro. He knows funny is funny. The great ones make fun of everyone. I'm telling you, Dice, he's gonna love you."

Not only did Gallin not love me, he didn't even look at me. I got to his office in a state of high fuckin' excitement. I was doing everything in my power to win this guy over, because this guy could turn me into a superstar. I was pulling out all the stops. But he was at the far end of a conference table talking on the phone while paging through a script. He barely nodded his head in my direction. When he finally got off the phone, he focused completely on the script. I did everything but tap dance on the table to get his attention. But I'm not sure he heard a word. He dismissed me with a smile and not a word of praise.

"Fuck him," I told Barry afterward.

"You can't tell with Sandy," said Barry. "He's not demonstrative. He was probably crazy about you. You'll probably hear from him next week."

"I ain't holding my breath."

I chalked up the meeting to just another example of Hollywood horse-shit. Barry meant well, but he didn't have the power to convince his boss that I was worth managing.

So it was back to the drawing board.

In my case the drawing board was always the Comedy Store, not only the best place for honing my material but the best hope that a director or producer or manager or any motherfuckin' *macher* might come in, see how I was slaying the crowds, and take me to the next level.

That *macher* turned out to be Rodney. A year or so after he saw me in New York, he showed up at the Comedy Store on the Strip. Word was that he was in the final throes of selecting the talent for his next installment of HBO's *Young Comedians Special*. With Rodney in the audience, I dug down deeper than usual and came up with the energy I needed to pulverize the room. When my half hour was over, they were standing and screaming for more. I would have given 'em a little more, but I wanted to get to Rodney before he slipped outta the club.

Like in New York, he was on his way out the door when I caught him.

"Rodney, am I on the special?"

"You're okay, kid. You're okay."

"But what does that mean?"

More tie tugs, more head jerks, and then, "You're a wild man."

"I think I did pretty good tonight, don't you?"

"Lemme talk to you later."

"You're always talking to me later, Rodney, but you're never talking to me at all. Just give it to me straight."

"You're gonna be okay, kid."

"I need to know. Am I on the fuckin' special or not?"

"You're a wild man, I'm tellin' you, you're really out there."

And that's all I got.

I was frustrated as hell 'cause I knew he was playing with me. Now he'd seen me twice. In New York I was good. In L.A. I was great. He knew goddamn fuckin' well that I was great. He had to let me on. But why couldn't he just say it?

A week later he didn't say it, but his rep did. I was on.

It finally happened November of 1987. Along with Robert Schimmel, Bill Hicks, Carol Leifer, and a few others, I'd been picked to go on the HBO *Young Comedians Special* that he was hosting. This was the moment I'd been waiting for. It was doubly sweet—and I was doubly motivated—'cause it was gonna happen on my home turf.

I prepared for this spot like a fighter going after a title shot. I worked out my material every night at the Store, honing it, tweaking it, weeding out anything that didn't kill, perfecting every punch line. I didn't care if I played in front of a packed house or five people. I went after them with everything I had.

I worked out like a fighter, too. I watched what I ate, hit the gym every day, and ran the Fairfax High track every night. I put every ounce of my energy and focus into getting ready for Rodney.

The night of the show I put on my clothes as if I was a soldier going into battle putting on a uniform. I got dressed slowly, deliberately, each item of clothing adding one more layer to the Dice persona—underwear, socks, black sweatshirt with DICE on it, pants, giant belt buckle, black boots, fingerless gloves with rhinestones, and the final two touches, my motorcycle jacket and my oversize shades. I checked the fluid in my Zippo lighter and made sure I had a full pack of cigs. Then I stared at myself in the mir-

TOP: The Originals: Jackie Silverstein, my mom; Fred Silverstein, my dad; Natalie Silverstein, my sister; and me.

ABOVE: Brooklyn's finest: Mom and Dad on their wedding day.

RIGHT: Mom looking like Liz Taylor at my bar mitzvah with her mom, my beautiful grandmother Shirley.

TOP: Dad helping me out, as he always did, at my bar mitzvah.

MIDDLE: The Originals at my high school graduation in 1976.

BOTTOM: At the Del Mar Hotel, practicing to be the next great rock drummer.

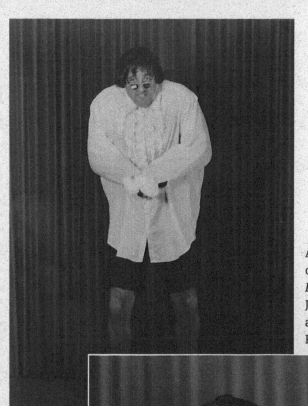

Andrew Clay, twenty-one years old, as Jerry Lewis from *The Nutty Professor* (top), transforming into John Travolta (bottom), performing at America's first comedy club, Pips, in Brooklyn, New York.

The famous Breakfast Sessions with Lee Musiker at the Del Mar Hotel in Loch Sheldrake, New York. The summer that changed my life.

As a prize for winning Joe Franklin's *Gong Show*, I got to perform on Franklin's TV show and also got a two-week engagement at the Fireside Lounge in Queens with Tiny Tim.

While I was working out material at the Comedy Store in LA, Andrew Dice Clay was born. Part James Dean, part Marlon Brando, part rock and roll, all Brooklyn.

Playing the godfather of stand-up, Rodney Dangerfield's club.
Courtesy of Joan Dangerfield

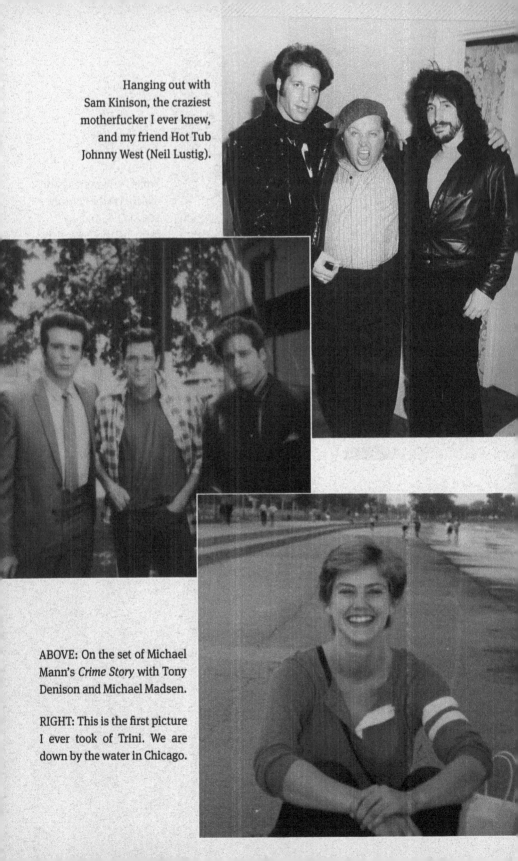

Hanging out with Sam Kinison, the craziest motherfucker I ever knew, and my friend Hot Tub Johnny West (Neil Lustig).

ABOVE: On the set of Michael Mann's *Crime Story* with Tony Denison and Michael Madsen.

RIGHT: This is the first picture I ever took of Trini. We are down by the water in Chicago.

Axl Rose and me the night we met at the Wiltern Theater in LA. Axl and the rest of Guns N' Roses came to see me perform that night. We've been friends for life since.

The Brooklyn Band that backed me up on the Dice Rules tour. From left: Frank Diorio, Horn Player, me, Richie Santa, Carmine Diorio, Robert Santa, and Sal Iuvare.

I NEVER STUDIED MUCH
IN SCHOOL,
(TOO BUSY DAYDREAMING)

BUT WHEN I TURNED
ON THE TUBE, THERE WAS
ELVIS THE KING,
BUDDY RICH WITH HANDS
LIKE LIGHTNING,
TRAVOLTA SANG & DANCED,
LEWIS MADE ME LAUGH,
SLY KNOCKED ME OUT,
BRANDO MADE ME POUT,
BOGIE TOOK BACALL,
DEAN HAD US ALL,
GLEASON WAS THE
GREAT ONE,
CAGNEY YOU WERE #1,
MURPHY AND PRYOR BOTH
GREAT NO DOUBT,
BUT IN '88 IT'S "DICE"
THEY'LL SHOUT.

I NEVER STUDIED
MUCH IN SCHOOL . . .

BUT I DID STUDY

ANDREW DICE CLAY

in

"RODNEY DANGERFIELD'S NOTHIN' GOES RIGHT"
HBO SPECIAL • SAT., FEBRUARY 13 • 10 P.M.

ABOVE: My dad and I took out an ad in *Variety* to announce the HBO Special and the coming of Dicemania.

LEFT: Meeting Sly Stallone on the set of *Lock Up*. Stallone's character "Rocky" was a huge inspiration. It was insane to then get to be friends with him.

ANDREW DICE CLAY

DICE RULES

IN CONCERT

This Concert is being filmed for the upcoming 20th Century Fox Feature Film

February 21
8PM

or Mature Audiences Only

TICKETS $25, AT THE MADISON SQUARE GARDEN BOX OFFICE AND ALL TICKETMASTER LOCATI

CALL TICKETMASTER: (212) 307-7171, (201) 507-8900, (516) 888-9000, (914) 965-2700 INFORMATI

February 21st and 22nd, 1990: I'd reached the top of the mountain. Two sold-out nights at the Garden.

Rodney, thank you for everything.

Mickey Rourke with my mom and my nephew Michael at Sly Stallone's birthday party.

It was a dream come true to have my original Brooklyn family always at my side and looking out for me.

It was an honor to get to meet and almost wo with the great Jerry Lewis.

The one and only Howard Stern. I am proud to call you my friend.

ABOVE: My family with Tom Jones at the Bally's Las Vegas Hotel. Great guy, great sense of humor, and always great to our family.

LEFT: At Radio City Music Hall doing my pre-show prayer.

The Three Amigos. Selling out the Garden was a big thing, but man, the birth of my sons Max and Dillon was ten times bigger. Getting to raise my boys has meant everything to me.

The Crew: Club Soda Kenny (Kenny Feder), me, Happy Face (Mike Malandra), and Details (Dave Schuller).

Michael "Wheels" Parise.

The night before the return to MSG: Max Silverstein with Club Soda Kenny, Happy Face, and Todd Rosken.

BEACON THEATRE SOLD OUT IN RECORD TIME!
BY UNPRECEDENTED DEMAND,
102.7 WNEW's OPIE AND ANTHONY PRESENTS

ANDREW
DICE
CLAY

On Sale
NOW!

"I'M OVER HERE NOW!"

OCT 26

MADISON SQUARE GARDEN.
The World's Most Famous Arena

October 26, 2000. The return of the Diceman to the Garden. Ten years after the original shows. Sold-out again. That night was for my boys.

"Uncle" Lee Lawrence. My uncle. My friend. My mentor.

Being on *Entourage* was the beginning of a great resurgence.

The day I got married to the incredible and gorgeous Valerie Vasquez.
© *Steven Shofner*

My boys, Dillon on guitar and Max on drums, in their band, L.A. Rocks, rehearsing at home. © *Joefer Bautista*

My amazing family: Max, Eleanor Kerrigan, me, Val, and Dillon. © *Joefer Bautista*

ror and took in the full effect of Dice. Yeah. I was ready. I was so fucking ready.

I walked from my hotel to the club. I wanted to feel the pulse of Manhattan and bring all that energy and aggressiveness with me. I felt people staring at me, this cocky half Elvis, half Terminator walking down the street like he owned the city. As I walked and smoked I thought, without an ounce of doubt, I was about to make comedic history.

When I got to the club, I found Mom, Dad, and Natalie sitting ringside. I said hello and then drifted over to the bar. After a while, Rodney came over. "How you feeling, Dice? You ready?"

I paused and looked at him through my dark sunglasses. "Ready? Tonight they pay. Tonight they get disciplined."

Rodney roared. "Tonight they pay. Okay, you're ready."

And I was.

When it was time for my set, Rodney introduced me this way: "This next gentleman comes from Brooklyn. Best way to describe him is to say he's the typical boy next door. Say hello to Andrew Dice Clay."

I got up onstage and took my sweet fucking time lighting my cigarette with a flick of the Zippo and an over-the-shoulder-back-of-the-head drag. I opened with the nursery rhymes.

"Little Miss Muffet, sat on a tuffet, eating her curds and whey. Along came a spider and sat down beside her and says, 'Hey, what's in the bowl, bitch?'

"Little Boy Blue, he needed the money.

"Was an old lady who lived in a shoe, she had so many children her uterus fell out.

"Mary, Mary, quite contrary, trim that pussy, it's so damn hairy."

From the rhymes I went to the audience. I spotted a guy sitting with a good-looking chick and started needling him.

"How long you been going with her?" I asked.

"Couple of weeks," he said.

"Is she nice?"

"Very nice."

"Bottom line, she suck a good dick? She suck the chrome off a trailer and lay back with a beer after? To me that's a lady. Today chicks don't suck dick the way they used to. They dabble at it. They lay there, they flick it, they smack it. They say, 'Ooh, look at the way it jumps.' I say, 'It can sing and dance too. *Now suck my dick,* honey.' Most of 'em don't know what they're doing. The minute they start sucking they gotta look right up into your eyes with this innocent expression. It's like you're staring down at a fuckin' gopher. 'Why you looking at me, honey? Don't look at me. Suck my dick. *Concentrate.* And jiggle my balls. What are they, orphans? It's a three-piece set. Work it, hone it, get it right. If you can't party with the big boys, don't show up.

"These days the chicks like us to go down on them. Ever seen a vagina up close? It's fuckin' frightening. It's a haunted house down there. It's covered with so much shrubbery and weeds, you gotta cut through with a machete. And depending on her moods, she'll just lay there like you're not even in the room. You gotta check in and say, 'Honey, am I in the right ballpark?' She says, 'No. A little lower. A little to the left.' I say, 'What are we doing? Backing in a truck?'

"Once you go down there, it's no five-minute trip. It's a fuckin' weekend. After ten minutes it gets boring. That's why I wear a Walkman."

The crowd was mine. I owned them. It's like my friend Lee Lawrence always told me: when preparation meets opportunity, it spells success.

The only thing I didn't like was the title that either Rodney or HBO gave the special. They called it *Nothing Goes Right*.

EVERYTHING GOES RIGHT

IT WAS 1988—A decade after my debut at Pips—and it was shaping up to be the biggest year of my life. Even though *Crime Story* wasn't picked up for a third season, my appearance as a cast member had given me a boost. I was also featured in a movie called *Casual Sex?* with Lea Thompson and Victoria Jackson where I played Vinny, a sexy thuggish guy who found his feelings and went around saying, "I'm the beast from the east. I'm a wild crazy beast. I'm the Vin Man." When the producer, Ivan Reitman, saw what the Vin Man was doing on-screen, he rewrote the script, turned me into the star, and changed the ending so that I went off into the sunset with Lea Thompson. Professionally, I was in good shape. Personally, my relationship with Trini was going great guns. When it came to women, I was no longer the crazy man I once had been. At least I told myself that. I told myself that the reality of having a beautiful family life was right around the corner. Trini and I were living together in an apartment in Hollywood.

On the night that *Nothing Goes Right* aired we were at home. We had a few friends over, and during the show we were sitting on the couch holding hands. Trini was laughing louder than anyone. After the show I told Trini and my pals I needed to go for a walk. I needed to be by myself.

It was a Saturday night in Hollywood like any other. Bumper-to-bumper traffic, music blaring from the cars and clubs that lined the Strip. As I made my way to the Store, I was smoking my cigarette and savoring the moment. I was about to break through the show business barrier. I was about to achieve what I had always wanted—recognition and fame. I couldn't remember feeling happier.

The special was the tinder that started my full-on inferno. I was playing Chuckles, a comedy club in Long Island, when Dennis Arfa, the greatest agent in the world, came in to see me. Dennis represented Rodney. He had been there the night of *Nothing Goes Right*. Rodney was actually the only comic on his roster. The other artists were Metallica, Joe Cocker, and Billy Joel.

Arfa was a complete hipster, a guy who had the balls to leave William Morris to do his own thing. The Morris office had been representing me for years for movies and TV, but not for personal appearances.

"Diceman, baby!" he said to me after the show. "I brought the papers."

"What papers?"

"I'm signing you."

"You are?"

"Tonight, baby, right now. I see your future, and it's all green. The minute you go on sale, it's like checkers, sweetheart. One jump, done. We're sold out. Just like that."

Naturally I was flattered, but I was also consulting with my father, who, now that I was taking off like a rocket, had become more involved in managing me. There was no one else I trusted more.

"There are bigger booking agencies than Arfa's," said Dad, "but you'll never find anyone as devoted as Dennis. This guy is ready to go to war for you. I'd sign with him." And I did.

A month later I was playing the Treehouse in Connecticut, a comedy club attached to a hotel. This was just after *Nothing Goes Right* had aired, and everyone and their mother was talking about my performance.

I was having a late breakfast at the hotel when the waitress said I was wanted on the phone by a Mr. Gallin.

Sandy Gallin? How the fuck did he know I was at the Treehouse? And what did he want?

"How are you, Mr. Gallin?"

"Fine, Andrew. Please call me Sandy. I'm calling to set up a meeting. When will you be back in L.A.?"

"Couple of days."

"Can we get together the first day you're back?"

"What's the hurry?"

"You must know that you're the hottest thing in the country right now, Andrew, and it's absolutely paramount that your next move is the right one. There's much to discuss."

Naturally I was jumping out of my fuckin' skin. Sly Stallone's manager had hunted me down and found me in Connecticut and was practically begging me to sign. If I was a putz, I would have said, *How 'bout last time I was in your office when you didn't even bother to look at me?* But I wasn't a putz. I was a guy who wanted a big career—so I didn't say nothing.

The afternoon I arrived in L.A. I ran over to his office. Unlike the last time when I met Sandy and felt like I was invisible, this time he greeted me like I was some kind of conquering hero. He started with a personal story of his own, about how he was from Brooklyn, how he loved the Dodgers when he was a kid, and how we had so much in common. Then he came right to the point.

"I want to do great things for you, Andrew. I want to be your manger."

"I already have a manager," I say.

"Who's that?"

"My dad."

"That's wonderful. I can work with your dad. I look forward to meeting him. I know you're lucky to have a father to look after your best interests. He adds to the strength of the team."

"And you know I got an agent."

"Dennis Arfa. The best."

"I can't lie, Sandy. I can't tell you that I'm not excited about having you as a manager. That's been a dream of mine. But I also have another dream. And before I sign with you, I need for that dream to come true."

"What is it, Andrew?"

"My own HBO special."

Sandy didn't say anything. I could see he was surprised.

"You get me that special," I said, "and I'll sign."

"Andrew," he said, his tone changing from light to dark, "I don't audition for anyone."

"Look, Sandy"—my tone totally sweet, not a trace of anger—"I know you're as big as they get, and I don't wanna show no disrespect, but the truth is that I had to audition for you. Last time I was here I came up empty. Then the Rodney special became my audition. You saw it, you liked it, and now I'm back. All that's good. But before I commit, I need to see you in action."

"You really are from Brooklyn, aren't you?"

"That's right. We come from the same place."

"Sheila," Sandy said into his intercom, "get me Chris Albrecht at HBO."

Thirty seconds later Albrecht was on the speakerphone.

"Chris," said Sandy, "I'm here with Andrew Dice Clay. Maybe you heard of him. Anyway, I want to sign him, and he's willing, on the condition that I get him his own HBO special. Can you help me out?"

"Give me twenty-four hours, Sandy, and I'll have an answer."

When Gallin hung up from Albrecht, he looked at me and said, "If the answer is yes, I'll have an eighteen-month contract ready for you to sign."

I smiled, trying to look cool, but my heart was pounding and my mind was racing. All I thought was, *So, that's your move, huh, Dice? You're gonna play two-handed poker, winner takes all, with the most powerful manager in the business?*

That was my move.

I went home to hang with Trini and my parents and my sister, who'd flown in for a few days. We all holed up at my place, not saying much, basically sitting on pins and needles, waiting for Sandy to call.

Later that afternoon, the phone rang.

Sheila.

Sandy's assistant. She told me that Sandy wanted me to come up to his house that evening. I explained that my parents and sister were in town and I didn't want to leave them alone. Sheila put me on hold and then came back on the line ten seconds later. "Sandy said to bring the whole family."

Around seven o'clock, we wended our way into the hills above Sunset Boulevard and pulled into the Sandy Gallin estate, an eighteen-thousand-square-foot palace only slightly smaller than the Ponderosa. A butler greeted us at the door with Sandy close behind. He welcomed Mom, Dad, Natalie, and Trini like family who'd just arrived from the old country and then took us on a tour of his mansion. Each room was more magnificent than the next, but one room absolutely floored my mother: a walk-in closet off the master bedroom suite that was the size of a bedroom itself. My mother froze and gawked at the rows of red underwear neatly draped on hangers. "Red underwear," she said. "Keeps away evil spirits."

"You got a smart mother," Sandy said to me.

After the tour we all went downstairs, where the butler met us with a tray of crystal flutes filled with champagne.

"A toast," Sandy said, passing out the flutes and holding his up. "To working together, and to the first of Andrew's many HBO specials."

I nearly fumbled my champagne flute and dropped it onto his marble floor. "You did it?"

"No," Sandy said. "I booked it. You did it."

CUTE LITTLE STORY

THE GALLIN/ARFA COMBINATION was nuclear.

Within a week, Dennis booked me at the Roxy on the Sunset Strip. Being the clever manager that he was, Sandy invited twice as many people as the place held. The overflow filled the street and made the news. This was the start of Dicemania.

A week later Sandy called and said, "Carl Reiner's hosting the annual Big Brothers banquet at the Beverly Hilton tonight. It's a twenty-thousand-dollar-a-plate men-only affair. I've talked to Carl. He'll try and bring you up if there's time. There's no guarantee. It's up to you whether you want to go, but I will tell you this—every producer, every power player, every talk show host, every important director in Hollywood will be there. We've already scored at the Roxy, but this will take you to another level. If you bomb, though, the consequences could be grave. Your exposure will be enormous."

"Are you kidding?" I said. "This is the chance of a lifetime. How can I not take this shot?"

"It's a risk," said Sandy.

"Risks are what I'm all about."

I knew what Sandy was up to. He wanted to put me on edge. He wanted to get me crazy so I'd outperform myself. Well, I hardly needed more motivation than God originally gave me. But if Sandy Gallin wanted to play God—as most managers do—I'd play along. I'd overmotivate and make sure that the fuckin' Big Brothers banquet was something no one would ever forget.

I was feeling great, but my stomach was in knots when Barry Josephson picked me up his black Corvette. When we arrived at the Beverly Hilton, I saw that every man was wearing a tux. Not me. I said, *Fuck the tux*. I was wearing my leather—crazy leather jacket, fingerless leather gloves, leather boots, tight black jeans. I had on my shades. I had on my attitude.

Eventually, after a crew of other comics, Carl Reiner finally got to me. "Gentlemen," he said, "let me introduce our next speaker, a man recently hired by the Bush administration as an adviser on foreign affairs. Please welcome Mr. Andrew Dice Clay."

I loved the intro. As I made my way up, I felt like Martin Scorsese was filming me in slow motion. I passed by Jack Lemmon and gave him a playful tap on his cheek. (Later someone said, "Do you understand, Dice, that no one has touched this man in thirty years?") This was it. Every power player in Hollywood was sitting right there. It was all or nothing. I had all these thoughts of what I had been through in the last ten years of show business. Then I thought of what my dad had said that day on the phone: "Don't hold back, sonny boy. Let them have it."

I stood at the podium. I gave the audience all the time they needed to take me in. I lit my cigarette, snapped my Zippo closed, and, looking to the left at Carl Reiner, said, "I noticed all night you've been telling little stories . . . Well, I got a cute little story . . . See, I got my tongue deep up this chick's ass . . ." The roof blew off. My insides were shaking from nerves, but they would never have known it. I held nothing back as I barraged them with my best material.

Those fuckers were falling on the floor. Literally. Near the end when I hit Sidney Poitier with a few oversized-black-dick jokes, Aaron Spelling, who was sitting next to him, got so worked up that he knocked Sidney out of his chair and was punching him on the arm. It was complete mayhem. Even one of my favorite clean jokes went over: "You know when you're standing on line at the bank and the guy says, 'Is this the end of the line?' 'No, asshole, it's the front. We're all standing fuckin' backward.' " I wasn't up there for more than ten minutes, but they were the best minutes of my life. The howling and screaming was beyond belief.

"I don't know what just went on here," said Reiner, "but I'm looking at a bunch of old farts who are laughing—really laughing—for the first time in twenty years. In this room tonight, right before your very eyes, Andrew Dice Clay has become a star."

Garry Shandling followed me and bombed. It was so quiet you could hear crickets. Shandling didn't work for another five years. After Gary, Red Buttons came on and said, "Wasn't Dice unbelievable? Big man, big star." Then Red looked over to me and said, "But, schmuck, next time wear a tux."

The phone woke me up the next morning. It was Sandy saying that my HBO special would be shot in Philly.

"What do you want to call it?"

"The Diceman Cometh."

"Great title. You certainly came up with it quickly."

"No, Sandy. I've had it picked out for years."

Amazing things were happening. Arfa booked me in Town Hall in New York. Half the borough of Brooklyn came to see me. Just for the hell of it, I had my buddy Robert Santa and his band back me up on the Elvis and Travolta stuff. We had become friends about seven years earlier at an audition for an Elvis off-Broadway show. They helped me fire up my passion. Felt even better when Hot Tub Johnny came along with Club Soda Kenny, whose real name is Kenny Feder, a gold shield detective who, at six foot five, is all muscle and a martial artist. I liked having an entourage—not so much for the protection, since I'm pretty good at protecting myself. I liked them for the Brooklyn that they brought with them. They brought the streets. If I'm not street, I'm not shit.

When the Santa Brothers opened for me with "That's All Right," I was feeling all the crazy energy of being a kid and wanting to make it—except this time me and my boys were onstage at Town Hall, where the night before there were ballet dancers and the next night there would be opera singers. But that night Elvis was rocking out and I was fucking up Mother Goose and they were falling out in the aisles, laughing so hard that they were pissing their panties.

I did stop for a moment and realize that after this, nothing would be the same. At age thirty-one my dream was actually coming true. I always wanted to be more than a club comic. I wanted to show the world that a comic could be as big as a rock star—and play the places that a rock star played. I wanted to show the world that, more than a comic, I was an actor playing the part of the funniest guy on the planet. I wanted to use my platform as a comic to become an actor and make movies, not as a bit player but as the main player, the driving force.

At age thirty-one, those goals were being attained. It was the end of one struggle. It was a clear victory, and it felt great.

DICEMANIA!

THE RODNEY SPECIAL was huge for me. But my performance was abbreviated, and I was sharing the bill with other comics. *The Diceman Cometh* would be my first solo shot, the moment I would take command.

I trained for it like I was Rocky taking on Apollo Creed.

I hit the gym with a vengeance. I went on a low-carb, high-protein diet, like I was a professional athlete. I tightened up my material at the Comedy Store, and then I ran the streets of Hollywood late at night, blasting my workout music through my Walkman.

The day of the special Johnny, Trini, and I slid into the back of a limo, left Brooklyn as snow fell, and headed down to Philly. Was I nervous? Fuck yeah. The driver knew it, Johnny knew it, Trini knew it. To relax me and make me laugh, Trini started singing. Every fucking song on the radio. All the fucking way to Philly. Amazing. She knew the lyrics to *every* goddamn song. She was like a human jukebox. And she put her heart and soul into every one. Plus she had pipes. It was like I had a private two-and-a-half-hour concert.

By the time I went out onstage for a quick walk-through rehearsal, my jitters were gone, replaced by a jolt of excitement. I stared at the unbelievable set—a pair of giant dice with my name in huge red letters. It felt surreal, and it felt so right.

Afterward we grabbed a quick bite and then we went to the hotel and I got dressed. I'd had a leather motorcycle jacket custom-made for the occasion by Jeff Hamilton, the guy who designed George Michael's jacket in a video I saw. I shrugged into my jacket, popped a cig into the corner of my mouth, and walked over to the mirror. I nodded at Dice staring back at me and headed out.

Back at the theater, I took a moment for myself in the dressing room. I had agreed to shoot two full shows and pick the best one. I took a deep breath, told myself to concentrate on just this one show. One at a time. Then I lowered my head, closed my eyes, and whispered a little prayer, my pre-show ritual, something I'd done before every show to that point and have ever since. Then I got up and opened the dressing room door.

My family came in first, followed by my team, then the director, then Trini, and then Sandy Gallin, wearing a wide smile. He'd flown in from California. He sat down next to my mom and dad, and the three of them started schmoozing about the Brooklyn background they all had in common. Sandy realized that for all his power, I wasn't gonna make a move without Dad. It was important to me that he treat my father with great respect—and he did. Sandy was also learning how to handle me.

"Dice," he said, "do you like good news before or after a show?"

"Before," I said. "I wanna hear good news the minute it happens."

"Okay. Three-picture deal. Twentieth Century Fox. Two theatrical features and a theatrical release of a concert film on the order of Eddie Murphy's *Raw*."

"You gotta be kidding."

"Barry Diller, head of the studio, signed off on it an hour ago."

First thing I did was turn to my parents and ask, "Do you hear what this man is saying? A major Hollywood studio is banking on me for three major pictures."

Dad smiled and said, "I think you better concentrate on going out there and destroying this crowd."

Which was just what I did. With the Allman Brothers song "Whipping Post" blasting through the speakers, I hit the stage. I lifted my collar and pumped my fist, and the crowd erupted, chanting, "Dice! Dice! Dice!" I slapped hands in the front row, pumped my fist again, lit a smoke, and started in.

I hit hard with the nursery rhymes, which, because of my appearance on the Rodney special, were already well-known. A lot of the fans had 'em memorized, like the way fans memorize hit songs. They recited them along with me and had a ball. For this show, I also made up some new ones.

"Stick these in your pocket," I told the crowd before launching into the fresh limericks.

"Little Jack Horner sat in the corner eating a pizza pie. He shit pepperoni, blew his friend Tony, wiped his mouth on his tie."

The crowd went nuts. With every poem, they were standing, screaming, yelling, and pumping their fists.

"Mary had a little lamb she kept in her backyard. When she took her panties off, his wooly dick got hard.

"Georgy Porgy pudding and pie, jerked off in his girlfriend's eye. When her eye was dry and shut, Georgy fucked that one-eyed slut.

"Hickory dickory dock, some chick was sucking my cock, the clock struck two, I dropped my goo, I dumped the bitch on the next block."

From there I thought it was time to go back to the beginning of the Diceman's days on planet Earth.

"I've had pressure my whole life," I said. "You know what they do the second you're born? They throw you in a nursery with thirty or forty kids you never seen before in your life. So I'm laying there, bored out of my mind. I ask this one kid, I say, 'Johnny, you got a light for me?' The kid's taking a dump in his diapers, drooling all over himself. That's when I knew that kid's got no fuckin' class. I put on my leather jacket, ring for a little service. This big blond nurse comes in and shoves a plastic nipple in my mouth. I look at her and say, 'Sweetheart, who you teasin'? Pick up the dress. We're gonna mow the lawn tonight.' " The crowd went nuts.

When it was over, I knew that this was the show of my life. I headed back to the dressing room, where I'd have an hour or so to rest before the second show.

"Great show," said Sandy. "But do the second show even faster. I think it'd be a good idea to pick up the pace."

Without losing a beat, I turned to him said, "Look, Sandy, you are one of the greatest managers ever. As far as Hollywood goes, you're in the history books. I respect that. But don't ever tell me what to do onstage. Because on that stage, I'm king. And as king, I gotta say that the first show was perfect. That second show can't be any better. The first show is what's going on HBO. This second show is just for fun."

Sandy had the good sense not to argue. He soon saw that, good as the second show was, it couldn't compare to the first.

The show was set to air at midnight on New Year's Eve. A few hours before it was to be broadcast, I had a gig at the Beacon Theatre with a viewing party afterward being thrown by HBO. What a way to ring in 1989!

The Originals—Mom, Dad, my sister, and me—plus Trini were in a cab from the Beacon on our way to the party. Dad reached into his coat pocket and pulled out a check. He kept staring at it.

"What is that?" I asked.

"The money for the Beacon show. Thirty thousand. You made thirty thousand for an hour's work."

"Ain't that beautiful, Dad?"

"Sure it's beautiful. It's just hard for me to wrap my head around the numbers. Do you know how many years of process serving I had to do to make that kind of money?"

"Don't even think about it, Dad, 'cause you'll never have to do a day of process serving again."

HBO had set up a wall of televisions in a restaurant so a hundred of us could all watch. The anticipation for *The Diceman Cometh* was tremendous. I was too excited to eat anything. New year, new career, new star shooting across the sky. Watching myself, I felt like I was kicking the doors down in every home in America that had HBO.

Next day I didn't wake up till one P.M. With the great Beacon show and the HBO special under my belt, I'd never felt better. And then I got a call from a "friend."

"You read the *New York Times*?" he asked.

"I'm more of a *Daily News* kinda guy," I said.

"Well, get the *Times* this morning."

"Why?"

"You'll see."

I ran down to the newsstand on the corner and picked up the paper. And right there, in a five-word description of *The Diceman Cometh*, I read, "The Demise of Western Civilization."

I was half amused, half amazed that the *Times* took me so fuckin' seriously. But I wasn't upset. I was actually glad for the attention. Let the press write whatever the hell they wanna write. I work for the fans, not the press. All the press could do was bring me more fans. I didn't see then—and remained blind for months to come—the power of the press to fuck me up.

A few weeks later—in between gigs at four-thousand-seat arenas—I was back in Hollywood on my way to the Comedy Store, just to drop in and let 'em know that I hadn't forgotten my L.A. roots. I was driving down Sunset when I stopped at the light at Vine Street. I heard a honk and looked over. Who'd pulled up beside me? Sam Kinison.

Sitting next to Sam was a hot chick with her huge boobs spilling out of her tank top.

"Dice!" Kinison screamed at the top his lungs. "Fuckin' Dice! I've heard all the good shit about you. Welcome to show business, baby!"

"Thanks, Sam."

And then he peeled off, him and his honey heading out into the night.

Living on both coasts, I'd been in and out of L.A. so much that I hadn't hung out with Sam in a while. But we were still pals, even though his career had taken off long before mine. Sam wasn't looking at me like a competitor at that moment. He was looking at me like a brother. In my naïve way, I presumed that was always gonna be the case.

Gallin had hooked me up with David Geffen. I was soon going to be making my first comedy album for Geffen Records, the same label that did Aerosmith and Guns N' Roses. The producer was set to be Rick Rubin, the guy I met back at Greenblatt's Deli, who I'd since learned was a genius in the studio and one of the hottest guys in music. I was also talking to Dennis Arfa about my upcoming tour. He carefully explained to me about the building blocks of a career.

"Look, baby," he said, "you start with a five-hundred-seater. You move to a thousand-seater. You slowly develop these markets and then move into the bigger venues."

"I know you're a genius, Dennis," I said, "but I don't think you're thinking right. You got to use your imagination. You got to imagine what it was like when the Colonel spotted Elvis. No one like Elvis had ever existed before. The old rules didn't apply. Same with me. I don't think we gotta worry about building blocks. I think we need to be bolder about the bookings. The demand is already there."

"All right, Dice," said Dennis. "I'll do it your way. I'll test it out with a thirty-five-hundred-seat theater. How about the Celebrity in Phoenix?"

I knew Dennis was challenging me with a tough one, because Arizona isn't New York, L.A., or Chicago, where my brand of humor had proven so popular. At the same time, I was sticking to my guns. I believed that even in Arizona I was catching on like crazy.

"I'll take the challenge," I told Dennis. "Book the Celebrity and see how the sales go."

A week later Dennis called.

"Were we able to sell out the Celebrity?" I asked.

"For the first night."

"What do you mean the first night?"

"Sales were so strong they added two others—all sellouts."

The result was an eighteen-city tour with major venues in every market.

"It's still not big enough," I told Dennis.

"How big are you talkin', Dice?"

"Madison Square Garden big."

FLEEBIN' DABBLE

THINGS WERE POPPIN' off fast and furiously. I was bouncing between both coasts. I was staying close to Hollywood, the place where my manager Sandy Gallin and my agent Dennis Arfa were planning my worldwide takeover. And I was staying close to Brooklyn, where my parents gave me the love and support that kept me grounded. In Hollywood, Trini and I moved into an apartment at Hawthorne and Fuller. In Brooklyn, I got my own apartment a block down from my mom and dad on Nostrand Avenue. I had all the bases covered.

My instincts about playing the Garden turned out to be doubly right. It wasn't just a one-night sellout. It was two. No comic had ever done this before. Leading up to that was a multicity tour that started in Providence in November 1989 and culminated in those two nights in New York in February 1990. I was modestly calling it the Dice Rules tour.

All this mega-success and these mega-plans had me feeling out of my depth. That's why I went to see the one man in the world who could settle me down: my dad. I went to the office of the Royal Process Agency at 16 Court Street.

I told Dad that I wanted him to manage me full time and that he didn't need to do the process serving any longer. His days of nine-to-five were over. I even had the name picked out for the new company: Fleebin' Dabble. It doesn't mean anything. It just sounded funny to me. I was over the moon to be able to do this for Dad and have him on my side even more. At first he tried to keep the business in the family, offering it to his brother-in-law, Ernie. But for some reason, that didn't work out. So Dad just padlocked Royal Process and, on the same floor in the same building, opened up an office with FLEE-BIN' DABBLE PRODUCTIONS written on the door.

I've heard it said that most highly creative, highly crazy entertainers like me are unmanageable. I basically agree. But if there was anyone who could keep me from going off the deep end, it was my dad—the steady, always-cool, always-loving, warm and wonderful Freddy Silverstein.

With Fleebin' Dabble attending to details and watching my back, I got ready to storm the country with the Dice Rules tour. To make sure the show was tight and right, I was rehearsing in a studio in Rockaway, Queens. I wanted to make sure that the music segment had the same nonstop energy as the comedy. That's why I was using a live band. A rock-and-roll comic had to have a rock-and-roll band. When other comics hit it big and went out on tour, they treated the theater like it was a small club. They stayed with that same tame-ass buttoned-down stand-up shit. Not me. I was thinking of when Elvis played the Astrodome. I was thinking of a gigantic, loud, raucous, balls-out, mind-blowing, blasting assault. I wasn't looking at these shows as a comedy routine to amuse the fans. I was seeing them as an experience, a once-in-a-lifetime event.

The band was all Brooklyn buddies. It was Robert and Richie Santa, but also my pals Carmen on lead guitar, Sal on bass, and Frankie, who left his UPS job, on drums. It was basically a bar band—but a kick-ass bar band—which was exactly what I wanted.

I bought one of those video recorders that were just coming out at the time. I was into it, recording everything, including the band rehearsals. I basically just started taking it everywhere I went. One night me and the boys drove over to Brooklyn and Pips, the comedy club where it all began. For the sake of good memories, I wanted to see what was happening there.

Minute I walked through the door, I saw this big man onstage. He had to weigh three fifty. His hair was worked up in a giant pompadour. Marty

Schultz told me the big boy's name was Michael Parise, but he called himself Wheels. And he was actually up there riffing on my material.

I didn't mind. Matter of fact, I wanted to record what he was doing, so I climbed onstage and moved around him with my video camera aimed at his head. No one seemed to mind—especially since there were only nine or ten people in the audience. Naturally he was shocked to see me up there, but everyone was getting a kick outta what I was doing. I was circling him with my camera and telling Wheels, "Breathe. Just breathe." In response, he picked up his game, revved up his rhythms. He liked to talk about his weight. He said, "Man, I'm bloated. You ever get bloated? That Chinese food will fuck you up. You can't eat that shit. They put that MSG in there and you swell up. I'm usually one fifty, one sixty. Then one beef and broccoli, and look what happens. It's not my fault. I like being fat. Fuck skinny people."

When his set was over, we walked off the stage together—Wheels the comic and me his videographer—and who was waiting for us at ringside but none other than Downtown Ronny.

"Hey, Dice," he said. "What do ya think of Wheels? I think he's gonna be a star, ya heah?"

"He's okay," I said. I was sounding like Rodney Dangerfield describing me.

"I think this Wheels is going places," Ronny continued. "I think you're the guy to take him places. He's a fuckin' perfect opening act for you. Ya heah what I'm saying, Dice?"

"I heah, I heah you, Downtown Ronny. But right now I got a lot on my plate. Besides, when did you get in the business? I thought you was in another business."

The business I was referring to was bookmaking. A few years back my mom had implied that Ronny was a good guy to know. She had said that in the future, if I became a big star, he'd be a good guy to have watching my back.

"I didn't realize you was in show business," I said to Ronny.

"I'm in fuckin' everything, ya heah? And this Wheels, he may not be no

Dice, but the fuckin' guy is going places. I see you think enough of him to put him on tape."

"I'm videotaping everyone. I'm videotaping life. I'm about to videotape you."

"What do you really think of him?"

"Like I say, Downtown, he's okay. But he's green."

"You could develop him, Dice. You could take him wherever you want. 'Cause right now I'm hearing that you're going to the fuckin' top, and you need all the friends you can get."

"Friends I already got."

"Now you got some more. Now you got me and Wheels."

"So you're managing him. Is that it, Downtown?"

"I'm seeing him where you were maybe six or seven years ago. A star in the making. Ya heah?"

I'm not sure exactly what I heard, except that I liked Wheels, and Downtown had always fascinated me. Besides, it was my mom who first introduced me to him.

Before long, Downtown Ronny became a part-time member of my entourage. Before long, I used his comic Wheels to open some of my shows. What I couldn't foresee, though, were the complications that came with Downtown's connections.

STERN

I LOVE HOWARD Stern. I think the guy is brilliant. I first heard him when he was just starting out in the New York market. Friends kept saying, "Dice, you got to do *Howard Stern*. You guys are two peas in a pod."

They were calling him a shock jock at the same time I was being called a shock comic. Like me, he loved talking about sex and wasn't afraid of where the conversation might go, and like me, he was looking to bust through boundaries. Because we were two New York Jews with chutzpah to spare, we could read each other's rhythms. We could bounce off each other's grooves. He was fast, I was fast, and together we worked up a superspeed banter that the listeners loved.

You couldn't exactly call Howard a straight man, but in some ways he played that role. I could bounce off his wit. We were a good combination, because Howard is essentially an inside man. His world is the studio, the safe cocoon where he does his thing better than anyone. I'm essentially an outside man. My world is the comedy club, the theater, and the arena. The bigger the live audience, the happier I am. Knowing these differences between us reinforced our relationship. If I was stuck in a studio all day, I'd go nuts. And if Howard had to do his act in front of eighteen thousand people, he'd have a hard time.

Given these contrasts, we appreciated each other. More than any other interviewer, Howard loved candid discussions about sex. He pushed the raunch because he liked the raunch. Howard became a fan and a booster.

He was more intellectual than me, but I was more street-smart. And all the way to this day we are absolutely magic on the air together.

We had this brotherly bond. He gave me his private number at home and even liked it when I called him late at night, just to fuck with him. Sometimes I'd have Hot Tub Johnny on one line, Howard on the other, and the three of us would make three-way prank calls to some poor schmuck in Queens just for kicks. We were like five-year-olds. Later when I started hanging out with Wheels and Downtown Ronny, I'd take them on Stern with me. Downtown Ronny's guttural super-street Brooklynese "ya heah" became a trademark that Stern taped and loved to play back. No radio personality was into the whole Dice thing as deeply as Stern.

As Stern was moving up, so was I. When it came to taking on the media hypocrites, we were like soldiers fighting on the same side. I loved having Howard as an ally. He was razor sharp and never afraid to call me on my shit. I liked the challenge 'cause it made me even sharper.

A little later in my life, Howard and me were such good pals that he thought it'd be cool if I lived close to him. We found a great place fifteen minutes away from him. Four acres. A four-million-dollar spread reduced to $900,000. I loved the layout and the style. I loved everything except the voodoo dolls sitting in the den.

"They aren't voodoo dolls," said Howard. "They're exotic African art."

"It looks like fuckin' voodoo to me," I said.

"You can't pass up the deal. You'll live here four or five months a year. Besides, it's a great investment. You gotta take it."

I took it. But when the papers were written up and I got to the lawyer's office, I couldn't sign. I kept thinking about the voodoo dolls. I tried, but I couldn't sign on the dotted line.

"You're crazy," said Stern.

"Maybe," I said. "But I'll sleep better tonight."

PANTIES IN A BUNCH

MY DEAL ON Geffen meant that my first comedy record would be coming out soon. I also learned that Joel Silver, one of the most powerful moguls in Hollywood and the guy who produced the *Die Hard* and *Lethal Weapon* movies, was set to produce *The Adventures of Ford Fairlane*. This would be my first starring vehicle, a film where Sandy Gallin had made sure that my name would appear above the title. The story revolved around a detective who was a variation of the Dice character. He was a hipster who hung out in the rock-and-roll world of L.A. nightclubs and rock arenas. Perfect for me. My costars were Wayne Newton, Priscilla Presley, Lauren Holly, and Maddie Corman.

Along with this superstar treatment came some nasty treatment from the press. But I didn't give a shit. The press had their panties in a bunch 'cause I was joking about women and gays in ways they didn't consider funny. Fuck the press. I wasn't putting on this act for the press. I was playing to the fans, and my fan base was growing by leaps and bounds. If the press didn't understand that the Diceman was a character who amplified certain attitudes that millions of people had—not only amplified those attitudes but actually made fun of those attitudes by making fun of himself—then the press had its head up its ass.

In the midst of my success, something happened that shouldn't have surprised me but did: my fellow comics started attacking me.

Ever since I started out at the Store, I knew that comics could be the most backstabbing, envious assholes in the world. But that always happened behind the scenes. When one guy did well, you'd hear whispers that he didn't deserve it. Or when a guy fell on his ass, you'd hear whispers that that was just what the motherfucker deserved. It was always behind-the-scenes shit. So when I was being called the biggest comic in the world, a couple of other dudes who couldn't stand it started badmouthing me to the press.

But when Sam Kinison lost his mind and became obsessed with my success, that got to me. Not because I felt it would hurt my career—his attacks actually brought me more attention—but because Sam and I had been running buddies. We'd gone through the wars together. I knew he was deep into coke, and that coke will fry your brain and scramble your soul. Given Sam's hyper energy, the last thing he needed was artificial chemical energy. Whatever it was, for a long time Sam was fixated on telling the world that I wasn't shit. He went on Stern and couldn't stop ripping me. He started calling me Andrew *Jew* Silverstein, like I ever hid the fact that I was Jewish. He told a couple of audiences that he was hoping I died of inside-out stomach cancer. It made him absolutely insane that I had leapfrogged over him and was playing huge arenas.

But because I knew Sam wasn't in his right mind, I didn't let it get to me. When I learned that his brother Kevin, a really nice guy, had committed suicide, I felt terrible. So when I saw Sam at a Bon Jovi concert, I went over to express my condolences. When I started to say something, though, Sam turned away, like I was dead meat.

I thought about it for a couple of weeks and decided to call him.

"The reason I came over," I said to him, "was to tell you how sorry I was about your brother. I don't have a brother, and I can't imagine the pain of losing one. When you wouldn't even look at me, I thought it was a pussy move on your part."

Silence. I could hear Sam thinking.

"You know what, Dice, maybe I been wrong about you. Maybe the thing to do is for the two of us to go out on tour together. We'll rent a bus. The two shock comics, the two screamers, the two rock and rollers who ain't scared of saying nothing to no one. What do you say?"

"I'm not sure that's a great idea, Sam. You got your audience and I got mine."

What I didn't say was something Sam already knew: I was playing twenty-thousand-seat arenas, and at best Sam was playing two-thousand-seat theaters.

Next time I saw Sam was the night before Rosh Hashanah, the Jewish New Year. I was at the Comedy Club with Hot Tub Johnny. When Sam saw me walk in, he ran over. Wearing his usual long coat and beret, he fell to his knees and started in with, "Oh, godfather, oh, great godfather, let me kiss your hand."

"Get the fuck up, Sam," I said. "That ain't even funny."

"Godfather," he continued, "will you grant me the extreme privilege of going on tour with you? Will you be kind enough to grant me my wish, godfather?"

"You don't gotta do this, Sam. You know that a tour with the two of us ain't in the works."

Without a word, he just got up and left. Next day Trini and I were coming from Rosh Hashanah services when she turned to me and said, "I got something to tell you, Andrew, but promise you won't get mad."

"How can I promise when I don't know what it is?"

"It isn't good. That's why I wanted to wait till the services were over."

"Tell me already."

"Last night after you left the Comedy Club and Hot Tub Johnny stayed behind, Johnny and Kinison got into a fistfight."

"What!"

"It got ugly."

"Who told you this?"

"Hot Tub."

"And why didn't he tell me?"

"He didn't wanna mess up your holiday."

That night I heard the story on the phone from Hot Tub Johnny himself. Kinison had come over to him saying shit like "You think I'm afraid of Dice? You think I can't kick Dice's ass?" Being a cool guy, Hot Tub ignored him. But Sam didn't go away.

"What are you gonna do," Sam asked Johnny, "if I decide to kick your ass?"

"Put your hand on me," says Hot Tub, "and find out."

Sam gave Hot Tub a shove and Hot Tub laid him out with a single shot to the mouth. Sam's bodyguard went after Johnny, there was a big scuffle, but no one was really hurt. This was all I needed to hear. I jumped in the car and roared over to the Comedy Store, where Kinison was doing a late set. On the way over, I got crazier and crazier. My ears were burning and my throat was dry. If Sam was angling for a fight, I was more than willing—I'd be fuckin' delighted—to give him one. I'd bash his fuckin' brains in.

When I got there, Hot Tub Johnny was waiting for me.

"No, Dice," was all he said.

"Get outta my way, Johnny."

"I can't let you do it."

"I said, *get out of my fuckin' way!*"

"This is what he wants."

"Fine, 'cause this is what he gets."

"He's setting you up. He'll take the beating so he can take your money. That's all there is to it."

"It'll be worth it."

"No, it won't. He'll win. He'll get the publicity, his career will get the bump he's looking for, he'll sue you for millions, and you'll wind up looking like a schmuck. Just go home and forget about it."

I thought about it for a minute. Hot Tub was right. Hot Tub was a great friend who wanted nothing for me but the best. "Thanks," I said before leaving the club and going home to Trini.

MEETING THE MASTERS AND THE MANIACS

"STALLONE WANTS TO meet you," said Barry Josephson, my day-to-day manager, who worked for Sandy Gallin.

I took it as a joke, but Barry's not the kind of guy who jokes.

"If you're pulling my leg," I told him, "I'll fuckin' kill you."

"He's making a movie called *Lock Up* with Donald Sutherland. He wants you to come over to the set."

"When?"

"Today."

"This is crazy."

"No," said Barry, "this is real. Sly is a Dice fan—simple as that."

I felt like a giddy little kid on his way to Disneyland. I could hardly concentrate on anything but this one amazing fuckin' fact—Stallone had asked to meet me. I always thought I'd make it big, but for all my certainty, I never thought—never even imagined—that one day I'd be sought out by Sly.

I pulled into the studio lot. The drive-on pass was waiting. I was directed to go straight to Stallone's trailer. I parked the car. Took a few deep breaths. Got out. Walked to the trailer. Took some more deep breaths. Knocked on the door. Waited a few seconds. Then that voice:

"Come on in."

I climbed up into the trailer, and there he was. He was smiling.

"Hey, man," he said, "glad you could come over. Just wanted to say congratulations on everything. You deserve it. You're breaking new ground. And you break me up, you really do."

I jumped in before he could go any further and told him how much *Rocky* meant to me, meant to all of us. How it was like nothing that came before it. How I used it to channel my energy and my character.

He laughed appreciatively and asked if I'd do my Rocky impression for him.

"Adrian!" I started screaming in my best Sly voice. I was performing before an audience of one, but it was the best audience of my life.

We hung around and shot the shit for a few more minutes before he was called to the set.

"I'm having a few friends up to the house for a little barbecue on Sunday," he said. "We'd love to have you and your girl come over."

When we arrived that Sunday, we weren't surprised that the place was palatial. But we were surprised that Sly was in the backyard flipping burgers. No cook, just Sly. He introduced us to his brother, Frank, and all his friends. It's like we were family. The conversation was low-key and easy. Everyone was treating me like I was the star, not Sly.

Among his pals was George Pipasik, the famous trainer who got Stallone in shape for *Rocky*. I'd been reading about this guy for years. He was Mr. Czechoslovakia four years in a row. He was all about building up your natural strength—no steroids, no nothing but working on the machines that he built with his own hands. At forty-five, he looked twenty years younger. In his Czech accent, he said to me, "They call you the Diceman, is that correct?"

"That's right."

"And do you know what they call me?"

"Mr. Pipasik?"

"No, they call me Filthy Dirty and Nasty Mouth. What do you think of that?"

"I like it. It sounds like a name I'd make up."

"Well, I'm happy to shake your hand, Mr. Diceman."

When we shook hands, everyone—including Sly—was looking at us.

They knew what was coming, but I didn't. He shook my hand with such brute unrelenting force that within a few seconds I was down on my knees.

"Holy shit," I said from my position on the ground. "You're the trainer I'm looking for. As long as Sly don't mind."

"If you can take it, Dice," Sly yelled from his position behind the grill, "be my guest."

A week later I was at Pipasik's gym, where all the machines, custom-constructed by him, were painted orange. I'm something of a gym rat. I've been to a thousand gyms, but nothing like this. Those machines were so quiet and smooth that it was a thrill to use them. I wouldn't call getting trained by Pipasik a thrill. It was more of a challenge. But I hung in. I was about to make a movie, and this was the man to get me in shape.

MY KIND OF GUY

JOEL SILVER DEMANDED respect. He got respect. He was the man who made a slew of tremendously expensive and successful action-adventure movies. Producers like him are army generals like Douglas MacArthur or George Patton. They're bigger-than-life figures—like Ivan the Terrible or Julius fuckin' Caesar—because they make bigger-than-life movies. If Joel didn't think he was getting the most out of you, he'd scream in your face. He was all about big passion. He'd love you, he'd hate you, he'd hug you, he'd rant at you like you were a piece of shit. Joel was my kind of guy.

Up until this point, Joel and I had had great creative meetings about the character of Ford Fairlane and my approach to the film. So I was a little puzzled when I got a call from his office saying that he needed to have an emergency meeting with me. I showed up with Hot Tub Johnny. Barry Josephson and a couple other reps of mine were waiting for me.

We were all called into a huge office, where Joel got up from his gigantic cherrywood desk, shook my hand, and then said to Hot Tub, "Would you mind waiting outside?"

"Not at all," said Hot Tub, who left me alone with Joel.

Now I knew something was wrong. Joel didn't want me to have my backup. He wanted me to feel unprotected.

"What's going on?" I asked him.

"We have a problem with the movie."

"What kind of problem?"

"Look, Dice, if you don't care about the film, then I don't care."

"What are you talking about, Joel?"

"I make movies every day," he said as his voice got louder and louder. "This isn't the only movie I'm making. Because I'm making movies—with or without you. You understand that, don't you, Dice?"

"Get to the point. Tell me why you're so pissed."

"You're too fuckin' fat—that's why. I'm not making this movie with a fat Ford Fairlane."

"What are you talking about, Joel? Last week you told me how great I look."

"That was last week. This week you look fat. I heard you been eating pizza. Get Hot Tub Johnny back in here."

Hot Tub came back into the office.

"Did Dice eat pizza last night," asked Joel, "or didn't he?"

I broke in before Hot Tub could answer. "Is this what this emergency meeting is about—pizza? I had one fuckin' slice."

"We start filming in less than two weeks, and you're out eating pizza!" Joel screamed. "Movie stars don't eat pizza!"

"One slice ain't gonna kill me . . ."

"I'll tell you something else, Dice. I fuck better-looking women than you do. I fuck *Playboy* Playmates."

"I'm not gonna listen to this shit," I said. "I'm outta here."

"Go ahead. Walk out, fat boy, and I'll pull the plug on this fuckin' movie."

"Who the fuck do you think you're talking to, Tubby? Any good-looking chick who'll fuck you is only fucking you for your money. They're fucking you to get into one of your movies. The chicks I fuck actually like fucking me. They like sucking my dick. After they fuck you or suck your dick, they're running to the bathroom to puke."

Joel ignored my last remark. In a weird way, it calmed him down. In a lower voice he said, "I got a doctor I want you to see in Pacific Palisades. He's gonna give you something to lose that fat before you start shooting."

"I ain't taking no fuckin' drugs. You know what, Joel—I ain't taking no more of this shit. Period. I'm outta here."

Joel turned to Barry and my other reps and said, "I'm not shooting this movie with some pizza-eating slob."

I made a move toward Joel and said, "I'll knock the fuckin' teeth outta your head."

Barry and his boys jumped up and grabbed me before I got to Joel. They dragged me out of his office while I was still yelling obscenities at one of Hollywood's biggest producers. No one was gonna talk to me like that.

On the way out to the parking lot, Barry was laughing.

"What's so fuckin' funny?" I asked.

"That's one of the best shows I've ever seen."

"You think so?"

"I know so."

Somehow Barry's laughter changed my mood.

"He just wants you to look your best for the film," he said.

The next day I went to see the doctor in Pacific Palisades, who put me on something called Medifast, a liquid diet. I started drinking this stuff on a Thursday—five times a day. By Monday I'd dropped twelve pounds. By the time we were ready to start shooting, I had the body of Atlas and the eye of the tiger. I was in the best shape of my life.

ROCK-AND-ROLL DETECTIVE

THE FILMING ITSELF went great. I was free to offer up suggestions to the writers, and the director, Renny Harlin, encouraged me to incorporate my Dice-isms and improvise many of my lines. Since I was a rock-and-roll detective, I figured we needed a big rock-and-roll number. That became "I Ain't Got You," produced by Don Was. The supporting cast was beautiful. Wayne Newton turned out to be one of the sweetest guys in the world. He was the complete pro—easy to approach with no attitude other than "How can I help?" Like me, he took his job seriously. So did Priscilla Presley. She was wonderful. I loved her sense of humor and her upbeat personality. We had some beautiful talks about Elvis. Just to talk to the King's former wife was a thrill, and when she told me that she could feel the influence he had on me, that's all I needed to hear. Harlin, who did *Die Hard 2* with Joel Silver, was great. I was able to get my friend Gilbert Gottfried into the movie, along with Uncle Lee Lawrence, the bandleader who I met in the Catskills when I was just a horny teenager beating the drums. There were parts for Sheila E., Morris Day, the rapper Tone Loc, and Ed O'Neill, who went on to star in *Married with Children* and *Modern Family*. Even Hot Tub Johnny had a cameo.

And I got to sing and dance in the film, and rehearsed for days with top-notch Hollywood choreographers. While I was singing and dancing and acting up a storm during the making of *Ford Fairlane*, Ed Weinberger, the big-time TV producer, kept coming by the set. I had just signed a sweet pay-for-play sitcom deal with him worth a potential quarter million an episode.

But I didn't wanna see Weinberger. I needed to concentrate on the film, so I had Joel Silver, now acting as my watchdog, keep him away. The more I heard about Weinberger—how he controlled every last bit of his sitcoms—the more leery I became of doing the show. Finally, in spite of the big money, I bailed on Weinberger. With my feature film coming out and the demand for me in ever-bigger venues, TV looked less like an opportunity and more like a prison.

THE BIG BAN

"YOU WATCH MTV?" asked Sandy Gallin.

"Who doesn't?" I answered. In the eighties, MTV was the hottest thing going. MTV was the center of red-hot pop culture. "They want me on MTV?" I asked.

"They want you as a presenter on the MTV awards. Prime-time national telecast. Arsenio Hall hosting."

At the time Arsenio was also riding high.

Naturally I accepted.

I got to the Universal Amphitheatre for the afternoon rehearsal. It was insanity. Because I was the hottest comic in the country, I had cameras chasing me everywhere. They were ignoring the rock stars and TV stars. They were after me for some crazy quote. I had nothing to say. My job was easy. I was introducing Cher. I was going to walk out, play with the crowd for a minute, and then say something like, "Ladies and gentlemen, the last Puritan—Cher!"

Rehearsal was a breeze. I figured the actual performance would be the same. Keep in mind, it was live, and there was no tape delay. What you said went out to the world.

The show started. This was the year of Madonna's "Like a Prayer" and Paula Abdul's "Forever Your Girl." Paul Reiser got up and did some shtick. He was promoting his sitcom—*My Two Dads*—but he was really digging himself a ditch. He was talking about all the different hats Sinatra wore. No one wanted to hear about Sinatra's hats. No one was laughing—not the six thousand people in the audience, not the millions at home. I was backstage thinking, *I gotta get this crowd going.*

Dick Clark, who was producing the show, called me over. I love Dick Clark. Like the rest of America, I grew up on *American Bandstand.* Far as I'm concerned, Dick Clark was cool his entire career. Besides, he looked younger in 1989 than he did in 1959.

"Look, Dice," he said, "Cher isn't ready to go on. So you go out there, say a couple of short things, and I'll send Arsenio out as well."

"Why?"

"So you can play around with him."

"I don't think that's necessary, Dick. I'm a stand-up. I can handle it alone. It's what I do."

"It'll be better with Arsenio."

"No, it won't. It'll be awkward. It'll be another one of those stupid award show encounters when two presenters trip over each other. I love Arsenio, but this isn't the spot for him. I don't need him."

I'm thinking, *My career's going through the roof right now, and the last thing in the world I need is to bomb with some dumb-ass banter with Arsenio. I need to do my job. And my job is to be fuckin' funny.*

As I heard my name announced, a huge roar went up. The last thing I did was tell Dick, "Don't send anyone out there." I said it with such fuckin' menace that even Dick Clark, great producer that he was, would not not challenge me.

In my animal-skin zebra-striped jacket, I swaggered out to the podium. I took my time reaching for my pack of cigarettes and lighting up. I wanted the anticipation to build. I was still pissed that Clark thought I needed help out there. But rather than let my anger distract me, I used it to motivate me. Come hell or high water, I was gonna say some funny shit.

"I met this chick last week," I said, "wheeled her back to my apartment, got her in bed, started brushing the hair on her back, braided it, spiked it, got her all excited. And you wanna talk breasts? Lemme tell you something—I grabbed on to a set of tits where I didn't know where the tits begin and belly ends. I mean, it was like one big glob of shit."

As you can imagine, the crowd was hysterical. To push the hysteria even higher, I went right into a rhyme: "Jack Splat could eat no fat, his wife could eat no lean. So Jack ignored her flabby tits and licked her asshole clean." All this before I introduced Cher.

When I got offstage, there was pandemonium. My man Barry Josephson had turned white.

"I don't know what's gonna happen," he said.

"What are you talking about? It's already happened. They loved me."

"Not MTV. MTV wants to kill you. They had to restrain Dick Clark from running out there and grabbing you."

After awards shows, the producers set up tents for interviews. That's when the press shouts out questions. Well, I went from tent to tent, and not a single reporter had a question. They were already writing furiously in their notebooks. It turned out that, in the end, I was the story. But they didn't want no comment from me. The story was better without any comment. The story was simple: MTV BANS DICE FOR LIFE.

When I got home that night the phone was ringing. It was Sandy Gallin.

"I saw it," he said.

"What'd you think?" I asked.

"It hit me so hard I actually started to believe that someone was playing a joke on me. Someone had messed with my TV and put in a tape. No one could have said on national TV the things you said."

"The things I said were funny. The audience went nuts."

"The audience always goes nuts, Andrew, but that's not the point."

"Then what is the point, Sandy?"

"Typically, an awards show incident is talked about the next day and then forgotten. But this incident is going to be talked about for years to come. MTV has never issued a lifetime ban before."

"And I'm supposed to feel sorry about that?"

"I don't know how you're supposed to feel."

"Well, I'll tell you how I feel. I feel that MTV can get fucked. Those videos are pushing the line as hard as they fuckin' can with tits and ass. Michael Jackson is grabbing his dick, and Madonna is practically grabbing her pussy. MTV is all about raunchy rock and roll. But if a comic gets on there with some raunchy rock-and-roll humor, that's no good? That deserves a lifetime ban? Well, good. Great. If MTV wants to go after me, I'm ready. 'Cause I'm going after their fuckin' ass. They're now a permanent part of my act. I'm the comic banned by MTV. That's gonna raise my price, it's gonna raise my profile, and it's gonna make me bigger than ever."

DICEMAN COMETH

BUT THE BIGGEST news of all had nothing to do with showbiz.

Trini was pregnant, and I was ecstatic. It was the best news I could have gotten—better than making a movie with Joel Silver, better than selling out arenas across the country, better than making money hand over fist. My dream of having a family—of being a dad and raising kids with a loving woman like Trini at my side—was coming true.

Family was also on my mind when I played the big arena in Miami. There are hardly any New York Jews who don't have relatives in Miami. And naturally mine came out in force. Besides Mom and Dad, they all showed up— Grandma Shirley, Uncle Ernie with his sister, Sandy, and her twin daughters, Dad's sister and his brother, Sammy Sunshine, who, at eighty, was so inspired by my act he started doing his own stand-up routine.

Some people asked me whether I felt bad about doing such blue material in front of my family. My answer was that my family didn't give a fuck how much I cursed, since they cursed up a storm themselves. They understood that humor is humor and entertainment is entertainment. Just as I entertained them when I was a little boy banging the drums, I entertained them as a grown man making funny jokes.

What I loved most about that night in Miami was the presence of the godfather. Rodney Dangerfield came to see me. Dennis Arfa, who booked Rodney as well as me, suggested that I call him up to the stage.

"As long as he'll like it," I said.

"He'll love it," Dennis assured me.

I went out onstage in my sleeveless Dice leather jacket with seven thousand studs and rhinestones. I drank in the thunderous applause. And then, before getting deep into my routine, I said, "There's a man here who's responsible for introducing me to the public. In turn, it's my honor to introduce him to you. He's the only man in America who had the balls to put me on TV. He never asked me to water down my material. All he said was, 'Be yourself.' For those words of wisdom and for the faith he had in my talent, I'll be grateful to him for the rest of my life. I consider him one of the greats—and I know you do too. Show the man who can't get no respect all the respect and love you got. Get up on your feet and salute the one, the only, the godfather—Rodney Dangerfield."

Rodney came out, gave me a hug, waved to the audience, and left.

The next stop was the L.A. Forum, and the stars came out. My shows became Hollywood events. Sly. Mickey Rourke. Cher. They all came out. And I wasn't just doing comedy. I actually sang a soul ballad: Major Harris's "Love Won't Let Me Wait." And if that wasn't enough, I got behind a drum set to do battle with Frank Diorio, a man who could rival any of the greats. We went back and forth on this double drum duel. If I got the best of him—which I did—it was only because Frankie let me. One night I even called to the stage Duff McKagan and Slash from Guns N' Roses. They were both huge Dice fans, and just for the love of it, they came out and pulverized the crowd with their searing rock-star riffs. For years I'd been calling myself the rock-and-roll comic; now I was proving it. The edgiest rock and the edgiest comedy were all coming together. The energy was unbelievable. With me behind the tubs drumming up a storm with Frank Diorio, with my bass player Sal Iuvare matching funky licks with Duff, and with my guitarist Carmine Diorio going toe-to-toe with Slash, we blew the roof off the fuckin' Forum. You had to be there.

You also had to be at the Nassau Coliseum.

When Dennis Arfa called to say I was booked into that huge arena on

Long Island, I predicted I'd sell it out in fifteen minutes. It pissed me off that the sellout took an hour.

"Schmuck," said Arfa, "do you realize what it means to sell out a venue like that in just an hour?"

"Yeah," I said, "it means it took forty-five minutes longer than I predicted."

It turned out to be another one of those nights. There was hysteria in the air. I felt terrible for my opening act, Lenny Clarke, a terrific comic. The crowd wanted no part of him. They just wanted me, and had no patience for anyone who stood between us. Fact is, at one point Lenny stopped standing and sat on a stool, where he started clipping his toenails—that's how he reacted to the boos.

Backstage, I felt bad for him, but what could I do? I kept pacing around the hallways as the crowd screamed, "Dice! Dice! Dice!" preventing Lenny from saying another word.

When the crowd saw me take the stage, they exploded; everyone was standing and screaming while I raised my arm in the air, my hand in a fist of recognition and defiance. They knew I was gonna say some shit. They knew I was gonna be raunchy and funny and not give a fuck who I offended. They knew the Diceman character was uncensored and unafraid. He said things they only said in their minds. When he said 'em out loud, they roared. They loved this character—not because he was the ideal American with the ideal American virtues. They loved him because he was honest. They loved him because he loved pussy and he was not afraid of saying so. They loved him because they loved being shocked.

A VISIT FROM THE PROFESSOR

THERE HAD BEEN blue comics before me, but none of them could have even imagined selling out arenas. I knew that the clubs and the theaters were too small. They couldn't contain me. I needed something bigger. But when I finally got something bigger, when the arenas started selling out left and right, the reaction during the shows—the stomping and screaming, fans standing on their seats and cheering like I'd just thrown the winning touchdown in the Super Bowl—those were things I hadn't expected, things I didn't see coming. The other thing I didn't see coming was how the critics were going to come after me.

But how could I worry about the critics when the only people who mattered to me—the fans—were running over themselves to get to my show? And how could I worry about the critics when the artists I admired the most—like Jerry Lewis—were coming to meet me? You heard right: Jerry Lewis.

When I had my manager tell Jerry's manager that I wanted to star in a remake of *The Nutty Professor,* my manager wasn't all that sure how Jerry—who wrote and directed the original and controls all rights to the story—would respond. Well, Jerry responded right away. He wanted to meet me and was willing to come to my suite at Bally's, where I was performing in Vegas.

Naturally I went nuts with anticipation. I knew I was perfect for the role—that was a given—but the idea of actually speaking with the great Jerry Lewis, whose professor character inspired my whole career, was too good to be true.

Remembering how on his telethon Jerry smoked like a fiend, I got Club Soda Kenny to fill my suite with bowls of cigarettes, all different brands, so Jerry would feel at home. This didn't turn out to be a good idea. When, accompanied by his people, Jerry entered the suite, he looked at the cigarettes and said, "Is this some kind of joke?"

"No, Jerry. I'm trying to be a good host."

"No one told you that I'm recovering from a heart attack?"

"I had no idea," I said. "Sorry."

Not a great start, but the mood turned better when we sat down to discuss the project. Then the mood turned great. I told Jerry about the beginning of my career and how for years I riffed on the nutty prof turning into Buddy Love.

"I see you as Buddy Love on acid," said Jerry.

"I love that," I said. "And I also wanna say, Jerry, that I know you got this reputation as someone who might be tough to work with, but I'm here to tell you that when we're working on the movie you can hit me in the mouth every day. You can kick me in the ass. You can do whatever the fuck you wanna do. You can't be too tough on me. That's how much I love and respect you. That's how willing I am to work with you."

"Who says I'm tough to work with?" asked Jerry.

"It's the general impression I've gotten by reading and talking to—"

"Let me ask you something, Mr. Dice. Is that the general impression you've gotten by reading about Barbra Streisand? Is that the general impression you've gotten by reading about Sly Stallone? Because if these people are tough to work with, these people are like me. These people are perfectionists. They're artists. True artists. They see a scene one way—the right way—and aren't happy until the scene comes to life in precisely the way it's been living in their imagination."

By now Jerry was up on his feet and yelling. Jerry Lewis was yelling at me about how the great ones are all perfectionists and the great ones are all difficult because great artists can't be compromised. Naturally I was a little taken aback that Jerry Lewis was standing in front of me screaming his head off. But who was I to argue? So I didn't. I was nodding my head and listening and letting him go off for as long as he wanted. Which was quite a fuckin' long time.

At the end of the meeting, Jerry had calmed down.

"You know what," he said, "I can see you seeing doing this movie. I can see it happening, Andrew."

"I can't tell you what that means to me, Jerry."

"What it means is that we'll have a meeting with the studio—that's what it means."

Less than a month later we were in the offices of New Line Cinema—me and my management, Jerry and his management, and the studio's top brass. As the meeting started, there was only one problem: Jerry was not being funny. He was stiff and withdrawn, and I could see the thing was not going well. So I excused myself and went to the men's room, where I put on a pair of nutty professor glasses and pushed my hair down over my forehead in the nerdy manner of the character I wanted to play. I returned to the room in character, asking everyone—in the professor's voice—whether they had a couple of quarters for the parking meter. The room broke up—even Jerry. The mood changed, and suddenly everyone was animated and excited.

At the end of the meeting, the man who ran the studio said, "We're making this picture. This movie's gonna happen."

I was over the moon.

Then came a strange call. It couldn't have been a month later when I was at home and Trini said, "Jerry Lewis is on the phone."

Naturally I jumped.

"Everything okay, Jerry?" I asked.

"No, everything's not okay!" he yelled. "And nothing will be okay until you get what you're supposed to get and I get what I'm supposed to get!"

The screaming went on for quite a while. I didn't know what to say. My managers hadn't mentioned anything about the negotiations. I had no idea what we were being offered, and Jerry wasn't being specific. He was just yelling about how neither of us should get fucked by the studio. I agreed, but

I was seeing what everyone meant when they said Jerry was tough to work with.

No matter; we pushed ahead. Turns out we were both booked in Atlantic City, performing at different hotels at the same time. I saw that as a good sign. I went to see him perform and, afterward, I told him straight from my heart that he was fuckin' brilliant.

"You're the best," I said.

"Thank you, Andrew."

"I'm wondering where we are on the movie deal."

"Where we always were," said Jerry. "We're holding our ground. You're gonna get what you're supposed to get. And I'm gonna get what I'm supposed to get."

"Well, I think I'm happy with what I'm gonna get."

"You can't be. You can't be happy unless I'm happy—and I'm not. I'm not at all happy."

In short, Jerry's unhappiness killed the deal. The studio got tired of his demands. They revered Jerry Lewis, but the simple truth was they didn't need him.

I wouldn't say that I was crushed—remaking *The Nutty Professor* was always a long shot—but I was deeply disappointed.

A FUNNY THING HAPPENED ON
THE WAY TO THE GARDEN

AFTER JERRY LEWIS there was one other person I really wanted to meet—and I knew the man who knew the man. I got close with Wayne Newton, a great guy, while working with him on *Ford Fairlane*. If his trailer door was open, I'd go in and start shooting the shit. One day I noticed a flashy diamond bracelet on his wrist.

"Man, that thing is gorgeous," I said.

"It was a gift from Frank," said Wayne.

"Sinatra?" I asked, knowing goddamn well that "Frank" meant Sinatra. But then again, talking to Wayne Newton like he was my costar—which he was—had me sounding stupid.

"Yes," he said, "Sinatra is such a generous guy. Wonderful friend."

All this Wayne Newton/Frank Sinatra talk got me excited and even more stupid, to the point where I asked Wayne an amazingly stupid question:

"Hey, Wayne," I said. "Do you think Sinatra likes me?"

"If he does, I promise you that you'll hear from him."

I didn't know what else to say. I felt like I'd made a fool of myself. I couldn't believe I'd asked such a ridiculous question—*Do you think Sinatra likes me?* Was I really that needy? I guess so.

That happened in the summer. At the end of the year I was headlining at Bally's in Vegas. I got to town with my crew a couple of days early. Not only was I being paid a ridiculous amount to play the hotel, I was also on a hot winning streak. First night out I won $69,000 at the blackjack table.

The cards were smiling at me like I was their best friend. Making me even happier was the fact that, come the weekend, Trini was flying in from L.A., and my parents were arriving from New York.

The day after my winning night, Hot Tub Johnny, Club Soda Kenny, and I piled in the limo. I was dressed in my usual sloppy gym clothes. I told the driver, "Take me to the closest Mercedes dealer."

The dealership wasn't far from the Strip. I got out, walked into the showroom, and looked over the new models. A salesman, young guy, approached me. He smiled and got red in the face. He recognized me and happened to be a fan. I walked around a gorgeous four-door sedan the color of champagne. I peered at the sticker attached to the passenger-side window. "So, bottom line, what's this gonna cost me, out the door?"

The guy cleared his throat and said, "Well, including tax, license, registration, other costs—a little more than sixty-nine thousand dollars."

"And for me?"

He laughed. "I'm a big fan, sir, but, yeah, sixty-nine thousand plus. That's all I can do."

"I had this dream ever since I was a kid," I said. "I always wanted to drive a Mercedes right out of the showroom." I reached into my pocket, pulled out my wad—sixty-nine thousand dollars in cash—and pressed the bills into the salesman's hands. "There's sixty-nine K even. Can you make my dream come true?"

I thought his jaw would drop to the floor. "Well, I think, since it's *cash*—"

"Bring the paperwork over to my hotel tomorrow," I said.

"Yes, sir."

We stood silently, awkwardly, for about twenty seconds, the guy's eyes wide and still looking at the mound of cash in his hand. Finally, I said, "You forgetting something?"

He blinked at me. "Sir?"

I held out my hand. "The key."

Five minutes later, me and the boys were cruising the Strip in the new champagne Benz. Next day I drove it to the airport and picked up my parents, my sister, and Trini. The girls all got in the back while my father sat up front with me. Beaming like a little kid, he caressed the leather on the seat. "What a gorgeous car," he said. "I've never been in one of these before."

"Whenever you want a ride, just ask Trini," I said.

"Me?" Trini said from the backseat. "Why me?"

I caught her eye in the rearview mirror. "Because this is yours, baby. Merry Christmas."

From there it only got sweeter. A couple nights later, Wayne Newton invited us all over to his fabulous house, treating us like we were family. One of the biggest stars in the history of Las Vegas was entertaining my parents and girlfriend, lavishing them with attention and talking about me like I was in the same league as him. I guess I was, but I still had to pinch myself to believe it.

"Hey, Dice," said Wayne. "Have you ever headlined in Vegas on New Year's?"

"This is my first time."

"That's what I thought. Well, after the show come to the Hilton. I wanna do something special for you. I wanna throw a party for you and your family. What do you say?"

"What *can* I say? Thanks, Wayne."

The party was beautiful. We loved being with Wayne. After about an hour of schmoozing, he took me aside and said, "Grab Trini and meet me outside. We gotta do a quick getaway."

I didn't know what he was talking about, but where Wayne led, I followed.

Downstairs he pulled up in one of his many Rolls-Royces. He had me get in front. Trini got in the back with Wayne's girlfriend.

"Where we going?" I asked.

"I made a promise to you a while back."

"What promise?"

"You'll see."

We drove along the Strip and pulled into the Sands. Right next to the hotel was a little Italian restaurant—nothing super-fancy, just casually elegant. A small private party was already in progress. There was a nice buzz. Naturally I had an instinct about what Wayne was up to. I was hoping my instinct was right, but I was scared that I was wrong and didn't want to be disappointed. As my eyes swept around the restaurant, I suddenly saw that I wasn't wrong.

He was standing by the bar with a drink in one hand and a cigarette in the other. He looked just the way you'd think he looked. Beautifully tailored sports jacket and matching slacks. Cool as a cucumber.

Wayne looked at me as I was looking at Sinatra.

"Ready to meet him?" asked Wayne with a big smile across his face.

"I been ready my whole life," I said.

We walked over to where he was standing. He turned to me with those piercing blue eyes and said, "So Wayne says you're wondering if I like what you do."

I was too nervous to say a fuckin' thing.

"Relax, kid," said Sinatra. "I think you're funny. You're funny as hell. Come meet the family."

Frank was with his wife, Barbara, her daughter, and some other people. After Wayne introduced me and Trini, Sinatra tapped me on the shoulder and said, "Come have a drink with me."

We went to a little red leather booth by the bar. The waiter hurried over with two glasses of champagne.

"Thanks for coming by, kid," said Frank. "I just wanted to congratulate you on all your success and wish you a happy New Year."

Sitting there with Frank Sinatra, I was still speechless. I'd never been this tongue-tied before. Finally I got out some words.

"I can't tell you what this means to me, Frank."

"You don't have to."

"I want to. I wanna tell you how my folks went to see you at the Main Event in the Garden and how much I wanted to be there."

"Why weren't you?"

"I was only sixteen, but I did watch it with my girlfriend and her hundred-and-ten-year-old grandmother in Sea Gate."

Frank laughed. God, it felt good to get a laugh outta Frank.

"I hear you're gonna be playing the Garden," he said.

"And you're my inspiration to do it."

"I know the media's been after you, kid. How you dealing with all that?"

"It can be rough, Frank, but nothing compared to what you've been through with the media."

"That's why I'm asking you. Because I know that those bastards can beat you down. It took me a long time to learn to ignore them."

"I'm trying."

"You work for your fans, not the media. The media gets their tickets for free. If your peace of mind depends upon pleasing them, you won't have peace of mind, Dice. But if you concentrate on your fans, and you keep entertaining them to where they're willing to fork over their hard-earned cash to see you, that's enough."

After a few minutes, Wayne came over to the table.

"Boss," he said to Sinatra, "would you like to borrow my plane to fly back to L.A. tonight?"

"No, thanks, Wayne. We're staying over."

I sensed my private time with Sinatra was up. But before I left, the Chairman said, "I wish you all the best, kid. And if you ever need anything, let me know." Then he hesitated and corrected himself with a little laugh. "Actually, if you ever need anything, let *Wayne* know."

I don't know what was crazier—the celebrity theater I packed every night at Bally's or the total insanity happening at the casino tables. Every part of my life was a whirlwind, a complete high.

Didn't matter where I played—Bally's or Caesars—I had my way at the tables. One night I got so hot I lost track of time. I was wearing my DICE RULES leather jacket with over ten thousand rhinestones and studs on it. Cost me over ten grand. I was starting to draw a crowd. Suddenly Club Soda Kenny rushed over. "You gotta get onstage, Dice. Your set is about to start."

"Shit, really?" I shrugged at the dealer, gave him a nice tip, swept up the rest of my chips, and headed into the theater. That night I did my show with three hundred and fifty thousand dollars in chips bulging in my pockets.

Yeah, those days, I couldn't lose.

Until, of course, I did.

TWO NIGHTS AT THE GARDEN

BEFORE I GOT to the Garden, something else happened that turned the industry on its head: against the advice of many, I put out a record called *The Day the Laughter Died*. But it is not the typical comedy album. My idea was simple: with no publicity beforehand, do a long late-night set at Dangerfield's and put it on tape. Little or no editing. Just me and a small crowd. Heavy on the intimacy but no restraints on the material. Dice being raunchy and real.

"This record will not work," said my original mentor, Mitzi Shore, when I played her a preview copy.

"Why not?" I asked.

"Because no one has ever put out a double-disc comedy record. It's too long, and this time you're just too offensive. It's gonna ruin your career."

"I don't think so, and neither does Rick Rubin. He thinks it's funny as hell."

"He produces music, not comedy. I know comedy," said Mitzi, "and comedy albums are short. They don't go on forever like this one."

For a second or two, Mitzi's comments gave me pause. After all, when it comes to comedy, Mitzi has heard it all. But my gut told me that I was right—that an after-midnight comedy set had the relaxed feel that fans would love.

And the fans did love it. After just four days on the market, *The Day the Laughter Died* went gold.

• • • •

In February of 1990, I felt like I'd reached the top of the mountain; the corner of Seventh Avenue and Thirty-Second Street was the summit. Far as I was concerned, the Garden was it. Naturally my folks felt the same. The Knicks played in the Garden. Elton John. Aerosmith. The Rolling Stones. Paul McCartney. Sinatra. Elvis. They held political conventions in the Garden. Ringling Bros. and Barnum & Bailey Circus played the Garden. Michael Jackson. Guns N' Roses. The biggest of the big. And yet not even the biggest comics had ever been able to sell out the arena. Until me. And not only for one night, but two.

It wasn't just a matter of getting up there and telling a few jokes. It was a matter of taking the already crazed energy of eighteen thousand fans who were on their feet—screaming, pumping their fists, standing on their seats, and waving their arms—and taking them even higher.

Because of all the other arenas I'd been playing across the country, I knew I was ready. But on that first night when I got out on that stage to the most thunderous ovation I've ever heard in my life, when I looked at the cavernous size of the place, when I realized I wasn't at Pips in Brooklyn or Dangerfield's on First Avenue or Rascals in West Orange but in the biggest entertainment venue in the biggest city facing the biggest, most enthusiastic, crazed crowd of my life, I felt my engine racing. They were roaring at me, and I was roaring back at them.

I kicked it off, and I kicked it hard.

"Korean delis, Indian newsstands, Greek diners, and ass-fucking parties every night—that's New York. *How are you?*

"What a fuckin' crowd! Madison Square fuckin' Garden! Top of the world, Ma.

"We got some cute-looking whores hanging out. I'm all about pussy, I'll tell you that much. I live it, I dream it, I fuck it. And we'll talk about it, because it's a new decade. It's the nineties. I got a whole new act of fuckin' filth right here.

"Because being back in New York, I feel that New York attitude all the time. Even birds—fuckin' birds—have an attitude here. They don't shit on you by mistake. They aim. You can be walking with your chick and some bird shits on your nose. And your girlfriend looks at you and says, 'Honey, you have shit on your nose.' And you give her your attitude. You come back with, 'So what? Maybe I like it there. Now shut your fuckin' hole!' "

From there it got better, racier, raunchier, more daring, more ridiculous, more of fuckin' everything.

After the second night, I knew that, no matter how long I lived, no other night would compare to those.

I also knew that, to keep myself from going completely bat-shit, I had to anchor myself. That's why right after the show I avoided the media and the after-parties and went back to the Brooklyn neighborhood where I'd been raised. Me and Trini went to the apartment that I'd bought a block away from my parents. I needed to come down, and there was no better way to do that than with Trini, who was radiantly pregnant. The two of us went to the 7-Eleven, bought some Breyers ice cream, and went home and made root beer floats. It was a sweet end to a very sweet run.

HEAVEN

I THOUGHT HEAVEN was 8667 Metz Place, a two-level fifties-style house that sat in the high-priced West Hollywood hills just north of Sunset, not far from the Comedy Store. I knew the territory well. When I first moved to L.A. I'd drive up and down those quiet tree-lined streets with their cool-looking houses and think, *One day this is where I'll be living.* Well, that one day had arrived. Back in the spring of 1989, a real estate agent was putting up a For Sale sign from the trunk of his car when Trini and I pulled up.

"Mind if we take a quick look?" I asked.

"By all means," he said.

It was love at first sight—the light and bright retro feel, the sliding glass doors, the rock fireplace, the pool that wrapped around the backyard, the relaxed California vibe that seemed perfect for having parties and also raising a family.

"You can throw out that For Sale sign," I told the agent. "We're buying it."

They wanted 1.6 million but accepted my offer of a million. A million dollars seemed the perfect price for my first Hollywood home.

Then came perfect joy: the birth of my first child.

The day he arrived was a wild scene at Cedars-Sinai hospital in L.A. Trini was in one of those fancy suites. The room was packed with people, including Trini's mom, my parents, and a bunch of my pals. My booking agent was on the phone making deals. I was running around filming the whole thing.

When I stuck the camera in Trini's face and asked her how she felt, she gave me a look that said, *Get lost.* We were having a party, and she was having a baby—a beautiful baby we named Maxwell Lee. I felt a joy and love like I'd never felt before. I'm not saying at that moment I could love anyone more than I loved my mom and dad and sister and Trini. But with that tiny child, the love felt different. The intensity was different. The connection was different. I'd long felt responsible for making my parents' life better and buying them things they'd always wanted. But in my gut I also felt it was my parents protecting me rather than vice versa. Now, though, I had this precious little boy to protect. And I swore I would. I made an oath to God that I would give my son all the love, attention, and care that my heart could command. Looking at my newborn son, I cried like a baby. Selling out the Garden was a big thing, but man, the birth of Max was ten times bigger. I was a dad! I had a family! I was fuckin' complete!

Things couldn't get any better or bigger. Until they did.

Axl Rose and Slash, two of my biggest fans, asked me to do a guest appearance at their Rose Bowl gig. So it was Guns N' Roses and Dice entertaining a hundred thousand screaming fans under the stars of Southern California. That shit was unprecedented.

BABS

NOT THAT THERE weren't difficult moments. One happened at a party at the home of Barry Diller, head of 20th Century Fox, the studio putting out *Ford Fairlane*. I was especially happy that night because, in addition to Trini, I brought Mom and Dad. We were chatting with Neil Diamond, a fellow Brooklyn Jew, who couldn't have been nicer, when I spotted Barbra Streisand, still another Brooklyn Jew. The Originals are big Streisand fans—the singing, the acting, the whole shtick. But when I went over to introduce myself and my family and let her know how much I admired her, she saw me coming, turned her back, and walked away. I'd never been snubbed like that before. Just to be pleasant, she couldn't give me and my folks thirty seconds? I guess not. I guess she couldn't say hello. That hurt bad, and years later on one of my specials, it caused me to put her in my routine.

"Fuckin' Babs," I said, "with that one wandering eye of hers. While she's getting fucked, one eye is on the guy fucking her and another is looking out the window to see if it's raining. And talking about guys who fuck Babs, she used to be married to Elliott Gould. Lemme tell you something right now. Guys named Elliott don't fuck good. The Vinnies, the Tonys, the Frankies . . . they know how to throw a good fuck. So maybe that's why she's so fuckin' cranky and gotta lecture you about politics. Far as I'm concerned, Babs is a babbling fuckin' idiot. When you go to her show and she starts in with her goddamn politics, you wanna scream, *'We didn't come to hear your bullshit. We came to hear you sing. So shut up and fucking sing!'"*

Turned out that Gould was in the audience that night, which made me feel terrible. I think Gould's a great actor, and I hated like hell that he had to hear that. If I had known he was there, I wouldn't have said it. Years later I was shopping in a furniture store in Sherman Oaks when Elliott walked in. I went right up to him and apologized.

"I respect you so much as an artist," I said, "and feel awful about how I talked about you the night of the special."

"Are you kidding, Dice?" said Elliott. "It was your act. You were funny as hell. You're a pro, and so am I, and I didn't take it personally. I think you're terrific."

And to be honest, I idolized Barbra. She hurt my feelings, that's all.

HAPPY FACE

I BEGAN RUNNING around the country, working my ass off and making bank. In between the arenas, I was also playing clubs, just to keep my chops sharp. Sometimes Wheels opened for me, which meant Downtown Ronny was part of the entourage. At one point Ronny showed up in a beard, which wasn't exactly his style. According to Wheels, Downtown had gone underground. Other times Noodles—another funny comic whose real name is Marty Levenstein—opened for me. The schedule stayed hectic because I liked it that way. Besides, I had all this nervous energy I had to work off. In just a few months, *The Adventures of Ford Fairlane* would be opening. Everyone—Sandy Gallin, Barry Diller, and David Geffen—was saying that it would be the kickoff of a spectacular movie career. They were already talking about two more starring roles for me: *My Cousin Vinny* with Marisa Tomei, and *The Gossip Columnist* with Daryl Hannah.

To make sure I stayed in shape, I was hitting the gym harder than ever. In fact, it was at Gold's Gym in Paramus, New Jersey, where I met the guy who'd be the newest member of my entourage. His real name is Mike Malandra, but I call him Happy Face.

Unlike Club Soda Kenny, who was six foot five and obviously powerful, Happy Face's strength was more subtle. He was five ten and extra lean. He didn't have bulging muscles, but the man was made of concrete. He was the owner of Malandra's Martial Arts Center. He'd been watching me work out while a particular asshole, a guy I'd never met before, was giving me a hard time.

The guy was the size of a mountain. Must have weighed three hundred. He was a linebacker, a professional football player. He knew who I was, and for some reason didn't like that I was working out at Gold's. I have no idea why. He kept saying shit like, "You talk big shit, Dice, but I see that you can't do shit with these weights."

Far as I was concerned, I was doing pretty fuckin' good with the weights.

"If you got a problem, pal," I said, "take it elsewhere."

"And who's gonna take me there, a big mouth like you?"

"Look," I said, "I know you're a big guy and you're a fuckin' football pro who destroys grown men for a living, but do yourself a favor. Do your workout and go home. You don't wanna fuck with me."

"For a little man, Dice, you talk big."

"I wouldn't say it if I couldn't do it."

"Don't make me laugh."

I went up in his face and said, "If you really wanna push it, make your move and we'll see who's standing at the end of this fuckin' thing. 'Cause there's no way my son's father ain't going home tonight in one piece."

That was how I was thinking—*This animal will not take down Max's father.* But I was also looking around for a ten-pound dumbbell. Because if we were going to go at it, I wasn't just going at him with my fists. I was gonna bust him in the head with a piece of iron.

Seeing all this, Happy Face stepped in and separated us.

"All right, Andrew, you made your point," he said. "But lemme give you a few tips about those stomach crunches."

Somehow Happy Face's calm energy neutralized the situation. The football giant backed off—and so did I. I let Happy Face lead me through the rest of my workout.

At the end of day, he and I got to talking. Happy Face asked if I needed a bodyguard. I told him, "The whole idea of bodyguarding a celebrity is that nobody gets hurt. But people get stupid drunk. Big guys, crazy guys, will stop at nothing to get past you so they can get to me. Can you stop them?"

Happy Face just smiled.

"You mind if I test you?" I asked. "You mind if I see how you'd handle a moose like me trying to get past you?"

"I don't wanna lay a hand on you, Dice."

"It's all right, Happy Face. I need to see you in action."

"I don't want to hurt you."

"You don't have to hurt me. You just have to stop me."

So I made a move at Happy Face, and the next thing I knew he had me by the wrist, and with this intense pressure had me down on my knees, but he picked me up before my ass hit the ground. It was amazing. I'd never seen anything like it.

After I recovered, I turned to him and said, "I'll pick you up here tonight at seven."

"Where we going, Dice?" he asked.

"The Comedy Alley."

"And what am I gonna do?"

"You're gonna work for me, Happy Face. You're on the team."

It took Club Soda Kenny a while to get used to Happy Face. There was always a little thing between the two of them. But when Kenny learned that Happy Face was an eighth-degree black belt who taught martial arts to the FBI, he had to be impressed. Besides, Dicemania was getting wilder every day, and everyone realized I needed extra protection.

HELL

THE PREMIERE HAD been planned months in advance. It was gonna be the most spectacular in the history of Hollywood—and that's saying something. It wasn't enough to premiere *Ford Fairlane* at some movie palace on Broadway or in Westwood. Nothing less than the eighteen-thousand-seat L.A. Forum would do. That's right—for the first time ever, a premiere would take place in an arena. Not only that, before the film started, I'd ride in driving a cherry-red Ford Fairlane and do a short stand-up routine.

"The film is going to break box-office records," said Diller. "You're raising the commercial bar for comedy movies. Dice films will be to the nineties what Jerry Lewis films were to the sixties. You'll be dominating for years to come."

To build up the buzz on the film, Lorne Michaels asked me to host *Saturday Night Live*. Naturally I knew about the show—who doesn't?—but I can't say that I was a fan. I didn't follow it religiously. Sketch comedy is fine, but it just isn't my thing. Actors adapt—and that's how I looked at it. Besides, I was curious to see how the *SNL* writers would play with the Diceman character. Since I made a living out of making fun of other people, I didn't at all mind making fun of myself.

When Michaels called me to his office for a Monday-morning meeting before starting rehearsals, I was in a good mood. My mood changed, though, when he made me cool my heels in his reception area for an hour. Was he playing some kind of power game?

When I was finally called into his office he didn't apologize for the wait. He just said, "Look, Dice, I need to tell you that Nora Dunn has decided she can't appear on the same show as you."

"Who the fuck is Nora Dunn?"

"She's a cast member. Don't you watch the show?"

"Not too much."

"Well, she's boycotting."

"I really don't give a shit."

"Sinéad O'Connor, who's slated to be the musical guest, is also boycotting."

"I don't really understand, Lorne," I said. "Hasn't your show always been about making fun of different shit?"

"Ostensibly, that is our purpose."

"And don't I fit into that kinda thing?"

"These women think you've gone too far."

"And what do you think?"

"I think you're funny—or I wouldn't have booked you on the show."

"Then what's the problem?"

"I just felt that it's fair to warn you that you'll be receiving an inordinate amount of bad publicity."

"What else is new?"

Later I learned the real truth behind the Nora Dunn boycott. Next season she was being dropped from the show, and she wanted to bring some positive attention to herself. She figured attacking me might help spin the story from "comic gets fired" to "comic attacks woman-hater." Far as Sinéad O'Connor, she just went along with what her management told her to do. She actually said on *The Arsenio Hall Show* later that if she had to do it again, she would have appeared on the show.

As you've probably guessed, the media shit storm boosted *SNL*'s ratings for the week. I had no problems with the skits, and there were nice compliments all around. But this anti-Dice thing didn't go away. Among certain critics in the media, it was getting stronger every day. The sharks were in the water, and the sharks were smelling blood. *My* fuckin' blood.

How to respond? I didn't have a clue. All I knew was that the Diceman would always be the Diceman. That's who the fuckin' character was.

Some people say it was the Nora Dunn incident that energized the anti-Dice forces. I don't know if that's true. I don't know if you can cite a date on which the media attacks turned from negative to out-and-out vicious. But it came with a vengeance.

There were signs of things to come. I'm talking literally. Wanted posters with pictures of Barry Diller were put up in the gay community. The rest of the Gay Mafia—David Geffen and Sandy Gallin—were also getting calls from gay activists. How could they, as gay men, support my career? They were being called traitors.

One day I had the most powerful team in Hollywood backing me. The next day that team was being threatened.

"You got nothing to worry about," said my dad, the only manager who would never drop me, no matter what.

"I got everything to worry about."

"These managers are making a fortune on you. They're gonna stick by you."

"I ain't so sure."

I was even less sure when Barry Diller called me to his office for what he said was a big meeting. For whatever reason, Gallin made an excuse and said he couldn't be there. That wasn't a good sign. I was so uneasy that I flew my dad in from Brooklyn so he could be by my side.

"It's gonna be fine," said Fred Silverstein, always an optimist.

"I got a lousy feeling," I said.

"The movie's done, Andrew. The premiere is set. The ads are already out there."

"That's just the point. All over the city people are out there destroying the posters. They're ripping them off the telephone poles and off the sides of buildings."

"It'll pass," Dad said, trying to reassure me. "It'll all be okay."

Remember—my guy Sandy Gallin was the most powerful manager in Hollywood; my record deal was with David Geffen, who had the hottest label; and my three-picture deal was with Barry Diller, who ran the behemoth 20th Century Fox. And, if you go by the numbers, I was easily the most popular comic in the world. In a single three-day weekend, I could sell sixty thousand tickets. I could command a half million dollars a performance. When I remembered this, I got to feeling that Dad was right. Why would the studio buckle under the pressure of a few angry nuts when my fan base had proven to be not only huge but loyal as hell?

All these thoughts were running through my head when Dad and I showed up at 20th Century Fox, where we were sent into Diller's office, an impressive suite befitting of one of the kings of Hollywood.

"This isn't going to be easy to say," were the first words Diller said, causing my fuckin' stomach to do flips. "But I've had to make some very hard decisions. Let me tell it to you straight, Dice."

"Shoot," I said, eager to get this over with.

"I'm canceling the premiere."

"That's crazy," said my father. "You'll be hurting your own movie."

"I'm afraid that's not all, Mr. Silverstein. I'm also going to buy your son out of the other two films left on his contract."

I stayed stone silent. I knew what was happening. Dad, though, couldn't believe it. He kept pushing Diller until Diller finally told us the real reason behind all this.

"The pressure is too much," he said. "I've gotten death threats. These people—these insane protesters—are dead set on ruining my life, and to be frank, it simply isn't worth it."

"But what about *Ford Fairlane*?" I asked.

"The film will be released, but I can't promise much promotion."

"Without promotion, what good is a film?"

"Good word-of-mouth can keep it alive."

But I knew it was dead. If they were pulling the premiere and killing the promotion, it didn't have a chance.

When the film did come out, the critics did more than attack the movie; they attacked me. It was personal and nasty as nasty could be. And it didn't even matter that it made $14 million the first week and by the second week had grossed $21 million. By the third week, it was gone. Diller did what the protesters demanded: he killed the fuckin' film.

The critics did everything but put a gun to my head. I didn't mind their criticizing the film—that's fair game—but they went after me personally. A publicist I hired at the time said, "I've never seen anything like it, Dice. It's an orchestrated campaign to knock you off. One critic is even screaming about how you're really not good-looking and everyone needs to realize that. Where the hell is he coming from?"

It felt like I was falling into lower and lower levels of hell.

One day when I was feeling especially pissed—my head aching and my heart heavy—I was driving up Laurel Canyon in the Caddy convertible that Rick Rubin had completely refurbished and customized for me. Suddenly I heard this car behind me honkin' like crazy. I turned around to see that it was Eddie Murphy in his Benz.

"Dice!" he shouted. "Pull over!"

I pulled over, and naturally I was glad to see him.

"Remember back at the Comedy Club when I was a little nervous, you'd come over and say, 'Hey, you got nothing to be nervous about. You're Eddie Murphy.' Well, I'm here to tell you, you're the Diceman. And don't let 'em fuck with you. For a long time, Dice, they fucked with me. Now they're fucking with you. But just don't let 'em get to you. Stay strong."

THE RETURN OF DOLLFACE

AROUND THIS SAME time, as if things weren't negative enough, here came more: Dollface—wife number one—decided to sue me, even though I had generously paid her off when we first got divorced. Seeing all this amazing money I was making, she figured that some of that belonged to her. How did she come to that conclusion? Simple: she was listening to super-lawyer Marvin Mitchelson, famous for crushing the nuts of husbands and inventor of the palimony suit. Dollface wanted millions. Why? Because, according to her, she helped me develop my act. This really made me laugh, because—and this is the goddamn fuckin' truth—I never made Dollface laugh. Not only did she, a hayseed from Iowa, have nothing to do with my act as a wiseass street character from Brooklyn, she never thought my act was funny!

All this was in my brain when I was having lunch at Caffè Roma in Beverly Hills with Mickey Rourke. Mickey's cut from a similar cloth as me; he don't go with the flow. That made him a great guy to talk to when the establishment was coming down around me.

"We're the ones with talent, and they're the ones with the swords," said Mickey. "But you know something, Dice, in the end talent is the sharpest sword of all. Talent cuts through everything. They'll never keep you down—as long as you don't forget how good you really are."

For me, Mickey was a real-life Rocky. And Rocky was just who I needed.

Mickey was also a good listener. I told him all the bullshit with Diller and how I knew it wouldn't be long before Sandy Gallin and David Geffen followed his lead and dropped me like a hot potato. I told him how Dollface was coming after me and how the Marvin Mitchelson firm even tried to serve me with papers when I was doing *SNL* but couldn't get through security.

"Don't look now, Dice," said Mickey, "but look who's looking at you from a table out there in the patio."

I looked around and spotted him right away. It was Marvin Mitchelson having lunch with Reggie Jackson's ex-wife. Soon as he saw me, he got up to make a call.

"You wanna split?" asked Mickey.

"Fuck it," I said. "They're gonna serve me sooner or later. Might as well be sooner."

Not twenty minutes later, the server came over to our table and handed me the legal document that said Dollface was going after my bread. Out of the corner of my eye I saw Mitchelson smiling. Well, guess what? I was smiling too, motherfucker. I got up and went over to the big-shit lawyer and said, "I know how big you are, and I know what you've done. But I'm gonna tell you right here and now—you ain't getting a fuckin' nickel outta me. So if you're doing it for the publicity, great. Smart move. Good way to keep your name in the papers. But if you're doing it for the money, you're fucked."

He didn't say a word.

After that, I prepared like crazy. I knew my case was ironclad, 'cause I already paid her all the alimony in full. I also knew there was no way in hell Dollface could prove that she helped me with my act, something I developed long before I ever met her.

When my deposition started, I walked in dressed as Dice, not Andrew. I had the leather and the fingerless gloves and even the Danny Zuko/John Travolta curl dancing off my forehead. Naturally that threw Mitchelson and his minions off their game. When I started answering their questions, they were even more bewildered, 'cause now I was talking like Andrew, a nice Jewish boy from Brooklyn, calm and polite and respectful. By the time it was over, my prediction came through. I had to pay my legal fees, but fuckin' Mitchelson and Dollface didn't get shit.

STILL ROCKING AND ROLLING

WHAT REALLY BROUGHT up my spirits was that, despite all the backlash, my fan base stayed strong. Not only could I still fill arenas for the rest of 1990, I could fill 'em for the next five years or so. I'm not saying that I didn't suffer a fall—but that fall was off in the distance. For the moment I was still rocking and rolling.

Now I gotta be doubly honest. Yes, I was happy that I could still work giant venues. But no, I wasn't happy that my movie career had been torpedoed before it got off the ground. And yes, I was still in love with Trini. In fact, we got married in 1992, when Max was two. Max went on the honeymoon with us. When I held my son in my arms, I melted. He was my everything. But I can't lie about the fact that my relationship with his mother was going through heavy changes.

Like all human beings, Trini had problems, but I don't wanna lay 'em out here. I wanna respect her as the mother of our children. It's easier for me to lay out my own problems.

Because Hollywood had kicked me in the balls, I was even more determined to get back up and fight. In a weird way, gambling became part of my fighting spirit.

This one time, for instance, I was at Bally's in Atlantic City with Grandma Shirley, Mom's mom. I loved Grandma Shirley, the coolest grandmother around. She had the gold lamé shirts and the designer slacks and the high heels. I loved being around her, especially that night, because I walked away from the blackjack table to the tune of $40,000.

When the cards are smiling in your face, it's the greatest feeling in the world. To take the sting outta the *Ford Fairlane* fiasco, I went after that feeling as much as possible. And when I hit a winning streak, I wasn't selfish. I spread the wealth. I heard stories of how when Sinatra was riding high, he always carried fifties and hundreds 'cause they were the tips he gave. I heard the same kind of stories about the beautiful way that Elvis took care of his people.

Let's say I was up two hundred thousand or so. After the big win, I'd go back up to my suite with Club Soda Kenny, Hot Tub Johnny, and Happy Face.

"You know the game, fellas," I'd say.

Then I'd grab a stack of chips and toss them in the air. It was all for my guys. They kept whatever they caught. Incredibly, they all came out about even.

It wasn't that my crew lived on tips. They got good salaries. When we were in Brooklyn walking through the Kings Plaza mall I bought tons of shit—everything from gold chains to sweatpants—and gave 'em to my guys, just for the hell of it. When I learned of a special occasion—let's say Happy Face was getting married—it was nothing for me to give him five Gs, just 'cause I wanted him to know how much his happiness meant to me.

In the early nineties, I went through some crazy gambling periods. I don't say this to shock you, but only to tell the truth: on three straight nights at Caesars in Vegas I lost $700,000 each night at blackjack. That's $2.1 million in less than seventy-two hours. Was I fucked up over it? Not really, 'cause back then I was my own bank. It bothered me, sure, but I had to try to wipe the loss away and start fresh the next time I hit the table. You can't gamble scared. You can't gamble weak.

I have three rules: I don't gamble when I'm tired, I don't gamble when

I'm angry, and I don't gamble when I'm drunk. In short, I keep my head clear. And I know the game.

One day I was back in L.A., in my tank top and shorts, about to go to the gym. On my way, though, I took a detour and headed to the airport instead. I jumped on a one o'clock flight to Vegas, landed at one forty-five, and ran over to the Mirage. My plan was simple: I was gonna win a hundred thou at blackjack and be home by dinnertime.

Except it didn't work out that way.

Still in tank top and shorts, I was at the tables at the Mirage when, by three o'clock, I was down a half mil. The Mirage, of course, knowing who I was, wasn't upset. They gave me the credit 'cause they knew I was good for it. I walked out of the hotel. Bright, clear, sun-drenched Vegas afternoon. Since no one knew what I'd just lost, I was still feeling in control. I went over to Bally's and walked up to the tables like I didn't have a care in the world. You can't let 'em see you as a loser.

"Hey, Dice," said the Bally's casino manager, "didn't know you were in town."

"Came in for some meetings," I said. "I was just working out and I figure I'll relax for a minute."

"No problem, Dice. How much you need?"

"Start me off with a hundred thou."

I took the hundred and started winning. I let the Bally dealers know not to fuck with me. I didn't want no chitchat. I didn't want no distractions. I wanted the same dealer and I didn't want him taking breaks. I needed to be serious. I needed to focus like a laser beam. And I needed to win. When I got to $550,000, I stopped.

"You're having a good day, Dice," said the manager. "Lemme buy you dinner."

We went to the Italian joint inside Bally's.

Soon as we were eating, I asked the guy, "Will you set me up with a limo and plane back to L.A.?"

"No problem. How you want the money?"

"Make a check to the Mirage for a half a million and give me the rest in cash."

"When where you at the Mirage?"

"Early today before I came over. Ran into some bad luck over there."

I could see the manager was about to kick himself. That's because if he'd known I'd been losing at the Mirage, he would have had his people mess with me at the table. Every third or fourth hand they'd have switched up dealers. They'd have found ways to fuck with my flow. He realized that, in my own way, I had played him.

But casino managers are reputable people, and this guy honored my request. I took the check and delivered it to the Mirage on my way to the airport. When I got home that night I was still wearing the same tank top and gym shorts, except that in my right pocket there was a bulge of cash that came to a cool fifty Gs.

Funny thing what your mind can do.

When things were going great, I couldn't be beat.

But when my movie career collapsed and my emotional pain started seeping inside my soul and taking over, I couldn't win a bet. It was uncanny. Every table had my number; every casino crushed me. Dealers couldn't lose. I'd pull two pictures, the dealer would draw a blackjack. I'd split aces, I'd get dealt a two and a three. Most dealers liked me and felt my pain. They'd shake their heads. Every blackjack session turned into a bloodbath. One morning, around four A.M., after getting absolutely annihilated at Caesar's, Kenny and I walked back to Bally's, our heads down, not saying a word. The world felt like it was closing in. To this day we call that morning the "losers' walk."

I shook it off—or tried to. Even after I lost a hundred grand at Bally's the following night.

The day after I was totally out of cash.

"How much money you got on you, Wheels?"

"Twenty bucks."

"Pay for the cab, okay? Let's go."

"Where we going?"

"The Mirage. My luck's gotta change."

It didn't.

I sat in front of a dealer with a shitty attitude as I dropped more than half of my seventy-five-grand marker. Finally, the shift ended and a new dealer and floor manager came on. The dealer smiled at me. "Archie," his name tag read. He was a quiet black man from Louisiana. I smiled back at him. I liked him. Liked his vibe, liked his manner, liked how he shuffled the cards. Soft hands.

Maybe. Just maybe . . .

Archie asked me to cut the cards in the shoe. I sliced the six decks in the middle with the yellow card and Archie tilted the shoe away from me. I turned to the floor manager, a short, stocky woman with beady brown eyes that looked like a couple of rat droppings. "Excuse me," I said. "Could Archie please face the shoe toward me?"

"No," she said. She didn't say, "And by the way, fuck you," but she might as well have.

I took a breath, closed my eyes, calmed myself. I was not going to allow this lady to ruin the new vibe I was feeling at the table. I took out a cig, flipped open my Zippo, lit my smoke with all the flair of the Diceman. Out of the corner of my eye, I saw the short, stocky floor manager frown and back up a step.

Unbelievable, I thought. *I'm losing my ass, and this one's giving me attitude.*

I blew a smoke ring, watched it rise and disappear into the chandelier above me.

I'm gonna change the energy right now. Not gonna let her get to me.

I smiled at her. "I'm playing over at Bally's. How'd you like a couple of comp tickets to the show tonight?"

She made a face like I'd just asked her to suck my dick in the middle of the casino. "No. *Thank* you," she said.

I looked up at Wheels. We both rolled our eyes. *Great,* I thought. *I'm forty-five K in the hole and I got a floor manager who's a Dice hater.*

I turned my attention to Archie. I held up a chip. "So, Archie, here's the deal. See this five-thousand-dollar chip? It's yours. No matter what. That's your tip."

I pushed that chip aside and then placed a five-thousand-dollar chip in each of the six circles in front of me. My last six chips. I stood up and spread out. The table was mine. A few people eased in behind me to watch.

"Let's do this, Archie. It's you and me."

He dealt my six hands. I stuck on each one.

Archie busted.

I was up sixty thousand.

I felt the floor manager shifting her weight. I refused to look at her.

I let the sixty ride.

I stuck again on all six hands.

Archie busted.

The crowd, growing behind me, let out a collective sigh followed by a small cheer.

I was up $120,000.

I let it ride.

I won all six hands.

I was up $240,000.

I counted out seventy-five thousand in chips, the marker I owed the Mirage, and put those chips aside. I was now playing with $165,000.

I played fast and loose for the next twenty minutes, building my stack to $250,000. The crowd behind me had now gotten two deep. I'd become the show in the casino.

I sat down in the middle chair directly facing Archie.

"All right, Archie," I said. "This is how I wanna do it."

I lit another cig, took a drag, allowed the smoke to fill my lungs. I never enjoyed a cigarette more.

"I promised you that five-thousand-dollar chip. I'm a man of my word. So you can take it. It's yours. Or . . ." I took another long drag, let the smoke out. "Or you can play along with me. What I want, right now, for both of us, is a blackjack."

He laughed and looked down at the green felt of the table. Then he raised his face and cocked his head as if we were a couple of gunslingers.

"I'm with you, Dice," he said.

"All right. But. There's a catch."

He raised an eyebrow.

"It can't be just any blackjack. Got to be the ace of spades and the king of spades. That's the only thing it can be. Can you do that for me?"

"Well, that . . . I don't know . . . I can't promise that . . ."

"What? You don't believe in me? You don't believe in yourself? Archie, you gotta *believe*."

I whirled on the floor manager, who was staring at me with some weird combination of amusement and disgust. "I'll tell you what I'll do," I said to her. "I'll bet everything in front of me against your entire salary for the next year that Archie will deal me the ace and king of spades. What do you say?"

"No. *Thank* you," she hissed.

I looked back at Archie. Now he was smiling.

"Do it, Arch," I said.

He slid the first card out of the bottom of the shoe.

Ace of spades.

The crowd behind me gasped.

I have to say, as Archie pulled the next card out in what seemed like slow motion, I turned away.

I didn't have to look.

The roar of the crowd behind me told me what it was.

"Holy fuck," Wheels said. "Holy fucking shit. I don't fucking believe it."

King of spades.

"You gotta admit, a fifteen thousand tip is better than five," I said to Archie, who was staring at the cards, his hand trembling.

Wheels and I gathered up the chips to more applause. I cashed out at the cage and handed Wheels ten thousand dollars. "Thanks for lending me the twenty," I said. "Cab ride back's on me."

Least I could do after winning half a million.

OLD SPICE

I LET WHEELS open for me at Caroline's in New York. I also took him into Radio City Music Hall. Before long he was touring the country with me, and Downtown Ronny, his manager, was along for the ride.

When we got off the road and returned to Brooklyn, I learned that Downtown wanted me to go to Bay Ridge and meet a friend of his.

I had no problem with that.

The guy was holding court at the social club where the wiseguys played cards and sipped espresso. He was wearing a silk suit and was smoking a good cigar, had a nice haircut, and smelled of Old Spice. I wanted to ask him, *Can't you afford nothing better than Old Spice?* but I kept quiet. We ate cannoli. We talked about Brooklyn. We talked about the weather. We talked about his country house upstate. He had fifty acres and a private lake with ducks. He loved ducks. Did I like ducks? Sure. Did I want to go upstate to see his ducks? Wish I could, but I gotta work.

"Dice," he said, "you're beautiful."

Then he leaned over and whispered in my ear, "From here on, your problems are my problems."

I went back to see Mom and Dad and told them where I been.

"*What!*" screamed Mom. "You went to the social club?"

"What's wrong with that?"

"That's no association you want."

"I got no association. I merely went and met a man. We didn't sign no contract. Besides, Ma, all this started when I was back with Dollface and brought her to Brooklyn and you took me to that gambling joint. That's when you said you wanted me to meet Downtown Ronny."

"I never said that, Andrew."

"Yes, you did. You were the one who said Downtown could help me."

"Not me."

"Dad," I said, "you were there. You remember what Mom said."

"I'm not getting in the middle of this," said Dad.

Mom said, "Go back there and tell him you didn't mean to go there in the first place."

I said, "That's a stupid idea. It'll make me look like a putz."

Mom said, "Better an alive putz than a dead putz."

I said, "What are you talking about? This guy loves me."

"Now he does," said Mom. "But what about tomorrow?"

"What's going to happen tomorrow?"

"Who knows? That's my point."

"My point is let's just forget about it. All that happened was that I had a harmless meeting."

Turns out I was wrong. I should have listened to Mom. Always listen to your mom.

ANDREW DICE CLAY

SAM

I BELIEVE IN the fairy tale, the everyone-lives-happily-ever-after, the scenario that says true love wins out and even old enemies become friends. It was my hope that would be the case with me and Sam Kinison. When he got a part in Rodney Dangerfield's *Back to School,* I was glad for him. His career took off before mine—and that was fine with me. That even inspired me, 'cause it showed that there was a future for rock-and-shock comics. I only wish he had felt the same way when my career went through the roof. It hurt me—and I believe it hurt Sam even worse—when he got consumed by jealousy and insecurity. But even that didn't matter, 'cause I never lost my respect for Sam's talent, not to mention the courage it took to do his material and do it so fuckin' brilliantly. I never forgot those struggling Store days when the two of us would steal pork chops from Ralph's and spend long evenings cracking each other up. So you can imagine my shock and horror and sadness when I got the news in April of 1992: driving to a gig in Laughlin, Nevada, Sam had been killed in a horrible car crash. Thank God his new wife, who was in the car with him, survived. They hadn't even been married a week.

I wept for Sam. I weep for him now. He was a crazy Christian from the Midwest. I'm a crazy Jew from Brooklyn. Our styles couldn't have been more different, but, on the deepest level, our comedy was connected. He didn't accept limitations. He didn't accept any rules. He said a stand-up could stand up and say funny and outrageous shit about anything or anyone. He thumbed his nose at the rules. He broke boundaries and caused a sensation. I know that his fans—and that includes me—will never forget him.

CONNECTED

EVEN AFTER THE shit storm of *Fairlane* I was still making good money. In addition to my million-dollar spread in L.A., I'd bought a four-thousand-square-foot house on Avenue V in the Bergen Beach section of Brooklyn. I liked it, but when Dennis Arfa saw it he said, "It's great, Dice, but it looks like it belongs to a successful dentist." Getting to the gigs wasn't bad either. I was flying coast-to-coast on MGM, a chartered luxury airline catering to the Hollywood set. The flights were beautiful, first class all the way. MGM set up the big stars in private booths where you could have a drink, hang with your friends, play a little cards . . . whatever.

Traveling with my entourage on one flight, Downtown Ronny was especially excited because Robert Wagner and Jill St. John were sitting in the booth across from us. Starstruck, Ronny kept eying them. He couldn't stop sneaking peeks. So when he got up and went to bathroom, Hot Tub and I decided to have some fun.

"Hey, Ronny," I said when he got back. "I was just talking to Bob Wagner. I told him you were a big fan, and him and Jill wanna meet you."

"Serious?"

"Serious. Go tell him hello."

"I don't know what to say," he said.

"You'll figure it out."

"I better go back to the bathroom and prepare, ya heah?"

Dressed in his polyester plaid sports coat, powder-blue trousers, and orange-tinted aviator glasses, Ronny made his way to the men's room, where he splashed on Aqua Velva and got his approach together before walking over to Wagner. Hot Tub and I couldn't hear the conversation, but a few minutes later when Downtown returned to our booth, he had the facial expression of a hound dog.

"So what happened?" I asked.

"Fuckin' guy," he said, "fuckin' guy."

"Fuckin' guy what?" I asked.

"I throw roses at him, ya heah? I go over and I says, 'Mr. Wagner. You're looking at your biggest fan. Ya heah me, Mr. Wagner, I'm Downtown Ronny, and I'm your biggest fan.' And Wagner, he's looking at me like *Who?* And I say, I tells him, 'I'm with Dice and I manage Dice's man Wheels, and I'm thrilled—ya heah?—I'm thrilled, pardon my French, but I'm *fuckin'* thrilled to be making your acquaintance and the acquaintance of your lovely lady here, because the two of you, I've seen the both of youse on the silver screen and I wanna convey my deepest congratulations on your career, and when you did that thief movie, the one with Audrey Hepburn, wow, Mr. Wagner, you was sensational, ya heah?' So I'm throwing roses at him, but I'm getting the idea that my roses are stinking up the place, 'cause him and his lady, they keep looking down into their drinks like they can't wait till I get the fuck outta there—ya heah?—but I keep talking 'cause, like you said, Dice, the guy knows I'm a fan and he likes to hear from a true fan."

"So what made you shut up?" I asked.

"I shut up when he says, 'Excuse me, but I have work to do.' No 'Thanks for stopping by.' No 'Nice to meet you.' No nothing. Ya heah?"

"Yeah, I heah."

But Downtown could be more than an amusing guy. There came a moment when I figured that he might also be a useful guy. I was working my ass off trying to maintain my status as the biggest comic in the world and working on my new special, called *No Apologies*—a title that explains just how I felt about my act. It was the first pay-per-view comedy event ever. I stood to make a fortune. But it needed to be promoted, and I was thinking that maybe Downtown could help hype it. After all, I was using his client Wheels on the pay-per-view, so maybe Downtown could use his connections to beef up my marketing.

Me and Downtown met at a coffee shop on Ocean Parkway near Pips.

"I want you to go to your guy for me," I said.

"Anything," said Downtown. "He likes doing favors for friends."

"This ain't a favor. This is business."

"He likes business even more than favors. What's your angle?"

"I got a good one. He's hooked up with the unions, and the unions control every truck in the country. I want every truck plastered with an ad for the pay-per-view. Will he do it?"

"Naturally he'll want something."

"Naturally he'll get something. He'll be in for a piece of the action."

"How much of a piece?"

"You'll work it out with my father. He's good with numbers. I'm not."

So they worked it out. The problem was that nothing really happened. The trucks didn't carry the posters, even though Downtown claimed there were thousands that did. I never saw one. Anyway, my father said it wasn't worth arguing about. So after the pay-per-view was aired and they came to our office to collect their cut, Dad gave them all that was coming to them.

This was when I knew it was time for me to break off my association. It wasn't doing me no good. But that break didn't prove to be all that easy.

CLUB 33

TRINI DECIDED THAT we'd be more comfortable if we also had a suburban place on the East Coast. We chose Saddle River, New Jersey, 'cause Trini's from Jersey and it was nice and quiet with a big yard in the back. We went east for the holidays and the summer. Back in L.A. we moved from Metz Place, as much as I loved it, to another big house in Beverly Hills, a two-million-dollar fixer-upper, 'cause it was a better school district for Max.

I remembered the day we moved from Metz Place to our house on Doheny, and how choked up I got that afternoon. All those memories at Metz Place, the parties, barbecues, dinners, Sunday afternoon hangouts, flashed in front of me like scenes from a movie, the movie of my life, my life of show-business success and sometimes even excess—Sly Stallone and his wife horsing around and laughing by the bar; Mickey Rourke diving into the pool with his clothes on; a whole group of us singing karaoke on Christmas Eve, Trini singing loudest and best of all; walking in on Rodney Dangerfield and his wife making it in the master bedroom, with Max, still an infant, asleep on the bed (Me: "Rodney, the baby's sleeping"; Rodney: "I hope he doesn't wake up"). But in the Doheny house I created what I consider one of my masterpieces. I called it Club 33.

That was Trini's age when I completed work on the project. My motivation was not only to have the greatest private party room in California, but to make sure that our marriage stayed fresh and strong. At first glance, you might think it was a teenage fantasy—and maybe it was. Maybe I never got past the teenage part of wanting to have a good time with the woman of my dreams.

A former guest quarters, the room was attached to the house but had a separate, apartment-like feel. I put in wall-to-wall tiger carpeting, a hundred-thousand-dollar sound system worthy of a Sunset Strip disco, and patterned puffy fabrics on all the walls, each wall a different wild color. None of it matched, which is just what I wanted. There were blackout shades. There were custom-made couches and lounge chairs and a hammock hanging from the ceiling. There was a Murphy bed that came out of the wall with a fur blanket. The lighting was spectacular: lava lamps in groovy shades of pink and blue and orange and red.

It's where I entertained my closest business associates and friends. For years I'd been going to Joe's Tape World in Brooklyn, where I created my own mix tapes. So you know that the sound track at Club 33 was sizzling. I don't care what kind of music you like, I had it covered. My specialty was disco—I'm a guy who never got over the get-down get-funky super-sexy disco—but I had big bands and Sinatra and Sammy and Aretha together with Led Zep and Aerosmith and the Stones.

Club 33 was my escape, but also the place where I struggled like hell to renew the romance with my wife. In that regard, I didn't do all that good. We had some great nights up there, beautiful nights I'll never forget. But the truth was that, no matter how hard each of us tried, we were moving in different directions. She felt that I was too wrapped up in my career to see who she was and what she needed; I felt she was growing distant and not giving me the support I needed. But because we both loved our Max, we weren't giving up. I clung to the vision that came to me years before in Chicago when Trini and I had seen an old couple holding hands and looking at each other like teenagers falling in love. That would be us—in love forever.

ELVIS CALLING

ON THE ROAD, I kept things light and easy. I kept myself going by goofing with the boys. My favorite goof had to do with my Elvis thing.

It started with Ed the Machine Regine, a guy who worked very blue and was very funny until his woman insisted that he work clean. That ruined his act. When Ed came aboard, though, he was still working dirty. Wheels set him up. He took him aside and said, "One thing you gotta know about Dice is that he's a little crazy. A little psychotic. Sometimes when we're on the bus, he'll go into his Elvis routine and start singing Elvis songs. That's okay. You just watch him and smile. But then he'll get angry and go into this fuckin' trance where he really believes that he's Elvis. That's when you gotta go along with the program. You just gotta humor him."

Next thing you know we're on the bus driving somewhere out west and it was the middle of the fuckin' night. Me, Hot Tub, Club Soda, Happy Face, and Wheels had it all planned. Ed the Machine went back to his bunk and fell asleep. The rest of us stayed up. At three A.M., I cranked up the monster sound system and started blasting "Hound Dog." The lights went up, the music was so loud that Ed fell out of his bunk, and there I was in the middle of the aisle doing Elvis while the boys were cheering me on. At the end of the song, I started calling Hot Tub "Sonny" after Sonny, one of Elvis's Memphis Mafia pals, and Club Soda became "Red," another Elvis buddy. I told Wheels to call Priscilla and tell her we'd be rolling into Memphis before sunrise.

Seeing all this, Ed the Machine couldn't believe his eyes.

"Is he serious?" Ed whispered to Wheels.

"Very serious," Wheels whispered back.

"He's out of his fuckin' mind," said Ed. "You gotta do something to help him."

"If you don't go along with him," said Wheels, "he gets even battier."

That was part one. Part two happened in L.A., where I was living in the house alone 'cause Trini and Max were back in Jersey.

Wheels and Ed the Machine were gigging at the Comedy Store.

"Dice wants us to come by his house," Wheels told Ed at the end of the last show.

When they got there, I was nowhere to be found.

"Where is he?" asked Ed.

"He sounded a little fucked-up on the phone," said Wheels. "I'm worried. Let's check the bedroom and make sure he's okay."

Wheels opened the door, and there I was—in bed in my underwear, a DICE RULES leather jacket, and big black boots.

"Everything okay, E?" asked Wheels.

"Why are you calling him 'E'?" whispered Ed.

"He's in his Elvis trance," Wheels whispered back.

I got out of bed and, in my best trancelike Elvis voice, said, "Sonny, can I talk to you, man?"

"Sure thing, E."

"Where's Priscilla?"

"She's back in Memphis."

"I gotta see Priscilla. I gotta talk to Priscilla."

"Well, E, she decided not to make the trip, remember?"

"Get her on the phone, Sonny. Get her on the phone now."

Wheels took Ed into the hallway and said, "Look, you go into the den, and when the phone rings, pretend to be Priscilla."

"Are you fuckin' kidding me?" asked Ed.

"Do it. I'm afraid of what Dice might do if you don't. Last time this happened he drove up to the house on Truesdale where Priscilla Presley actually lives and nearly broke down the gate. They called the cops, and we just got outta there in time. I can't let that happen again."

So Ed went into the den, and when the phone rang I said, "Cilla? Is that you, baby?"

In a ridiculous high-pitched voice, Ed said, "Yes."

"Cilla, baby, I'm just calling to say I love you and I miss you and I can't stand being without you."

Silence.

"Are you there, Cilla?"

High-pitched Ed: "Yes."

"Good. Now put Lisa Marie on the phone."

Pause before high-pitched Ed said, "She's asleep, Elvis."

"Just tell her Daddy called, Cilla. Tell her I'll be home tomorrow. Love you, Cilla."

Pause. High-pitched Ed: "Love you too, Elvis."

TERI AND ME

IN 1993, I made a movie called *Brain Smasher . . . A Love Story*. The ad line said everything you need to know: "Rescue a supermodel. Battle killer ninjas. Save the world. No problem."

This wasn't a zillion-dollar Hollywood production, but it wasn't shabby by early nineties budgets. And I had some killer lines in it. Plus my name and Teri Hatcher's were above the title. At thirty-six, I was looking to keep my mug on the silver screen. And Teri, a talented twenty-eight-year-old actress, was happy to have nailed her first starring role in a feature. It was good to be back in the Hollywood game, and besides, it was a cute story. I played a nightclub bouncer who turned into a hero, rescuing Teri, the damsel in distress.

Naturally I'd heard of on-the-set romances between the leading man and leading lady, but that wasn't gonna happen to me. Even though I was going through hell with Trini, I was still determined to work it out and keep my family together. My live-happily-ever-after family dream would never die.

The film was shooting in Portland, and the minute I met Teri in the producer's office I knew there could be a problem. The vibe between us was powerful. Whether on purpose or not, the producer put her hotel suite next to mine. That first night she came over to rehearse in my living room. She wanted to go over the lines of the script we were set to shoot the next day.

I couldn't keep my eyes off her: she had a gorgeous face, thin frame, big luscious boobs, and a perfect butt. Every move she made was sensual. I loved the way she stood with both hands on her hips. I loved her little-girl laugh as she brushed one side of her hair behind her ear. I could feel her nervousness, so I said, "Sit down, relax. I'm not what you heard I am."

"What do you mean?"

"I'm Andrew. Not Dice. Unless you want me to be Dice."

"What's the difference?"

"Dice just wants to get it on. Andrew will take you to dinner first."

"I'll take Andrew . . . for now."

That was Teri—a mix of coyness and vulnerability, a flirt but also a great professional. She was serious about her acting. She came to read her lines with me—and that's all we did. Naturally I wanted to do more, but I remained a gentleman.

After we rehearsed, she suggested that we take a walk to the set, where they had already begun filming ninja stunts. The soundstage was cold and we sorta huddled together to keep warm. Already we felt attached to each other.

Walking back together, we took our time. We lingered. She laughed at my little jokes and I laughed at hers.

Before she disappeared into her room, Teri said to me, "Can you believe that our beds are back-to-back and separated only by a wall?"

Because the question made me uneasy, my answer was stupid.

"That's weird," was all I could say.

"Maybe you'll dream about me."

She went to her suite and I went to mine. I lit a cigarette, and before I could take a puff, the phone rang. My heart started beating: *Could it be Teri?*

It wasn't. It was Trini.

"Just checking in," she said. "I was just wondering if Teri Hatcher got in yet."

Women's intuition is something you never wanna underestimate.

"She's here," I said.

"You sound tired, Andrew."

"I'm bushed, baby. Early call tomorrow. Gotta sleep."

"Okay. Hope it all goes well."

Next day the filming began. Except for the nonstop flirting, crazy-intense eye contact, eating together alone in her trailer, taking walks between scenes, teasing, taunting, and toying with each other—on set, in the gym, and in my suite—we had nothing to do with each other. Yet I was guilty as hell because, any way you look at it, I was pursuing. With Trini and little three-year-old Max back in Jersey, I felt like garbage.

Fortunately, in between filming I had some concert commitments that got me and my entourage out of Portland. I needed a break from my obsession. To make the dates they rented me an eight-person private plane, a huge perk that I absolutely loved until it nearly killed me and my boys.

We were hopping around the country in this sports car of a jet, having a ball and doing terrific until Iowa. I have a thing about Iowa 'cause that's where Dollface comes from. But what the hell—we had two Iowa dates, Des Moines and Cedar Rapids, with Kansas City and Detroit in between. No big deal.

It was all good until the flight out of Des Moines. We flew into storm clouds and then got hit by a thunderstorm. The little jet started rocking and rolling. Out the window we saw bolts of lightning. It was raining and hailing, and the way we were dipping and diving all of us were scared shitless except Club Soda Kenny, who, with his feet propped on the seat in front of him, stayed cool as a cucumber. I held on until the descent, when, about five hundred feet from the ground, we hit these unbelievably fierce winds. That's when the plane literally turned on its side—and it's also when I was certain it was curtains. I knew I was done, and started seeing my whole stupid unimportant life flash in front of me. I thought about how the asshole media would poke fun at me and say I had it coming. Except for Stern. Stern would say some nice things about me. But maybe Stern wouldn't be nice; maybe he'd also goof on my crazy death, because Stern will goof on anything—which is why I love him. As we were plummeting to the ground, I had quick conversations in my head with Mom and Dad and Natalie and Trini and Max. I'd never see them again. But the worst thing—and the clearest and strongest thought—was imagining my boy growing up without his dad. The one thing I needed to do right in this world was to raise my son. With the plane still doing flips, I crawled to the cabin and told the pilots to fly wherever they needed to fly—fuck the gig—which was when they told me that they were gonna approach the airport from a different direction and to get my ass back in my seat and strap on the belt. Seconds later, we dove into another shit storm of hail and rain and lightning until somehow the genius pilots got the plane on the ground with all of us intact.

I don't gotta tell you we were fucked-up by it. Nonetheless, the show must go on, and we drove over to the gig, where a big crowd was waiting. I was with Club Soda Kenny, Hot Tub Johnny, and a new comic opening for me— Eric Edwards. Like Ollie Joe and Wheels, Eric had a big weight problem—at five foot four, he might have been four hundred pounds—but he was funny as hell. He was a young man in his early twenties with a great personality. I took a liking to the guy and wanted to see if I could help him, not only pro- fessionally but health-wise as well. Ollie Joe had died of a stroke only two years before—still a young man—and I didn't want that to happen to Eric. He became my protégé. At the Des Moines show Eric had risen to the occasion. I was taking him virtually overnight from playing a room of fifty people to a venue of five thousand. I was proud to see that he could do it.

Backstage, Eric was in the dressing room, where he couldn't stop sob- bing. I felt like shit myself, but I went over and put my arms around him.

"Crying like this," he said, "I feel like a pussy."

"Pussies can't cry. Pussies just get wet."

The little joke made him feel better. "Look," I said, "these people have paid their hard-earned money to have a good time. We got this gift to make people laugh, and that's we gotta do."

As I watched, I was proud to see that Eric put away his fears and made 'em laugh. When I got out there, I did the same. The crowd loved us. But after the show was over and our job was done, I realized how much emotion I had suppressed. The near-crash had shaken me up worse than anything I could remember.

Rather than get back on that jet and fly to Detroit, I had Club Soda Kenny rent us a bus. I also called Dad, told him what happened the night before, and asked him to cancel the second gig in Iowa. I'd had enough of Iowa. Turned out there were a lot of reports about our near-fatal landing in the newspapers. Even Stern was talking about it.

Next day Hot Tub Johnny came into my room and said, "Dice, you know how I respect your dad, but I gotta tell you, he just ripped me a new asshole."

"About what?"

"Canceling Iowa. He said, 'Fuck the private plane. Fly commercially. I don't wanna have to give money back to the promoters.' "

"And what did you say?"

"I told him what you had already told him—how we'd almost died in a wreck and were in no mood to fly in any kind of plane."

"And then what did he say?"

"He said, 'Cut out the bullshit and just get the job done.' "

I thought about this for a while. My dad loved me, and I loved him. We were as close as close could be. He always had my back. He also had to make an adjustment from heading a process-serving agency to dealing with big shots like Sandy Gallin and Barry Diller. He'd done a great job. But like everyone else who gets a taste of show business, he could get greedy—not for himself, but for me. After haggling with promoters to get me top dollar, he couldn't stand the idea of giving back any of the money.

At this point, though, I didn't give a shit. I needed my peace of mind. So not only did I cancel Detroit, I canceled the eleven gigs that were booked after Detroit. The cost to me was over a quarter of a million dollars. My dad thought I was crazy. I thought I was finally sane. The pressure of these tours was making me crazy. If I went back to Portland and concentrated on the movie, I might be able to calm down and keep from going nuts. Besides, my mind was back on Teri.

Filming resumed in Portland. Everyone had been reading about the near-fatal crash and was asking all sorts of questions, especially Teri. We talked for a long time my first night back. I described the whole incident to her. I also poured out my heart about how I had canceled the tour and infuriated my father, something that did not sit well with me. Teri was a sympathetic listener. She knew that I was torn up with conflicts and let me rattle on as long as I wanted. And still, at the end of the day, when we returned to our hotel, she went to her suite and I went to mine.

In bed, with one thin wall separating us, I couldn't get her out of my mind.

Unable to sleep, I got out of bed and reached for a cigarette.

Andrew, I said to myself, *don't get involved with Teri. It's wrong. Fix your problems at home. Make it right with Trini.*

And then the phone rang. This time it was Teri.

"What are you doing?" she asked.

"Was gonna ask you the same thing," I said.

From there we went into the whole what-are-you-wearing, what-are-you-thinking, what-are-you-wanting routine. She was both playful and nervous. When I suggested we have phone sex, she went for it. I led it off with a long, long monologue that had her excited out of her mind. But before she came, I asked a simple question: "Do you want me to come over?"

She got quiet. She didn't know what to say or do. That's when I knew she was mine. If I sound bold, I'm sorry, but that's me. I know what I can do to a woman. Doesn't matter if it's on the phone, in the bedroom, in the bedroom closet, the bathroom, tub, shower, while she looks in the mirror putting on her makeup, in an office building stairwell, a hotel lobby men's room, a parking lot, a dressing room in a department store, a baseball field, the front of a car, the back of a car, a bus, a plane, in the kitchen while her mom is sleeping in the living room, in the guest room while her husband or boyfriend is sleeping in their bedroom, in the basement, in the ballroom, even in the back room during her kid's birthday party.

I was now sitting on the couch across from her bed and smoking a cigarette. I stared into her gorgeous eyes. I knew this was wrong. I knew I was fucking up big-time. And I also knew that, way beyond sex, I was developing feelings for Teri. My heart was flipping as I leaned back and took her in. She was wearing nothing but a tank top and panties. We didn't have full-blown sex, but her moans were delicious and deep and by the time it was over she was completely and absolutely satisfied.

I left and went back to my room, where I was up all night, smoking, pacing, thinking. *What do I do now? What's gonna happen?* The only thing I knew for sure was no matter what happened, I was fucked.

Next morning I got to the shuttle van, which was made for twenty people. It was empty except for Teri. I took a seat next to her. For the first few minutes it was awkward.

Finally I asked, "Did you sleep good?"

She turned to me, put her arm through mine and said, "I slept great."

Over the next couple days, we grew even closer together. We stole kisses whenever we could. During one sweet kiss, I saw that there were tears in her eyes.

"I can't do this," she said. "I want to, but I can't."

"I understand."

I tried to stay away. I went to the gym with Club Soda Kenny and Hot Tub Johnny. I didn't call her room at night. Come Sunday the boys and I planned to have dinner at an Italian restaurant. Then, by chance, Teri got on the elevator with us and Kenny invited her along. At first she said she had planned on eating alone in her room, but Kenny persisted and she changed her mind. After all, we were going out as a group.

It was a great restaurant, more Brooklyn than Portland, and I felt right at home. It rained that night, making everything that much cozier. The only problem was my neck. All the touring and stress had given me chronic neck pain. Teri saw something was wrong.

"You look like you're hurting, Andrew," she said.

"It's my neck. My neck's killing me tonight."

Without my asking, she got up, walked behind me and began rubbing and digging her fingers into my shoulders and neck. At one point I put my hand on hers. It was very tender and very touching and I was getting real emotional. This woman was doing everything she could to relieve my pain. But my pain was still there. Not just my neck pain, but my heart pain, 'cause I was falling for a woman who wasn't mine while trying unsuccessfully to forget about the woman who was. I was thinking that I always wanted to look at Trini the way Rocky looked at Adrian. Adrian was always there for Rocky. He might have been getting the physical punches, but she felt the pain as much as he did. No matter how beaten he was, he could get up and keep fighting 'cause he knew his woman was by his side. I no longer was sure I knew that about Trini. I didn't know that she'd always be in my corner. And now I also didn't know if I could trust myself. I never saw myself as a married guy with a chick on the side. After meeting Trini, I'd passed up hundreds of hot groupies. Yet here I was, staying behind at the restaurant with Teri as the other guys went back to the hotel.

"Your neck feel better?" she asked.

"Much better. Let's just have a cup of coffee and talk."

We talked about the movies, her life, my life. We talked about everything. I liked her humor. She liked my humor. I liked her smile. She liked my dumb way of talking. I liked everything about her.

When we left the restaurant, the rain had stopped. Hand in hand, we walked back to the hotel. We rode up in the elevator together. When we got to my suite, I said, "I wanna do this so bad, but I'm all torn up."

"I know," she said. "I can feel what you're feeling."

She just stood there, running her hands through her hair. I walked over, put one hand around her waist and kissed her deeply. She responded by holding my face with both her hands. Lust was there, but love was in the middle of the thing. The lovemaking was out of this world.

The day before Thanksgiving was the final day of filming. It was rough. The next day I'd be flying home to Trini and Max in Jersey. This was the end of the affair we'd been having in the movie as well as in real life. Both of us knew it couldn't go on. I was still too attached to my family to ever leave them. Teri knew that from the beginning.

What was weird was that the director saved the last scene in the story for the last day of shooting. That's unusual, because films are shot out of sequence. But somehow things had worked out so that the climactic scene—in which we both finally say "I love you"—was being shot the day we parted.

To make the scene even more romantic and personal, I'd rewritten it. Everyone on the set knew what Teri and I knew—that these two adventures, the ninja killers/bouncer/model story and the real-life Andrew-Teri story, had come together.

On camera, I confessed my love and she confessed hers.

The make-believe story was over, and the next day I was on a plane to Jersey, my heart torn into a million pieces.

TWO WORDS

THE HOLIDAYS WEREN'T easy. I'd vowed to give up Teri, and Teri had vowed to give up me. We kept our vows, no contact, no more nothing. But my mind was cloudy and my heart was heavy with guilt, and even though I did my best to bring my attention back to Trini—I even bought her super-expensive lingerie to rekindle our romance—Trini wasn't all that interested. The fact that she had made friends with a woman who I respectfully call the Fat Ox didn't help matters. Why do so many fuckin' wives have fat ox girlfriends whispering bullshit in their ear and turning them against their husbands? This particular fat ox was the worst. Her whole thing was being the best friend of Andrew Dice Clay's wife. She had her nose in her everyone's business—especially Trini's—and she had the sensitivity of, well, a fuckin' ox. She came to our New Year's party, which was fine, but at four thirty in the morning the Ox was still there, drinking my booze and bullshitting with my wife. This was when I wanted private time with Trini. We needed to be alone. We needed to get rid of the Fat Ox, but the Fat Ox wouldn't move her fat ass off the couch, and Trini wouldn't kick her out. I ended the year in a state of deep fuckin' depression.

As 1994 began, I was positive that my marriage couldn't survive another week. But then in less than a second, my attitude went from dark and negative to bright and positive. It took only two words from Trini to renew my hope and warm my heart.

"I'm pregnant."

BOCA

SOMETIME AFTER TRINI told me I was going to be a dad again I was down in Florida visiting my parents.

"Diceman, baby," said Dennis Arfa, "you don't sound good."

"I don't feel good."

"The bookings are still strong," said Dennis.

"I'm not worried about the bookings. I'm worried about my family."

"Why? What's with the family? I thought you said Trini's having a good pregnancy. Aren't the two of you getting along?"

"No. We're always at each other's throats, but that ain't the problem. The problem is my mother and father."

"What? Jackie and Fred Silverstein? They're your rock."

"They are. I love 'em to death. But they're so fuckin' involved in my career that it's driving me crazy. My dad has become so over-the-top hard-core about me making more and more money that I don't even wanna discuss business with him. And my mom—well, it's like she's the one who became one of the biggest entertainers in the country, not me. I think my success is making them both nuts."

"I thought the whole idea was that buying them a condo in Boca Raton was your way of being closer to them."

"I bought it because they wouldn't move out to California."

"But then you bought your own condo in Boca only a few blocks away."

"Maybe that was a mistake. I'm not sure. I'm not sure of anything now."

"Something just hit me like a ton of bricks," said Dennis. "I just remembered a friend of mine in Boca who can help you out."

"Who?"

"His name is Frank."

"How can he help?"

"He's a psychiatrist."

"You gotta be fuckin' kidding. Can you see me going to a shrink?"

"Yeah. You'll like Frank. He's a regular guy. I can see you talking to him. You're a smart guy. He's a smart guy. You've got problems. He's a guy who helps solve problems. That's all there is to it."

"So you're saying that you think I'm crazy."

"No, I'm saying that I think you don't wanna go crazy. Which is why I think you'll call Frank."

I called Frank.

On the day of the appointment I went over there with Hot Tub Johnny and Club Soda Kenny, who waited for me in the reception area while I went into the lion's den.

The shrink looked the way shrinks look: Dead serious. Frown on his face. Thick glasses. Lace-up shoes. Severe.

"I've never done this before," I said, "so I don't know how it works."

"It works the way you want it to work."

"I want to stop feeling so fuckin' guilty and pressured about everything."

"Where do you think the guilt is coming from?"

"I moved my parents down here to Boca and then I moved down 'cause Mom said I didn't see her enough."

"Are you close to your mother?"

"Extremely."

"With few arguments or fights?"

"With many arguments and fights."

"Beginning when?"

"A few seconds after I popped outta the womb."

I figured I'd get a laugh out of the shrink, but nothing doing. He was just sitting there taking notes.

"Going back to your childhood, was there one major argument with your mother that you can remember?"

"I remember them all."

"If you don't mind, let me hear one or two of them."

So for the next forty-five minutes, I went back to the beginning in Brooklyn and started telling stories of me and my mom. Most of the stories had to do with how Mom always protected me. But some of the other stories were about how Mom got involved in every detail of my life. That got even crazier when I got into showbiz, because Mom loved showbiz so much. She was beautiful enough to go into showbiz, but it just didn't work out that way.

I finally paused, tired from telling stories, figuring Frank would finally jump in and say something insightful, or . . . anything.

"So, that's it, there we are," I said. "What do you think?"

Frank shut his notebook. "Unfortunately, we're out of time."

Over the next month or so, I went back to Frank the shrink a couple of times, and it was always about my mother. When I was talking to my friends about my life, I noticed I started saying shit like "My shrink says this" and "My shrink says that." When I'd heard other people refer to their shrinks, I'd always thought it was bullshit—yet here I was doing it. I couldn't believe I was a guy who was going to a shrink, but I was. In the meantime, I was getting more pissed about everything.

"You have a lot of rage in you," said Frank during one of the sessions. "It feels like you're angry at women."

"Are you kidding? I love women."

"When you've discussed your early relationships—Dolores; Sylvia; your first wife, Dollface; your current wife, Trini—you become enraged. You get furious. I wonder if that rage can be traced back to some unexpressed anger at your mother."

"That's bullshit. The anger I'm feeling has to do with what's happening right now."

"Would you like to be more specific?"

"Yeah, I'll be very fuckin' specific. I came to Boca to relax. That's the whole point."

"I thought the point was to be close to your mother."

"Right. Because if I'm closer to her, she'll stop nagging me about how I never see her, and I'll be able to relax. For me, a bike ride is relaxing. So yesterday I decide to ride my bike over to the Seven-Eleven and buy a Slurpee. But when the elevator opened up and I started walking through the lobby, the security guy at my building said, 'No bikes through the lobby.'

" 'Fine,' I said. 'Next time I'll go down through the garage.'

" 'No next time,' said the guy. 'This time.'

" 'Look, pal,' I said. 'I'm five fuckin' feet away from the front door. There's no one here but you and me.'

" 'Rules are rules,' he said.

" 'What is this—fuckin' junior high? I'm walking my bike through this lobby, pal, and if I were you, I'd get the hell out of my way.'

"The guy gets outta my way and I ride down to Seven-Eleven. I buy my Coca-Cola Slurpee and take it back to the pool area in back of the building, where I'm gonna sit in a lounge chair and relax. That's why I'm in Boca—to relax. But no sooner do I sit down than this old cocker on the other side of the pool says, 'Sorry, no food at the pool.'

" 'This isn't food,' I said. 'It's a Slurpee.'

" 'No food or drinks.'

" 'I understand, but I'm gonna sip on this thing and be through with it in two minutes and everything will be fine.'

" 'Everything is not fine,' said the old man. 'Take your drink and leave the pool area right now.'

"You gotta understand," I told the shrink. "I'm a guy who respects my elders. You know how I feel about my grandparents and my dad and mom."

"Actually I think your mom has a lot to do with this story."

"My mom has nothing to do with this story. My mom wasn't there. You ain't listening to me."

"I'm listening closely. Under the rage—"

"Before you tell me what's the under the rage, let me get done telling you the story."

"Go ahead, Andrew."

"So I'm sitting there with my fuckin' Slurpee and the old cocker keeps giving me a hard time. I figure the best way to handle it is to ignore him. Let him yell. I need to relax. But here he comes. He actually gets out of his chair and walks over to me. He gets right in my face and, with his garlic breath hitting me in the mouth, says, 'Look, wiseguy, I told you to move.'

" 'Why don't you do yourself a favor,' I said, 'and get the fuck outta my face?'

"That's when he starts shaking my chair. Now, you tell me," I said to the shrink, "what am I supposed to do? Hit an old man? I ain't gonna touch him, I'm just gonna say, 'Move away from me before I drown you in the fuckin' pool.' Well, just as I said that, Trini and little Max showed up.

" 'What are you doing to this nice old man?' asked Trini.

" 'It ain't what I'm doing to him,' I said. 'It's what he's doing to me.'

" 'If this is your husband,' said the old man, 'he's being disrespectful.'

" 'The fuck I am,' I said. 'This asshole—'

" 'Look how he talks to me.'

"At this point there ain't anything to do but get outta there. I can't win.

" 'Where you going?' asked Trini.

" 'Out,' was all I could say.

" 'While you're out, don't forget you promised Max a TV for his room.' "

Hearing this story so far, Frank the shrink said, "At this point I understand how you must be feeling outraged."

"You don't understand shit," I told the shrink. "Because you've haven't heard the whole story. It gets worse. At this point I figure there's no way I can relax, so I might as well just go to the store and get my kid a TV so he can watch cartoons in his room. I might as well make myself useful. At the store, I go over to the TV department and the salesman—a big muscular guy—said to me, 'I know who you are. You're the Diceman.'

" 'I am the Diceman, and I'm here for a TV for my son.'

" 'You must have a lot of people threatening you.'

" 'Not a lot. Some.'

" 'You must need a bodyguard.'

" 'I got a bodyguard.'

" 'I should be your bodyguard.'

" 'Like I just said, pal, I don't need a bodyguard. I got plenty.'

" 'But not like me.'

" 'No, better than you.'

" 'There can be no bodyguard better than me.'

" 'Do me a favor. Help me buy a TV and lemme get the fuck outta here.'

" 'How 'bout we fight?'

" 'Fight? Are you crazy?'

" 'The store's empty right here. We can do it right here. Not a fistfight, but a little wrestling match. If I pin you, you make me one of your bodyguards. If you pin me, you walk outta here with a free TV.'

" 'I don't need a free TV.'

" 'Then you just walk outta here. But that's not gonna happen. 'Cause I'm gonna pin your ass.'

"I look this guy over. He's taller than me. He's got bigger muscles, but I don't see him as tough. And tell him so. I said, 'I've had my ass kicked by some really tough guys, but you ain't tough. You might be strong, but strong isn't tough.'

" 'Then prove it, asshole.'

" 'Now you're calling me—a customer who's about to buy a TV—an asshole.'

" 'An asshole loudmouth clown who acts tough but underneath all the big talk is scared shitless when it comes to a real-life situation.'

"Well, Frank," I said to the shrink, "that's all I needed to hear. He punched all my buttons. Him and the security guard at the building and the old man at the pool. I'd had it. I was gonna show this salesman he fucked with the wrong guy. I was gonna show him that he'd made a mistake that he'd never forget. So right there between the stereo components and boom boxes and the VCR tape recorders, we went at it. A bunch of the other salesmen, who'd been listening to us, made a circle around us. We started dancing around each other, feeling each other out. What this guy didn't know, of course, was that I'd been working with Happy Face, a martial arts genius teacher. A quick jab instantly threw him off balance and twisted his whole body around until he wound up on his stomach on the floor. I jumped on his back and put my arm around his throat. 'Next time,' I said, 'I'll break your fuckin' back.' I threw seven twenties on his head and walked out with a TV. The other salesmen applauded me on the way out."

For a long time, Frank the shrink didn't say nothing.

Finally he said, "I can't help wondering about what incident in your childhood may have triggered this and how your mother—"

I lost it. I moved to the edge of the couch. I felt myself burning up.

"Forget about my mother! We're through talking about her. But I will tell you one thing I got from my mother—my mouth. How to speak my mind. So, that's it, Frank. We're done. But I have good news for you. After only two months of therapy, I've had a breakthrough. You know what it is? You haven't done *shit.*"

ANOTHER BEAUTIFUL BLESSING

THE POSITIVES OUTWEIGHED the negatives. I gotta say that, for all the crazy shit that has come down in my life, the positives have always outweighed the negatives. That was true in my childhood when the Originals—me, Mom, Dad, and Natalie—were together and making our way through the streets of Brooklyn, Staten Island, Miami, and then back to Brooklyn. It was true when I went to California to hustle and scuffle at the Comedy Store. It was true when I started hitting it big. And it was true after my showbiz star started to fade—mainly because of my boys. My second son, Dillon Scott, was born in 1994, and, like Max, he won over my heart the second I laid eyes on him. I called him my blond angel. We loved Matt Dillon's name. I always said if we had another son we'd have to name him Dillon. And Trini agreed.

He was a sweet, sweet baby, and holding him in my arms, I vowed that I'd care for him and his brother no matter what insanity came into my life. The feeling of being a father was the most powerful emotion I have ever experienced.

After my boys made their appearance in the world, I wasn't just living for myself; I was living for them. I was determined to be a man they'd look up to and be proud of. Every day I let them know—even before they knew what the words meant—that they were the most beautiful blessings in my life.

My professional life was definitely taking a downward dip. When that happened, one of the characters who disappeared was Downtown Ronny. Much as I liked him, I was half-glad that he was gone.

There were moments of light in the professional dark, though. While *Brain Smasher* was hardly a big hit, two years later Warner Bros. and CBS television still had enough faith to cast me in the starring role in *Bless This House*, a sitcom costarring Cathy Moriarty, who was brilliant as De Niro's wife in *Raging Bull*. I played a working-class hero, a postal worker struggling to make ends meet. It ran for sixteen episodes, and I hated practically every minute of it. The writing was shit, and the character they tried to develop for me had no soul or depth. The day it was canceled, I rejoiced. I was so miserable I'd been gaining five pounds a week. The only happy moment came when, dressed in a Santa jacket, I got to sing a full version of "Blue Christmas" Elvis-style.

The show did bring a little heat back to my career, which was why Downtown Ronny was suddenly showing up at my stand-up gigs in L.A. He immediately started in on problems booking Wheels.

"I can't do nothing with Wheels," I said. "Wheels gotta roll on his own."

But just when I thought that Ronny was finally getting the picture, he showed up at Mulberry Street Pizzeria in L.A., where I was having lunch with friends.

He took me to the side and said, "Don't worry, Dice, it ain't about Wheels. It's about our friend in Brooklyn."

"What friend?"

"Our best friend."

"Maybe your best friend, Downtown, but not mine."

"He sends his regards."

"Fine. Give him mine."

"He wants your regards in person. He would very much like for you to come by and see him."

"I got no reason to see him."

"You got every reason, Dice. He's your friend. He's just looking for you to pay your respects."

"I already paid. You got your pay-per-view money."

"It ain't about money. It's about honor."

"Look, Downtown, I'm an honorable Jew from Brooklyn. I worked my way up legit. I ain't ever lived that life, and I ain't living it now. I met the man once. I had one little piece of business with him. The account was settled. End of story."

"He won't like hearing this."

"You'll tell it to him nice. You'll give him my apologies."

"You need to do that in person. He wants a sit-down."

"No sit-down. No stand-up. No nothing. There's nothing between us—not between him and me, not between you and me. You get it? That was the past. I've been raising a family now, Ronny. Not that I don't love you, but people change."

He got up and left.

A month went by. I thought the problem was over, but then Downtown and a group of his guys showed up when I was working the Store. They were sitting at front-row tables. Sometimes they'd laugh, sometimes they didn't. Mainly they stared. What was I supposed to think?

"I need to talk with you, Dice," said Downtown after I got offstage.

"I gotta get home."

"We'll be back tomorrow night."

They were back the next night and the night after. They were staring at me harder than ever. I was on the verge of a nervous breakdown.

I told my wife what was happening, but she said I was imagining things.

"I ain't imagining shit," I said. "This shit is real."

"Go to sleep and forget about it."

I couldn't sleep. The next morning I called my mother.

I said, "Ma, don't start up. What am I gonna do?"

"Call your uncle Jay."

If you're a Jewish family with a wiseguy problem, you gotta be awfully goddamn lucky to have an Uncle Jay, a Jewish defense lawyer for the mob. Jay was a huge guy with a huge head and a huge reputation for keeping the wiseguys out of the can.

So I called Uncle Jay and explained the problem.

"And that pay-per-view deal you made with them, they got paid?" asked Uncle Jay.

"Every last dime."

"You sure?"

"Positive. Ask my father. Can you help me, Uncle Jay?"

"Give me a couple of days."

During those days, I thought about the stories Jay used to tell. The one I remember most is about when he was with the most ferocious wiseguy of all time, the nutcase Joe Pesci played in *Goodfellas*.

"This guy—let's call him Al—wanted to meet me for lunch at a steak joint in Canarsie," Uncle Jay told me. "I got there first, ordered a martini, and waited. Al arrived a half hour late. He was wearing a green felt Borsalino fedora with a fancy red feather sticking out of the hatband. On his way to the table he passed by a man at the bar. Nursing a beer, the guy looked up at Al's hat and said, 'Nice feather.' Then Al joined me at the table.

"He said, 'Jay, see that lunch box at the bar'—by 'lunch box' he meant a nine-to-five guy—'when he leaves here I'm whacking him.'

" 'Why would you want to do that, Al?' I asked.

" 'Because he made fun of the feather in my hat. He questioned my fuckin' manhood.'

"I didn't argue with Al. I knew him too well. I trusted that his anger would subside. But as he started downing scotches, his anger grew.

" 'It was a personal insult,' Al said. 'Not only was he insulting me, he was insulting my mother, who gave me the hat for Christmas. This bum is mincemeat. After our steaks, we'll have coffee and dessert. Then I'm taking him out back and busting his fuckin' head wide open.'

"We ate our steaks, we drank our coffee, we had cheesecake for dessert, and just when Al was about to walk over to the bar and make his move, I made my case.

" 'Al,' I said, 'you called it right. You saw this guy accurately. He's a lunch box. In your world, you're a star. Why should a star bother with a lunch box? You're a bigger man than that. Just think of the heat you'd be bringing. Right now I have your legal affairs in order. Right now everything is beautiful. Don't let the lunch box throw you off.'

" 'Is that your professional opinion, Jay?' Al asked.

" 'It is,' I said.

"With that, Al got up, walked over to the man at the bar and put his arm around him. I didn't know what to expect. Al was a wild card. Al was an impetuous murderer.

" 'Look here, pal,' Al told the man. 'When I came in, you said something about my hat, didn't you?'

" 'I don't remember,' said the guy.

" 'Yes, you did,' said Al. 'You said, "Nice feather." '

" 'Maybe I did,' said the guy. 'So what?'

" 'Here's what,' said Al.

"That's when I held my breath.

" 'Here's my hat,' said Al. 'Take it. If you like it so much, it's yours. And all your drinks are on me.'

"Al came back to our table and said, 'Jay, no matter what you've done in your life, you're going to heaven because of what you did for me today. I was about to whack that bum for nothing. You showed me why, next to a dog, a smart lawyer is man's best friend.' "

That was Uncle Jay, the guy you want on your side.

Meanwhile, for those two days when he was trying to work out my mob problem my stomach was in knots. Finally the phone rang.

"Sorry," said Uncle Jay, "it's going to take a little more time."

"What's the problem?"

"Long Island is fighting Brooklyn. Long Island is claiming you."

"How can Long Island be claiming me?"

"They said you were with them before you were with Brooklyn."

"Uncle Jay, I wasn't with anybody—ever. You gotta believe me."

"Of course I believe you, Andrew. But they have their own way of thinking."

"Get 'em to think different."

"That's difficult. It's better to think the way they do. Long Island likes you. Long Island wants to protect you. Harry from Long Island will be coming to you."

"Who's Harry?"

"A man who likes you."

Harry from Long Island came to see me. He was bigger than Wheels. Haven't any of these guys heard of Weight Watchers?

Harry said, "You want to carry something?"

"No, I don't want to carry anything. I'm not a killer, I'm a comic."

"Because if you carry, Dice, and they cross your property line, you can unload on them."

"Who's crossing my property line? Isn't it your job to keep them from crossing my property line?"

"We'll do our best, but you never know."

That "never know" line had me half-crazy.

I called Uncle Jay and said, "If Brooklyn gets past Long Island's protection, what are they gonna do to me?"

"They may hurt you, but they won't kill you."

"Uncle Jay," I said, " 'hurt me' is no good."

"I understand, but I have confidence in Long Island. Stay strong, Andrew."

For the next four years I stayed strong. But every time I got a haircut I worried. In fact, I stopped going to barbershops, 'cause I remembered how much the boys with itchy fingers liked barbershops. I didn't really stop worrying until Uncle Jay called me with the news I'd been waiting for.

"Brooklyn is no longer a problem," he said.

"How can you be sure?"

"The man from Bay Ridge is gone."

"What do you mean by 'gone'?"

"Real gone. Permanently gone."

So gone they never found the body.

And that was the end of me and the wiseguys.

SLIM SHADY

BY 1995 THE road had broken me down. I felt physically and emotionally destroyed. I had done over three hundred arena shows alone, performing in front of an average of ninety thousand people a week. It was exhilarating, and it was killing me. I ate all the wrong foods and started to balloon up. When I got to Vegas, I hit the tables hard, losing more than I won. And whenever the press had an opportunity to slam me, they fucking killed me. After *Bless This House* ended, another HBO comedy special came along called *Assume the Position*, which, frankly, blew. When that nightmare ended, all I wanted to do was celebrate. Then in 1997, I landed a role in a sitcom called *Hitz* about the record business. *Hitz* was a flop.

But the upside of my so-called sitcom career was that I got to spend more time at home with the family. And even during those dark days, we had plenty of good times.

One night I'll never forget was the night that Eminem came over.

When his *Slim Shady LP* came out in 1999, he was the hottest thing in music. I loved his shit. He was a brilliant storyteller inventing all sorts of whacked-out characters and describing them in rhymes that set the world on fire. Max, who was turning ten, also loved him. Turned out that Eminem loved the Diceman, 'cause one day I got this call from his manager saying he wanted to meet me and give me a multiple-record deal on his label. Even more exciting, Em personally wanted to produce. He was flying in from Detroit to meet me. I suggested he first catch me at the Comedy Store and then come to the house afterward. Trini would throw some steaks on the grill. The manager said cool.

In the articles I read about Em, it was like they were replacing my name with his. They were calling him homophobic and misogynistic just like they called me. Every chance I got, I defended him—and this was even before I learned that he was a fan of mine—because I recognized that he was just creating characters. Rap's a little like stand-up: because the creation is coming out of your own mouth, everyone presumes you're that guy. Well, you are and you aren't. You understand him, or you couldn't create him. And part of you has to identify, or you couldn't make him real. But another part of you has nothing to do with him. In the end, that character—whether Eminem or the Diceman—is something you've invented.

Em showed up at the Store with his bodyguards—each one the size of a barn door—and laughed his ass off at my act. Then he and I rolled back to my crib. My kids were huge Eminem fans, and Max was waiting for him at the door. Dillon had fallen asleep in the master bedroom, but I got Em to sit on the bed while I tried to wake him up.

"Open your eyes, honey," I said, "and see who I brought home to meet you."

Dillon wouldn't stir. The kid could sleep through a tornado blowing through his room. After a few more not-so-gentle shakes, I gave up, bringing personal meaning to the expression "You snooze, you lose."

A half hour later, at three A.M., Eminem and Max were outside playing hoops and I was videotaping the whole thing. Eminem took the game seriously, playing like he was getting paid. It was a good lesson for Max: no matter what you do, do it all the way. After the game, he gave Max a huge hug, and Max couldn't stop grinning. The kid wore that smile for a week.

Up at Club 33, we made plans. Eminem was dead set on producing a series of albums with me. I also suggested that the two of us go into a big venue, like Giants Stadium, under the banner of Comedy, Rap, and Roll. He dug the idea. When the evening was over, we hugged. This is one great guy, a real artist and a true mensch.

Ultimately, though, our plans went awry. I thought it was because he went off and did the movie *8 Mile*. But I learned later that the money men behind his record label didn't like the idea of his producing Dice and killed the deal. I was disappointed, but it never killed my respect for Eminem and my gratitude for the respect that he showed me and my kids.

THE RETURN
OCTOBER 26, 2000

AFTER THE DEAL with Eminem fell apart, I felt empty. I needed to do something else, something special. What motivated me were my kids. Every time I looked at their faces I felt a rush of so many things—unconditional love and undying devotion, of course, but also this feeling of overwhelming responsibility and this absolute drive to accomplish something for them, just for them. Even though they were young, they knew I was different. Hey, when your father's name is Dice and not Steve or Bill or Eddie, and he wears leather motorcycle jackets to work, you know he's not just some *guy*.

At this point, I'd started appearing regularly on this FM radio show out of New York, an afternoon drive time, with these two wild guys, Opie and Anthony. They were outrageous and funny, and they were starting to make some noise. I'd call in from L.A. and we'd riff, but it was even better when I was in New York and I'd go into the studio. Anthony started doing an impression of me, and I had to say, he was kind of brilliant. He'd get into my character and in my voice say, 'Yeah, this weekend I'm gonna be at the Garden . . . the *Olive Garden*. Ohhh!' Club Soda Kenny heard that and got pissed, but I thought it was funny. Opie and Anthony grew in popularity, and the three of us got tight, both on and off the air.

One night, Max, who was about ten, and I were watching 'N Sync doing a show from Madison Square Garden. My son knew I'd been the first comedian to sell out the Garden, and he just said, innocently, "Hey, Dad, why don't you play the Garden again?"

The question tore into me. I took a few seconds before I answered. Then, in the best way I could, I tried to explain that I had a different career now and that I didn't play places like the Garden anymore.

"But you could if you wanted to, right, Dad?"

I looked at my son and bit my lip. "Yeah, Max. Sure I could."

After he went to bed, I started pacing through the family room like a caged animal. It got dark outside, but I didn't want to turn the lights on. I stopped pacing, looked into the night, and stood in the shadows of the room. I paced again, and then I put the lights on dim and started looking at all the framed photographs spread around the family room—pictures of Trini and me; shots of my mom and dad and Natalie; photos of the biggest moments of my career, including me at the Garden. And then I sat down at the big redwood and oak bar and chain-smoked. I don't know how long I sat there, but I finally forced myself to my feet and wandered into Club 33. I stared at the tiger carpeting, the puffed-out velvet walls in different vivid colors, the spa I'd put in that was equal to the ones in any health club in the city, the sound system as primo as in any recording studio, and I thought, *What the hell good is all this? This stuff don't matter. None of it.* There were only two things that mattered.

I went back into the family room and picked up a picture of Max and Dillon, ten and six, and I looked at them, and I started to lose it. I shook my head to fight off tears and I spoke directly to their little faces in the photograph: "You want to see me at Madison Square Garden? Is that what you want? Okay. Then I'm gonna get it done."

I went after it, but I went after it smart. I bided my time. I waited until my new album came out, *Face Down Ass Up,* which I recorded at the Roxy and would promote like a maniac on Opie and Anthony. I did new material about how the digital age was driving everyone bat-shit. I also had a lot of stuff about how because the guys are all getting to work at home, they're missing the office, where they used to dream of getting the receptionist with the big fat tits up against the copying machine and banging her wet pussy while she was screaming, "More dick! More dick!" The record also included a killer collaboration with Snoop Dogg, who, along with a whole gang of other rappers, happened to be a Dice fan. We called the song "Club 33."

Back in New York, the day the album broke, Dennis called me in my hotel room. "Sales are strong," he said.

"That's good, real good."

"So, Diceman, what do you think the move is?"

"Book the Garden," I said.

Silence.

"I'm serious, man," I said.

"Diceman, the album is selling, but it's been out exactly one day. I love your passion, you know that, but—"

"The Garden. It's time to go back."

He sighed through the phone. "How about we book the Beacon first? See how we do."

"We'll sell that out in twenty minutes."

I was wrong.

It took thirty-five minutes.

But it was fast enough to convince Dennis to go after the Garden. He didn't think we'd sell out, though. He was right. The Garden holds eighteen thousand. We sold ten thousand tickets. Not bad considering that the night of my Garden show the Mets were playing the Yankees in their first-ever subway World Series.

But ten thousand fans? Yeah. Not bad.

Well, ten thousand and *two*, counting Max and Dillon.

I swore I'd give them a night to remember.

Like always, I trained. I hired George Pipasik, Sly's guy, who beat the shit out of me. We focused on my lower body, building up my legs—three sets of twenty reps each on three different machines. Fucking ridiculous. Fucking torture.

At night I ran, either into the Hollywood Hills or sprints around the track at Fairfax High. I wanted my mind to be clear and positive. As I ran I listened to tapes I'd made for Trini, songs she loved, music that reminded me of our happiest times. I'd picture her dancing to Janet Jackson, Trini's face a full-on smile of joy and abandon and love. And then sometimes I would get sad in the middle of my workout, thinking of how difficult things had gotten between us now. I would break out of it by thinking of Max and Dillon. They were my heart. I could never—would never—fail them. I would push through the pain and the sadness and confusion and focus everything in my entire being on them. And on the Garden.

I kept pumping up my upcoming Garden party on Opie and Anthony. Their ratings soared. The hype built. I marked the occasion by having special jewelry custom-made. I created a big medallion to put around my neck with MTD spelled out in diamonds—for Max, Trini, and Dillon. The T was in the middle and stood over the M and D the way a mother should look over her kids. Then I made dog tags for Mom, Dad, Natalie, and the boys. They had the same MTD with little red sapphires underneath spelling out "Daddy Dice."

By the middle of October, I was ready mentally and physically. I'd trimmed down and felt stronger than ever. I flew my dad up from Florida. My mom had to forgo the trip. Her health was starting to fail, and she couldn't fly. I made sure that Trini, Max, and Dillon were backstage when Opie and Anthony introduced me and then arranged to have Happy Face and Club Soda escort the kids out once I got into the raunchy stuff in my act.

The night of my return to the Garden, I went into a little room backstage, closed the door, and, as I always did before every concert, prayed. First, I said a prayer for my mom's health. Then I thanked God for everything I'd achieved and for allowing me to find the strength to never give up and to fight back. I'd been knocked down to my knees, and I thanked Him for giving me the power to stand back up. Finally, I thanked God for allowing me to appear once again front and center in the greatest arena of them all, in the greatest city on earth. And then I went backstage to find my family.

I saw my father first, that sweet, wonderful man, my rock, who always had my back, and then I swallowed the emotion rising up when I realized that next to him was an empty space where my mom would always be. I felt the space filled with my mom's energy and power, even though she was thousands of miles away. Then I hugged Natalie, my loving sister, my most passionate fan, who had encouraged me every minute of every day from childhood. I hugged Trini, my wife, the mother of my children, the woman who gave me the two greatest gifts I could ever receive. And then I gathered up my sons, the only fuel I would ever need to keep me going, my reasons to live.

The crowd started chanting, "Dice, Dice, Dice!" but all I could see were those two precious faces, my sons, Max and Dillon, looking at me with pure love and adulation.

"Told you I'd get back here," I said. "I'll never let you down." I squeezed my sons with every ounce of love I felt, and then I stepped away. I hiked up the collar of my leather jacket and, with the crowd growing into a fever, roaring, *Dice, Dice, Dice!* I started toward the stage. I stopped before I hit the spotlight, turned back, and pointed at both my sons.

"Boys," I said, "this one's for you."

EPILOGUE
THERE TO HERE

TRINI AND I kept trying to work on our marriage. We spent time alone. We went into counseling. Nothing helped. The truth is we were trying to fix something that was beyond repair. But every time I faced calling it quits for good, I fell apart. Finally, painfully, we made the decision to split in 2002. We officially divorced in 2005.

I hoped that for the sake of the boys there would be a minimum of bloodletting. Sadly, working out the financial settlement took years and turned into a brutal war. The whole thing ripped a hole in my heart. At least Trini agreed to allow the kids to live with me full time. I was a mess through those years, but without my boys around me, I would've been worse.

And of course my life would have been much worse had I never met Rodney Dangerfield. He changed everything. I loved the guy. I remember being in Rodney's hospital room right before he died and telling his wife, Joan, that this man gave me the shot of a lifetime. And it would never be forgotten, ever.

Rodney Dangerfield will go down as a giant and the godfather of stand-up comedy. I'll always be grateful to him.

There's someone else I'll always be grateful to—a great lady named Eleanor Kerrigan.

I've known Eleanor since 1993, when she started working at the Comedy Store as a waitress. Eventually she worked her way up to become Mitzi Shore's assistant. Everybody loves Eleanor. She calls herself a "hood rat from South Philly." She's one of ten kids brought up by a single mom. Eleanor is tough as nails but sweet as sugar. She's also super-hip. There wasn't a comic who passed through the Comedy Store who didn't adore her, and she adored them right back. Once she said to me, "The thing about you comics is that you have beautiful spirits."

Eleanor had great relationships with so many comics because she was smart enough not to sleep with any of them. She wanted to be their friend and not fuck up things by fucking them. I had to respect that, but I didn't like it. I was attracted to Eleanor and wanted her in the worst way, but she kept putting me off. She knew I was getting divorced, but that wasn't good enough for her. She'd have nothing to do with me romantically until I moved out of the house and filed papers.

That didn't stop me from hitting on her. Yet the more persistent I was, the more resistant Eleanor became. She'd be my friend. She'd go out with me and my boys. She and the boys were crazy about each other. But as far as my goal of getting her into bed—no Dice.

When I did move out and file papers, Eleanor and I started dating. In 2005, we got engaged. Then almost immediately a series of tragedies hit her like a wave. First, her dear friend comic Freddy Soto died. A week after Freddy died, Eleanor's beloved grandmother passed away. She went from one funeral to another. She stopped eating, lost weight, went down to 110 pounds. I was worried sick for Eleanor, and it affected us as a couple.

During the summer of 2006, I got a show on VH1 following me and my family. They called it a reality show, but the reality was it was shit. With my career not exactly soaring, I couldn't be choosy, so I took it. Eleanor and the boys were in the show, but the show went nowhere. Then that August, Eleanor said the words that I knew were coming.

"I'm always gonna love you and the boys," she said. "I'm always gonna be part of your life. But I can't marry you. If I do, it's not gonna work. And then we won't be friends and I won't see the boys and I won't see you, and I can't stand that thought."

I held her and kissed her and told her that I understood. I respected her honesty. I respect everything about Eleanor, who is one of the most beautiful people I've ever known.

Eleanor Kerrigan—who has turned into one of the best female stand-ups out there—is still opening for me. And we've stayed best friends.

On Super Bowl Sunday in January 2008, I scored an invitation for me and Max to the Playboy Mansion. I was happy to go, but Max, now eighteen, was *dying* to go.

The Playboy Mansion is pretty much what you'd imagine—a huge house packed with gorgeous chicks who happen to be unbelievably stacked. Max was running around having a ball getting his picture snapped with a bunch of Playmates. I staked out a spot on a couch so I could enjoy the view.

I kept noticing this one particular woman passing in and out of my sight line. I found myself staring at her. She wasn't dressed like a Playmate. She was wearing blue jeans and a purple polka-dotted tube top. Her body was incredible. She wore her hair pinned up high on her head. She had gorgeous brown eyes and a radiant smile. Her skin was dark; she was maybe Italian, maybe Middle Eastern, maybe Latin. Whatever she was, she was a total knockout. And then, suddenly, she appeared right in front of me.

"I'm Dice," I said.

The name didn't ring a bell for her. She said her name was Valerie. She just wanted to tell me that she liked my oversized aviator glasses. Before we could really talk, a couple of chicks came over and asked if they could take their picture with me. I stood up and posed with them, and when I sat back down, Valerie was gone.

I couldn't get my mind off her. After a while, I gave Max a mission: find Valerie. Couple of minutes later, Max returned and whispered her location to me.

I found her in a corner by herself, sipping a drink. We started talking. I told her what I did and she told me she worked as a hair and makeup artist. Then she asked me to guess her ethnicity. I gave it a shot. "Persian? Haitian? Hawaiian? Canadian?"

"Mexican," she said, laughing. "Actually my mother is Italian and Jewish. Her father is Italian and her mother is Jewish. My dad's Mexican."

The more we talked, the more I felt myself falling. I invited her to meet me the following night at the Comedy Store.

That's when I brought Valerie Vasquez into my world. I'd been focusing so much attention on raising my sons that I almost forgot what it was like to be in a relationship. I missed having a woman in my life. And Valerie was special—an entrepreneur designing her own clothing line, attentive to me, wonderful with the boys, a truly caring human being who happened to think I was funny as hell (a plus), and have I mentioned she happened to be fucking gorgeous?

Val and I got married in Vegas on Valentine's Day 2010. Soon after she moved in, her best friend moved in, too. Her mother. Wild, huh? I love her too. She is an incredibly sweet, loving woman and a helluva cook who ran a concession stand at Dodger Stadium.

I've had setbacks in my life and people close to me have passed away, but nothing hit me harder than losing my mom and dad.

Jackie Silverstein went first. And then not so long after, Fred Silverstein passed away.

Just writing those words—

I can't really write much more without crying.

When I lost them, I fell apart. I didn't know how to process it.

I just . . . cried.

And cried.

I felt as if I'd lost a piece of my soul. I didn't imagine I could miss two people so much. I wanted to call them. I wanted to laugh with them again.

I wanted to see their faces. I wanted to hear their voices. I wanted my mom and dad to comfort me, to protect me, to cheer me on, to push me, to stand by my side, to take on the fucking *world*, the way they always did every day of my life. When they passed away, I felt so alone. I was a little boy again, back in Brooklyn.

I refuse to say I miss them.

Because that doesn't come close to describing how deeply I feel their loss.

Not close.

I stopped smoking for ten years. But after my father died, I started again. I also stopped gambling. I took that up again because I had to.

The recession hit me hard. The ex was still throwing lawsuits at me. Attorneys were at my throat. I was about to lose the house where this new modern family of mine was living.

I said to Val and the kids, "Look, you know I gave up gambling. That was a good thing. But right now things are real bad. I'm down to fifty thousand dollars in cash. My debts amount to a lot more than that. It sounds crazy, but I'm gonna take that money and go to Vegas and come back with a pile. I can't you tell why I know I can do it, but I can. I'm saying all this so it's not a secret. I don't wanna do it on the sly. I want you guys to know what I'm doing."

I drove to Vegas and played blackjack with a focus and a vengeance until I turned that fifty thou into one million. I paid off the debts and bought Val her first Mercedes.

Back in Brooklyn so many years ago, I'd sat at my drum set, blasting the *Mod Squad* solo, my head and heart disappearing in the blinding flurry of my drumsticks, losing track of time, aware only of the time I was keeping.

And now, my son Max, twenty-three, drum master, drum *monster* (and stand-up comic and actor), and my son Dillon, nineteen, who plays guitar, writes, and sings (and is also an actor), have their own band, L.A. Rocks.

They were into music since elementary school. I'd wake them up, get them dressed, make their lunches, and herd them into the car for the drive to school. Once they were belted up in the backseat, I slipped in a cassette tape—a custom mix, of course—and did the announcing.

"Ladies and gentlemen, live from the Sands . . . it's Frank Sinatra with the Count Basie big band!"

Or, "In one of his last appearances, live from the Hilton, the King himself, the one, the only, Elvis Presley!"

The kids went crazy listening to the music, and I went even crazier. We'd sing along to Guns N' Roses and Led Zep and Aretha and Sammy Davis and Kool and the Gang and Aerosmith and Pearl Jam and Ray Charles and every great song you can think of. Driving my kids to school was the highlight of the day.

My kids are talented and tough and motivated, but if I've taught them nothing else, they know all that's not enough.

"Here's how you make it in show business and in life," I told them. "You go out and get it. You let nothing stop you. You just take it."

That's what you do.

That's what I did.

That's what they'll do.

Then there was the career, which had—for lack of a better word—stalled.

One day, I went to Starbucks to grab a coffee and tried to figure some shit out. Truth is, I had a lot of time on my hands. I took a table outside and a few tables away I saw an old friend, Bruce Rubenstein, who had worked for Mickey Rourke and wrote *Bullet*, which stared Rourke and Tupac. We shot the shit, and then Bruce, who'd become a building contractor as well as a manager, asked me the inevitable question. "So, Diceman, you busy? What've you been up to?"

"The truth? Not that much."

"Maybe I can help," Bruce said. Two days later he and I were sitting with Doug Ellin, the producer of the HBO show *Entourage*. Right after that meeting, I got a call. Doug had cast me to play myself. I wound up doing five episodes in the final season. In the show I played sort of a role model to Johnny Drama (Kevin Dillon). The mantra I gave to Johnny is one I'd adopted for myself. It became an *Entourage* battle cry: *No one fucks with me; I do the fucking.*

Entourage turned out to be a game changer. My shows got good ratings and I got critical raves.

Even better, Woody Allen saw the show, liked what I did, and contacted Bruce Rubenstein—now my new manager—to ask me to read for a part in his movie *Blue Jasmine.*

I have to say, I was a little nervous. But I was also cool. When I saw Woody, the first thing I said was, "I want you to know that you're not meeting the Diceman. You're meeting Andrew."

"I appreciate that," Woody said. "I'm hoping you won't mind reading a few pages for me."

"No problem. That's what I'm here for. Would it be okay if I looked them over for a few minutes?"

"Of course," said Woody. "Take your time."

I went into another office with the casting lady and read over the lines for about ten minutes. "Okay, I got it," I said.

I went back to Woody. "Don't worry about reading them verbatim," he said. "Feel free to change whatever you want."

The part was not comedic. The role was for an unhappy working-class guy who got screwed out of money by his sister-in-law and was royally pissed at her. I knew this guy. I could feel him.

A week later word came from Woody that I got the part. I shot scenes in San Francisco with Cate Blanchett and Sally Hawkins, and then I went to New York, where the cast included Alec Baldwin. It was exciting, and I felt in my element. The acting came naturally. Woody is one of those directors who expects his actors to come prepared and to *bring* it. That's just what I did.

The film was a hit, and the reviews were sensational. For the first time in five decades, I didn't get one negative notice. And—just like that—I was back, only this time not only as a comic, but as an actor to take seriously. The gigs started coming in again. I got a chance to do a Showtime special for New Year's Eve that I called, fittingly, *Indestructible*.

Since I returned to the Garden fifteen years ago, I've refined my act. It's now funkier and harder-edged. And I'm talking about the new generation of wild women. I call it the most aggressive fuckin' animalistic generation you ever met in your life. And I don't say that with disrespect. I've been waiting for this generation. This is the generation finally meeting me on my own turf. This is the generation that says you don't care about her if you don't come all over her on the first date. When she says that to me, I say, "Relax, honey, 'cause on the next date I'm gonna blow my wad so big that it'll be like putting your head under a yogurt machine and pulling the fuckin' nozzle." This generation of women don't wear nice little earrings in their ears. They put piercings in their pussies. They BeDazzle the pussy. When they take off their jeans, you could go blind from the diamonds and rubies. Some chicks have a string of pearls hanging on their asshole lips a mile long. In this recession you can go down on a chick and come up a wealthy fuckin' guy.

I talk about women today being so sex-crazy that the asshole has become the new pussy. This is the same asshole they used to hide from us. They actually bleach out their asshole and put it on their Facebook page as their profile picture. This is a mistake. No guy wants to go down on a chick and smell Ajax.

This generation doesn't know how to have a good time. When they go to a party, all they do is go around saying, "Did you get my text? Did you get my e-mail?" I'm like, "Fuck face, you're right in front of me. *Just tell me!*" Then they gotta tell you everything that their smartphone can do. "When your smartphone starts sucking dick," I say, "I'll be impressed. Until then, shove your smartphone up your ass."

In my day back in Brooklyn, we knew how to party. You went for the chick with the biggest, fattest fuckin' tits in the room. You hoped she was as horny as you were. And if she was, you took her into the master bedroom, where you fucked her on top of all the coats and jackets piled on the bed.

During the fuck, you moved your jacket out of the way so she was driving home with your load on her boyfriend's jacket. Now that's a fuckin' good time.

This new generation is Internet crazy. The Internet changed everything, 'cause these days even the shyest chicks have seen guys with giant schlongs. The humongous big dick has come to life before their very eyes. So they'll say shit to you like, "Whip it out." Well, nice Jewish boys from Brooklyn don't whip anything out. We'll bring it out. We'll take it out. We'll put it on a bed of lettuce for you and make a beautiful presentation. But there'll be no sound effect. It's not gonna sound like London broil hitting the kitchen counter . . .

So the Diceman keeps going.

You've seen it time and time again in these pages—knock me down as hard as you can, it don't matter. I'm gonna get right back up and come at you harder.

The Diceman ain't fading away, 'cause the Diceman is *indestructible*.

And with his family by his side, Andrew Dice Clay is *just that fuckin' good*.

ACKNOWLEDGMENTS

SPECIAL THANKS TO my sister, Natalie Michael, who kept me grounded through the brutal process of writing this book; and, more importantly, for her support, love, and encouragement that was there all the way back to our Brooklyn apartment, where the Originals would be up until all hours of the night—the only apartment in a six-story building with the lights on until after midnight, with us eating, laughing, and loving our little family.

Thank you to my gorgeous wife, Valerie Silverstein, aka Mrs. Dice Clay (@mrsdiceclay), who met me and believed in me at a time in my life when I wasn't so sure I myself believed that I could do it again—a young girl who stood by me and hasn't left my side, pushing me, like Adrian did for Rocky, to reach my potential. Once again, I truly love you.

Thank you to Eleanor Kerrigan (@ejkerrigan), one of the world's greatest people. The woman, girlfriend, fiancée, and friend who always encouraged me, who raised my sons with me, and who is now one of the strongest, funniest, most fearless stand-up comedians I have ever worked with. Thank you for always being there.

To the loves of my life, Max and Dillon, whose young faces were all I had to look at during my lowest times. I knew then, without any ifs, ands, or buts, that I would have to prevail and teach them by example to never back down and to believe in their God-given talent. They made me challenge myself again. Now, they challenge themselves. Max and Dillon, you are the two best guys I ever hung with. www.soundcloud.com/larockstheband

ACKNOWLEDGMENTS

Thank you to Michael "Wheels" Parise (@wheelslive) for your friendship, guidance, counseling, and talent. Twenty-five years of laughs. Your comedic timing and delivery is a force to be reckoned with.

An Un-Be-Liev-Able thank you to Bruce "Ruby Tattoos" Rubenstein (@rubytattoos) for believing when nobody in Hollywood did anymore. Not since my father, thirty-five years ago, have I met a man who not only believed in my talent but understood it, way deeper than my comedic persona, as where I could go as an actor. Hands down the greatest manager (other than my dad) that I ever worked with.

Thank you to Uncle Lee Lawrence for thirty-eight years of encouraging, loving, and being there to pick me up when I was down for the count. You just wouldn't have it.

To Michael "Happy Face" Malandra, thank you for twenty-three years of friendship, loyalty, and protection. Let's do another twenty-three.

To Jeffery Abraham, aka Jeffery A, my publicity monster, thank you for knowing when and how to make me move, and for your friendship and dedication.

Thank you to David Ritz for dealing with my craziness. You are a true master and have captured the essence of who I am.

Special thanks to my agent, Pete Pappalardo, for your friendship and dedication, and for the rebuilding of the Diceman.

Special thanks to Dennis Arfa, the agent who had the vision twenty-six years ago. What a vibe, my friend.

I also want to thank Simon & Schuster, Matthew Benjamin, Rick Rubin, Daniel Hayes, Arsenio Hall, Whoopi, Eminem, Nikki Sixx, Alec Baldwin, Roseanne, Ice-T, and Doug Ellin for your friendship, the beautiful foreword, and for igniting the fuse that catapulted me once again.

Thank you to all my boys back home: Neil "Hot Tub Johnny West" Lustig, Kenny "Club Soda" Feder, Jim Norton, Jim Florentine, Don Jameson, Eddie Trunk, Howard Stern, Opie & Anthony, Mancow, John Mulrooney, Robert and Richie Santa, Frankie and Carmine Diorio, Sal Iuvare, Tommy Scrow, Larry Winocor, Tony the Brush, Manuel and Lori Vasquez, Uncle Ronnie and

Grandma Charlene—now your name is in a book, James Messinian, Steve Arnold, Mike Tricharichi, Joel Goldstein, Todd Rosken, Tom Green, Mike Morano, Laurie Brockway, and Hank Gallo.

Special, special thanks to the millions of fans who have always backed me up.

INDEX

ABOUT THE AUTHOR

ANDREW DICE CLAY is a stand-up icon, actor, and the most controversial and outrageous comedian of all time. He even holds the distinction of being the only performer to have been banned for life from MTV. Dice is also the only comedian to perform in front of 100,000 people, opening for Guns N' Roses at the Rose Bowl. He starred in the cult classic films *Casual Sex?*, *The Adventures of Ford Fairlane*, and the concert movie *Dice Rules*; headlined several HBO specials; released bestselling DVDs and multi-gold-and-platinum CDs; and was nominated for a Grammy Award. In 2012, his first stand-up special in seventeen years, *Indestructible*, was Showtime's highest-rated comedy special to date. Once again and forever, Dice Rules.